'I *love* the process of designing and creating a brand-new space and I really *enjoy* the full range of change in the garden, from *building* walls and *laying* paths to seeing the first snowdrop emerge and unfurl.'

Monty Don

Gardeners' World
GARDENING
FROM BERRYFIELDS

Monty Don

Horticultural researcher: Phil McCann

contents

Welcome to Berryfields	6
The Long Borders	10
The £20 Border	42
The Courtyard Garden	54
The Cottage Garden	72
The Dry Garden	90
The Herb Garden	106
The Kitchen Garden	124
The Greenhouse	150
The Fruit Garden	172
The Spring Garden	194
The Pond	212
The Lawn	236
Index	250

THE **GARDENER'S**
WORLD GARDEN

1   Long borders
2   £20 garden
3   Courtyard garden
4   Cottage garden
5   Dry garden
6   Herb garden
7   Kitchen garden
8   Greenhouse
9   Fruit garden
10 Spring garden
11 Pond
12 Lawn

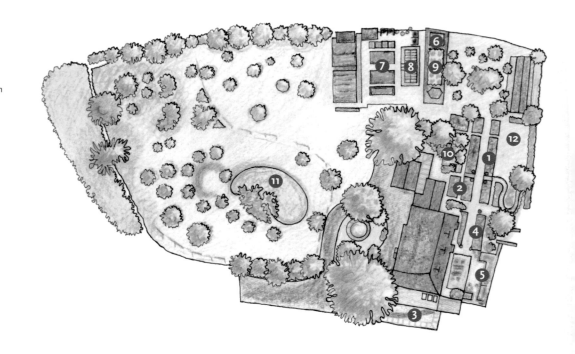

welcome to Berryfields

I FIRST VISITED BERRYFIELDS ON A cold, grey, wet November afternoon in 2002. *Gardeners' World*, one of the great institutions of British horticultural and television life since the late 1960s, was undergoing huge changes. I was one of them. When Alan Titchmarsh decided that it was time for him to move on after seven years at the helm, I was offered the chance to take over. I pondered long and hard for about two seconds before accepting gratefully, but I was fully aware of the scale of the task of stepping into shoes previously worn by such loved and respected figures as Alan, Geoff Hamilton and Percy Thrower.

We also needed a new garden. Until then *Gardeners' World* had always been presented from the home garden of its main presenter, but it was decided – not least by my family – that now, after thirty-

odd years, it was time for the programme to develop its own garden. My own garden was too mature, too far away and too much mine. We wanted somewhere that we could shape and develop to suit the needs of the programme and our viewers. We thought it should be in the Midlands so that it would be closest to most people's experience of gardening across the whole of the country, and also so that it would be accessible for the greatest number of people involved with the programme, which is produced from Birmingham.

And so, having looked at a great many possibilities, we decided upon Berryfields. Despite the horrible weather that November day and the almost total lack of colour in the garden, there was something about the place that just felt right. We knew that over the coming years we could make a garden there and

– just as important – make a good programme in the process.

Berryfields is in Warwickshire and is 2.5 acres in total – with the garden surrounding a large house. Of that area the vast majority was grass when we took it over. Despite our work over the past few years, there is still plenty of it left, providing a blank canvas for us to develop. Its boundaries are a neighbouring house, a road and fields. It is screened from the road but we often delay filming as buses and lorries roar by, light aircraft drone over or, as on one memorable occasion, a combine harvester starts up just the other side of the hedge and covers the whole garden in chopped wheat straw! The garden had very little in the way of structure – no internal hedges and just one small concrete wall – but it did have the glorious advantage of a number of mature trees including some superb hornbeams, poplars and Scots pine. There was an orchard that had fallen into dissarray but included mature apples and pears.

The soil at Berryfields is heavy and very compacted, with a solid pan about 15cm (6 inches) down. To improve the soil structure we have had to double dig, which is slow, laborious and not consistent with the demands of fast-turnover telly. But the dividends will be paid in years to come. When we did a pH test we found that it had a range that varied from 7.5 in the dry and cottage gardens, to 6.5 in the vegetable garden, and down to 5.7 in parts of the woodland area. This offers us opportunities to grow an unusual range of plants.

When I took over *Gardeners' World* I had long been an organic gardener – inspired originally by Geoff Hamilton – and there was never any possibility that Berryfields would not be run organically. We use no artificial pesticides, fungicides or herbicides. Wherever possible, plants that have to be bought in are sourced from nurseries that do not use peat. Wherever possible, plants are grown on site. We make a great deal of compost and leafmould and wherever possible use our own home-made potting compost.

The programme is largely shot on the Thursday and Friday a week before it is broadcast, with the weather voiceover and any bits and pieces added the following Thursday. A day can vary, but officially it starts at 8 a.m. and finishes at 6 p.m. – although we often go on filming till 8 p.m. In Percy Thrower's day the crew went to the local pub at lunchtime and the director and producer sat down to a three-course meal with Percy and his family. But at Berryfields sandwiches and a Thermos of soup are bought in from a local shop and lunch is always eaten outside, whatever the weather, in the dry garden. Filming carries on whatever the weather, too, and rain has never held us up for more than an hour, although we can have fun and games with keeping continuity from one day's filming to the next. I often walk out of a sunny shot and into another with the ground – and my clothes – wet from rain as in real life I move from Thursday's sunshine into Friday's squalls. The feature inserts, when a presenter goes off to visit a garden or plant specialist, take another day each.

Work begins weeks ahead, with some filmed sequences shot months ahead, but each programme is finalized on the Friday before filming, and on the Wednesday we tighten up all the details according to the weather so we know exactly what we are going to be shooting the next day. On Thursdays I film all the pieces that do not involve the others, and it is a relatively straightforward process, whereas on Friday we have Chris, Rachel, Sarah and any guests, a second crew, plus the team working on next week's programme and often journalists or visitors. It can be hard for outsiders to work out what is going on when television is being made, and there seems to be a surfeit of people and a huge deficit of activity. But making a programme is like piecing together a jigsaw, ensuring each piece can fit perfectly together – and very often not in the same order as originally intended. It is a technical process and often the more natural and relaxed it appears on telly, the more complex and difficult it is to film.

At the heart of the programme is the need to incorporate day-to-day seasonal tasks with the bigger projects of making and changing areas of the garden. In our first year at Berryfields we concentrated on making the areas that we knew we wanted to include as part of the existing garden. This involved creating the dry garden, the long borders, the spring garden, Rachel's garden, the vegetable garden, the greenhouse and the pond. Not a bad tally for seven months' work! But then, for a programme looking back over the history of *Gardeners' World*, I paid visits to Percy Thrower's garden 'The Magnolias', Arthur Billet's 'Clack's Farm', Geoff Hamilton's 'Barnsdale' and Alan Titchmarsh's 'Barleywood'. This taught me an important lesson. A *Gardeners' World* garden could not just be one integrated garden, however lovely. It had to have small, independent areas that reflected the interests and lives of our viewers and explored possibilities that perhaps they might be inspired to follow. In short, a television garden has to be rather different from a private garden if it is properly to reflect a full range of private gardens. So we made the three small fruit gardens, the cottage garden, the £20 border and the peony garden. More small gardens will follow. When making new gardens we do not set a specific time limit for their completion and are not seeking an instant effect. We are making spaces that can grow and develop into maturity. However, I love the process of designing and creating a brand-new space and really enjoy the full range of change in the garden, from building walls and laying paths to seeing the first snowdrop emerge and unfurl.

The garden will continue to change and develop, but certain things will remain constant. We shall continue trialling plants, equipment and techniques. We will continue to relish the day-to-day jobs of gardening that I love, from weeding and deadheading to mowing the grass. We will remain honest. This means that we do what you see and never cheat. After all, we can learn much more from our mistakes than our successes, so if things go wrong we share them with the viewer – and things do go wrong, often. That is gardening. That is life.

'We have used the whole gamut of plants for these borders, including *bulbs*, *annuals*, herbaceous *perennials*, *shrubs* both deciduous and evergreen and a variety of *grasses*. I think that it has been an unqualified success that will only get *better and better*.'

the long borders

AS I WRITE THIS, TOWARDS THE END OF THE SUMMER,
the long borders at Berryfields are looking magnificent.
At the pale end of the borders, nearest to the house, the
artemisia, melianthus, cardoons and ornopordums dominate
with their lovely ghostly silvers and dusty blue foliage; the
viticella clematis add height as we go down the borders
towards the old apple tree at the other end, and the towering
rudbeckias, heleniums, dahlias, cannas and gingers are filling
the hot end of the borders with every shade of yellow, orange
and crimson. The area is packed with colour and yet nothing
feels crowded. After just eighteen months, these borders are
undoubtedly the stars of Berryfields.

The long borders were there when we came to Berryfields, but after a short time it became apparent that their contents needed a radical revamp. The planting consisted almost entirely of very old hybrid tea roses, forget-me-nots and daffodils, with a few clumps of pinks and irises along the way. None of these plants was undesirable in its own way, but they did not begin to fulfil the potential of this magnificent space.

Not only was the planting potential of these borders undeveloped, but also it did not take much to discover that the soil was exceptionally compacted and poor. So we decided to take everything out, dig to break up the soil's compaction and incorporate plenty of organic material to improve its structure.

While this was going on I spent many days planning the planting. In the end I decided that the borders should be symmetrical, if not exact mirror images of each other. The planting of the long borders has followed a colour scheme that changes as you move away from the house. In the area nearest to the house it is dominated by whites and glaucous leaves, and then, as you progress down the path dividing the two borders, it moves into blues, purples, lemon yellows and burgundies, before exploding into a final burst of crimson, orange and chrome yellow at the far end. We have used the whole gamut of plants for these borders, including bulbs, annuals, herbaceous perennials, shrubs both deciduous and evergreen and a variety of grasses. I think that it has been an

unqualified success that will only get better and better. The cool and hot ends are in fact pairs of separate borders, divided from the main, central section by paths that cross through the borders, but I always intended the whole thing to be considered as one planting scheme.

We planted yew hedging along the back of the borders to provide a backdrop of dark green. To protect this young hedging and also the growing plants until the hedge got established, we put up hazel hurdles. This had the immediate effect of focusing and drawing the eye down the borders.

Hazel hurdles are fantastically useful when establishing a young garden. They are beautiful, robust and very effective at filtering the wind. They are made from hazel coppice that is cut every ten years or so as part of a cycle that can last for hundreds of years. The hurdler uses no nails or attachments of any kind, but simply weaves the split lengths of hazel to form the lightweight but very strong panel.

SITE

The total length of the long borders, including the cool and hot end beds and pathways, is 18m (59 feet) and the width is 4m (13 feet). They are aligned lengthways in a north–south orientation, with one end of the borders reaching the metal gates that lead to the cottage and dry gardens. The other end opens into the orchard and the views of the fields beyond. Trees in the woodland garden shelter the borders from easterly winds, although they also cast some morning shade. A central pathway of grass divides the two borders. This pathway is just wide enough for a fully laden wheelbarrow to pass without damaging the edges of the paths or the surrounding beds.

BACKBONE SHRUBS

If herbaceous perennials, annuals, grasses and bulbs are the flesh of a long border, the shrubs make up the backbone. In the growing season they play a part in the overall identity of the border, and in winter, when many plants have died down, they provide structure and interest. They also act as conduits for the different colours of the border to move seamlessly along the border. Among many shrubs, the purple-leafed shrubs play a major part in knitting the border together.

◆ *Corylus maxima* 'Purpurea', or purple hazel, will quickly reach a height of 6m (20 feet) with a spread of 5m (16 feet), when given the space to grow and not overcrowded by surrounding plants. Plants prefer a sunny or partially shaded spot in well-drained soil. On mature plants purple catkins are produced in late winter. Edible nuts occasionally mature in autumn. The young plant must have plenty of sun and air if it is to grow strongly, but the mature plant will take more shade. If coppiced back hard every few years, it will produce wonderful, outsized leaves.

◆ *Cotinus coggygria* 'Royal Purple', or smoke bush, has deep wine-red leaves that intensify in colour throughout autumn, before falling in winter. The flowers, which appear on unpruned shrubs in summer, are individually

small, but in large collections look like a cloud of smoke over the plants. Unfortunately the flowers are deep pink, which has no place in the Berryfields long borders. Pruning not only results in non-flowering, but also ensures that new leaves are formed and the overall shape of the plan is retained. If left unchecked, plants grow 5m (16 feet) high and wide and produce their best-coloured foliage in a sunny position.

◆ *Sambucus nigra* f. *porphyrophylla* 'Gerda' (often mislabelled *Sambucus nigra* 'Black Beauty'), or purple-leaf elder, is a shrub with deep purple leaves. It thrives in a sunny position and well-drained soil. To get the best from your plant, cut half of the branches back to ground level every spring. This continually rejuvenates the plant and ensures a good display of leaves. Plants will grow to around 3m (10 feet) high and wide.

◆ *Stephanandra incisa* 'Crispa' is a tough shrub. It will thrive in any soil type, in any conditions, and will tolerate the most heavy-handed pruning. It's actually best to cut older branches back to ensure plenty of side branches and fresh growth.

We planted box balls in each of the corners where the central grass path and the brick paths cross. The best time to clip box is when it needs it, but also on a dull, damp day. Light drizzle and hand shears are the two best tools when tackling clipping. The damp atmosphere will stop the cut edges of the leaves from turning brown, something that is a problem in hot, dry weather, and the hand shears will give you more control than electric hedgetrimmers.

The leaves are oval, wavy-edged and deeply lobed. Curious little greenish-white flowers are produced in early summer. It grows only 60cm (2 feet) high with the potential for 3m (10 feet) of spread.

OPPOSITE The inflorescences of *Pennisetum* are like iridescent foxtails and are wonderfully soft to run your hands through as you pass.

RIGHT Not all grasses are green. The leaves of the Japanese blood grass, *Imperata cylindrica* 'Rubra', turn a deeper red as the season progresses, adding as much brilliant colour as any flowering plant.

The initial planting of the shrubs in the long borders included many more plants than are there now in the borders. Inevitably plants were put in the wrong place, as happens in most gardens, and some were the right shrubs but in the wrong garden. *Griselinia littoralis* has fleshy green leaves with variegations and is a tough shrub. It thrives in seaside locations, where salt-laden winds can be a problem, and can make a very good evergreen hedge, but it just didn't look right in the planting scheme half-way up the borders. The jury is still out on the *Choisya ternata* Sundance with its almost day-glow yellow leaves. (Colour intensity is best in a sunny position. The foliage colour can bleach in intense sun.) In autumn and winter it screams out from its central position in the borders. However, from late spring through to early autumn the intensity of colour is

perfectly balanced by the hot colours of other plants around it.

We also have eight box plants, *Buxus sempervirens*, clipped as balls, marking the four corners where the two paths cross the borders.

GRASSES

Grasses are invaluable in the Berryfields long borders. The evergreen types add structure in winter, and the flower spikes add interest from flowering time, but above all grasses add texture to a border. Texture in plants is a funny thing. There are the obvious attractions of handling wispy or soft leaves, but it works in a more abstract way than that: the eye can

on the programme. Berryfields was one of the first gardens to obtain and grow *Pennisetum glaucum* 'Purple Majesty', and since it was featured in 2003 it has become a best seller. It is raised from seed and produces burgundy foliage and flowers. It grows best when planted in early spring with no check to growth. It also branches from the base, making slender clumps quickly within the year. Plants grow to around 1m (3 feet) high and some were planted in the area where the warm colours melt into hot, and others in the ends of the borders. It is not hardy enough to survive a Berryfields winter, so in exposed areas it is best to lift the plants in late autumn, pot up and protect in a cold greenhouse over winter. Other grasses in the long borders at Berryfields include:

somehow absorb and appreciate textures even though they are well out of reach. It is an important component in any planting scheme.

Of all the grasses in the long borders, it's *Stipa tenuissima* that has been the most filmed. In summer it's impossible not to caress or stroke the fluffy flower-heads. The delicate strands of evergreen foliage are soft green and the flowers, produced from June and lasting into winter, are lighter green. The grass grows 60cm (2 feet) tall with a similar spread. *Stipa tenuissima* is planted at the front of the borders, half-way along, to act as a resting point for your eyes. It works.

A purple grass, or ornamental millet, caused quite a stir when it was featured

◆ *Briza media* 'Limouzi', or quaking grass, has blue-green foliage and delicate, quaking flower-heads. It's a short-lived plant, lasting three or four years, but self-seeds freely in the garden. Best grown in sun or light shade, it is semi-evergreen and grows 60cm (2 feet) tall.
◆ *Stipa gigantica* is a majestic plant. With its great leaning stems of flowers (they start out standing straight but wind and weight bend them) they blow and glow like triumphant golden flags in the border. Catch them backlit on a midsummer evening and you see floral firecrackers. It needs well-drained soil in a sunny, open position.
◆ *Miscanthus sinensis* 'Silberfeder' is a whopper, reaching 3m (10 feet) or so with silvery flowers – although, looking closely at one before me, it is actually a pale

gold, flecked with bronze and green, crimping firmly up and out, whereas later, when fuller, these will fall gracefully down towards the ground. These look good in the border and even better in a vase, corkscrewing away from the leaves that bear them in a kind of final abandoned flourish.

◆ *Miscanthus sinensis* 'Ferner Osten' is planted in the pale end of the borders and adds a plum-coloured tone with its burgundy seed heads and glaucous green leaves. A very good border plant, it looks dramatic but not too big and, like all miscanthus, it will grow in almost any conditions but is especially good for a dry spot.

◆ *Molinia caerulea* subsp. *arundinacea* is an exceptionally graceful grass, growing tall and elegant and able to withstand quite a lot of rough treatment from the wind. Good for any soil including wet, acidic conditions.

◆ *Hakonechloa macra* 'Alboaurea' is a magnificent, gold-variegated grass with ribbon-like foliage forming superb mounds. Tiny flowers are formed in summer. It is deciduous, grows best in sun or partial shade and reaches 35cm (14 inches). It can also thrive in a container, but, wherever it grows, don't let the soil dry out.

◆ *Calamagrostis* × *acutiflora* 'Karl Foerster' produces mounds of green foliage with spectacular vertical flower stems, bleaching from white to straw in late summer. It's best grown in a sunny position where plants grow to around 2m (6 feet).

◆ *Eragrostis curvula* 'Totnes Burgundy' has leaves that mature to a deep burgundy from their tips down. It also produces long arching sprays of creamy flowers from midsummer. Plants thrive in a sunny position, are deciduous and reach 1m (3 feet).

◆ *Carex muskingumensis* produces slowly increasing clumps. The semi-evergreen leaves are narrow, light green and complemented by brown flower-heads in summer. Grows well in sun or partial shade, reaching 60cm (2 feet).

◆ *Imperata cylindrica* 'Rubra', or Japanese blood grass, is a grass with foliage that turns from green to blood red as the year develops. It's deciduous, thrives in a sunny position and grows to 40cm (16 inches).

Grasses from cool climates, such as *Deschampsia*, *Festuca*, *Helictotrichon* and *Stipa*, come into growth in late winter and flower before midsummer. They are divided in autumn or late winter to early spring. It is often preferable to divide frequently, to avoid the difficulties of congested roots and to keep plants growing vigorously.

Grasses from warm climates, such as *Miscanthus*, *Panicum*, *Pennisetum* and *Spartina*, come into growth in late spring, flower after midsummer and are usually cut back in late winter. They are best planted or divided in late spring. These grasses do not usually need such frequent division.

HEIGHT
Adding climbers to a border adds another dimension and enables you to sprawl colours through other plants. In keeping with the hazel hurdles that

VOCABULARY

What plants are called on camera and screen can cause discussion at Berryfields. There is a school of thought (of which I am the chief proponent) that holds that common or popular names should be given first, followed by the botanical name. Others feel that the botanical name should take priority over popular names. The fact is that botanical names are known universally and popular names can change not only from country to country but indeed county to county. *Viola tricolor* made a welcome appearance in the long borders. Or should that be wild pansy, love-in-idleness, loving idol, cuddle me, call-me-to-you, jack-jump-up-and-kiss-me, godfathers and godmothers, heartsease, stepmother, pink-eyed John, flower o' luce, bullweed, bird's eye or even kiss-her-in-the-buttery? That's a lot to put on screen for six seconds. Botanical names it is, therefore, followed by the most popular of the popular names, and all names are checked using an up-to-date edition of the *Royal Horticultural Society Plant Finder*.

There are other words we use that can cause confusion. The *Gardeners' World* audience ranges from experienced gardeners to others who are new to the pastime. If you know all your gardening

definitions, please skip this list, or use it to check that you're not rusty.

◆ ANNUAL: a plant that germinates, grows and sets seeds in one growing season.
◆ BIENNIAL: a plant that completes its life cycle in two years.
◆ PERENNIAL: a plant that lives for more than two years, often flowering every year once established. It doesn't mean that a plant will live for ever – every plant has a natural lifespan.
◆ HARDY: describes plants that can withstand frost.
◆ HALF-HARDY: describes plants that do not survive frost.
◆ TENDER: describes plants that need warm weather to grow.
◆ BULB: a swollen underground bud with fleshy scales. The scales are storage organs and may be enclosed in thin papery scales.
◆ CORM: a swollen underground stem. A papery covering makes many corms look like bulbs – but botanically they are different.
◆ TUBER: a swollen underground root used for the storage of food and the production of shoots.
◆ MULCH: a layer of material used on the soil surface and around plants. It conserves moisture, reduces weed growth and adds structure and fertility to the soil.

surround the borders, wigwams were made from hazel poles and planted with clematis. This was partly due to the lack of clematis elsewhere in the garden, but all clematis make superb border plants and especially the later-flowering varieties, which can be pruned hard each year. The varieties chosen include:

◆ *Clematis* Victor Hugo is a free-flowering clematis producing violet-coloured flowers with darker stamens from midsummer through to autumn. It's a vigorous grower reaching 3m (10 feet). It needs to be tied to supports as it is non-clinging. Group 3 pruning (see page 21).

Lower a 30cm (12-inch) length of clay drain-pipe over newly planted clematis. The clay pipe rests on the soil, where it keeps the base of the plant cool, prevents accidental damage when weeding and, if a band of petroleum jelly is smeared up the sides of the pipe, will stop slug and snail damage. Take care not to damage any of the young shoots when placing the pipe over the plant.

◆ *Clematis* 'Chinook' is another non-clinging variety, producing violet-blue, nodding flowers with twisted sepals. Flowers are produced from midsummer to early autumn. Plants reach around 2m (6 feet). Group 3 pruning.

◆ *Clematis* 'Gazelle' produces slightly scented, white, nodding flowers with twisted sepals. Only reaching around 1m (3 feet) high, it is ideal to clothe the lower areas of the supports. Flowers are produced in midsummer. Group 3 pruning.

◆ *Clematis* 'Polish Spirit' is one of the easiest clematis to grow, reaching 4m (13 feet) high and producing masses of nodding, intense purple flowers in July through to September. Group 3 pruning.

◆ *Clematis* 'Perle d'Azur' is a popular clematis for its mass of violet flowers, on plants 4m (13 feet) high, throughout late summer into autumn. Group 3 pruning.

◆ *Clematis* 'Marie Boisselot' is an early-flowering variety, producing white flowers in early summer. Plants quickly reach 3m (10 feet) high. Group 2 pruning.

◆ *Clematis viticella* 'Purpurea Plena Elegans' is one of my favourite clematis, with fully double flowers in violet-purple.

It is a very old variety dating back to Elizabethan times. Plants reach 3m (10 feet) high, and the flowers are produced in summer. Group 3 pruning.

◆ *Clematis* 'Princess Diana' produces nodding bell-shaped flowers in orange-pink. Its leaves and stems are waxy and the plant can reach 2.5m (8 feet). Group 3 pruning.

◆ *Clematis* 'Daniel Deronda' is a vigorous variety producing double and semi-double, deep purple-blue flowers early in summer. Semi-double flowers are produced early in the year and single flowers in late summer, which are then followed by perhaps the most amazing seed heads of any clematis. Plants grow to around 3m (10 feet) high. Group 2 pruning.

◆ *Clematis* 'Niobe' is an early-flowering variety, producing large, rich, velvety red flowers from late spring right through to autumn. The hotter the weather, the darker the shade of flowers. Plants grow to around 3m (10 feet) tall. Group 2 pruning.

Pruning clematis seems to cause more problems than almost anything else in the garden, but in fact it is easy enough. The easiest way to tackle it is simply to remember, 'If it flowers before June – don't prune.' But if you want to be more specific, clematis are divided into groups and each group has a slightly different pruning regime.

Clematis Groups

◆ GROUP 1: Clematis in this group produce flowers in spring on wood produced the previous year. So if you

OPPOSITE Clematis are an essential part of the long borders, where we grow them up wigwams of hazel bean sticks. They provide height and colour from midsummer right through to autumn. All the varieties in the border are late-flowering, so are pruned back hard each March, when we can replace the support if necessary.

TOP LEFT *Clematis* 'Perle d'Azur'.
TOP RIGHT *Clematis viticella* 'Purpurea Plena Elegans'.
BELOW LEFT *Clematis* 'Abundance'.
BELOW RIGHT *Clematis* 'Niobe'.

prune them in spring they will not have any flowers. They do not need to be pruned at all, but if you wish to reduce their size, clip them back immediately after flowering. This group includes *Clematis alpina, montana,* 'Ville de Lyon', 'Nelly Moser' and 'Barbara Jackman'.

◆ GROUP 2: These are all large-flowered hybrids that produce their big flowers in spring and often another crop of smaller flowers in late summer. Prune all dead or damaged growth in early spring and cut all healthy growth down to the top pair of buds. Examples include 'Miss Bateman', *henryi* and 'Vyvyan Pennell'.

◆ GROUP 3: Produces only flowers on the current season's shoots, so in early spring (when you see new growth) cut back all the previous year's growth to a set of healthy buds 15–45cm (6–18 inches) from the ground. This group includes all the *Clematis viticella* types, as well as 'Jackmanii' and 'Etoile Violette'. Whichever pruning regime you are tackling, prune only to a pair of healthy buds, always use clean, sharp secateurs and if in doubt – don't cut.

Clematis will grow without much help, but to get the best from them make sure the roots are cool and the stems are in a sunny position. It is essential to plant them deep with up to 15cm (6 inches) of the stem buried. Plant them with lots of bulky organic material added to the planting hole (to help hold moisture rather than to feed the roots) and add a thick mulch of compost or manure every year. However, striped varieties will flower well in shadier positions. Mulching with organic matter is

important, as this helps water retention in the soil, keeps roots cool and gradually improves the structure of the soil.

Some clematis are prone to clematis wilt, a fungal infection that can cause the whole of the growth above ground to brown and wilt within hours. In this case remove and burn all affected growth. If the clematis has been buried deep at planting, it will nearly always regrow unharmed. None of the species clematis or any of the *viticella* types is prone to wilt.

THE COOL END

Looking up the middle of the two long borders, you can see a temperature rise from cool to hot. But the journey starts at the cool end. The area is two beds, both 4m (13 feet) long and 3m (10 feet) deep. Backing on to one of the borders is Rachel's garden, whose pink, burgundy and white colour theme complements the cool end of the borders, and, if you look across the cool end of the border towards Rachel's garden, it all appears to be one garden.

The planting is essentially pale, with a few ruby and burgundy colours highlighting the ghostly pallor around them. These are a selection used:

◆ *Cerinthe major* 'Purpurascens' is a stunning addition to any garden and is easily grown from seed. Seed can be sown in peat-free multipurpose compost in March and plants will be flowering in July. It thrives in a sunny position and any well-drained soil and will self-seed or over-winter in a sheltered spot. It has

OPPOSITE *Cerinthe major* 'Purpurascens' is one of my favourite annuals. It has a deeply satisfying balance of ghostly glaucous leaves and a purple depth to its flowers that adds substance. Although not officially hardy, it is tough enough to withstand winters at Berryfields … so far.

Plant names are often the subject of disagreement. Some say clem-ah-tis and others clem-ay-tis. I have heard broccol-aye, but I say broccol-ee. Is it hel-een-ium or hel-enn-ium? The spigelia in the hot end of the long borders was cause for consternation. Is the 'g' in spigelia hard or soft? Does anyone really care, so long as everyone knows what it does and where to get it? Well, apparently they do, as we had emails and letters pointing out that in one programme I pronounced spigelia in two different ways. It was a brand-new plant, after all. For the record, the 'g' is definitely soft.

stems that are prone to dropping over the edges of beds and over neighbouring plants and produces yellow flowers, tipped violet, surrounded by purple bracts. Plants grow to around 60cm (2 feet) tall and wide.

◆ *Melianthus major*, or honey bush, has magnificent pale greeny-blue foliage that will reach 3m (10 feet) in a long growing season. It is a native of South Africa and will be damaged by frost unless it is in a very sheltered position. It can produce flowers, but only in exceptionally hot summers and autumns, so it is primarily grown for its foliage – which is more than reason enough to include it in any garden. I mulch it thickly in autumn to protect the roots and leave the top growth all winter and then cut it back in spring. Cuttings can be easily taken from new spring growth.

◆ *Hosta*, although generally thought of as either water- or shade-loving, will grow perfectly well in an open, sunny border as long as the soil is enriched with plenty of organic, moisture-retentive material. As a rule, hostas produce better flowers in sunnier positions and better foliage in slightly shaded positions. 'Snowden' is a slow-growing clump, forming enormous, thick (and slug-proof), glaucous, grey-green leaves. The white flowers are produced on spikes around 45cm (18 inches) high. *Hosta sieboldiana* grows to around 1m (3 feet) tall with oval, puckered, grey-green, thick leaves 25–50cm (10–20 inches). And just in case your garden is infested with slugs and snails, one of the best varieties to grow that doesn't seem to get eaten like most is the vast, yellowy-green *Hosta* 'Sum and Substance'.

◆ *Artemisia ludoviciana* 'Valerie Finnis' has been one of the success stories of the long borders. It has grown like crazy. The trick is to cut down newly planted plants to encourage bushy growth, and to plant in a sunny position in well-drained soil. Flowers are yellow but rather insignificant. Cut them off for better foliage. Plants grow 60cm (2 feet) tall and wide, producing a thicket of silver-grey stems. I divided this in late summer 2004 and replanted the division in the matching cool border.

◆ *Onopordum acanthium*, or Scotch thistle or cotton thistle, is a staggering, monstrous thistle with great, antler-like branches covered in a white film and topped with flowers. It is biennial. It germinates in late summer and produces a rosette of modest leaves. In the following spring it develops a huge tap root and enormous growth. It is beautiful and sculptural but very spiny. Plants grow to around 3m (10 feet) with a 2m (6 foot) spread.

◆ *Eryngium giganteum* thrives in well-drained soil and a sunny position. The leaves are shiny and dark green, the flowers blue, but the part of interest for the cool end of the border is their combination with the broad, silvery bracts that seem to support each bloom. Flowers are produced in late summer and, after flowering, plants often die. However, self-sown seedlings always appear. Plants grow to around 1m (3 feet) high with a spread of 75cm (2½ feet).

GETTING WARMER

Once the brick pathway is crossed, the colours graduate from the whites, cool blues and purples of delphiniums, monkshoods, *Anchusa* 'Loddon Royalist' and *Eryngium* × *oliverianum*, to yellows, oranges and, eventually, reds. We have work to do yet on this blue section, blending it in with purples that can act as a link to the reds as the border heats up towards the 'hot' end. In fact the warm russets and hot reds at the end of the long borders have worked well from the very beginning and are getting better and better.

◆ *Rudbeckia*, or coneflower, is a perennial from the prairies of America and is great at providing colour in mid to late summer. *Rudbeckia fulgida* var. *deamii* grows to around 1m (3 feet) tall, producing daisy-like, yellow flower-heads with central black cones. The narrow leaves are mid to dark green and plants thrive in moist soil. *R. laciniata* 'Herbstonne' has the same kind of proportions and style, but the flowers' central cones are green. *R. laciniata*

'Goldquelle' is the same again except that the flowers are fully double. All require a sunny position.

◆ *Kniphofia*, or red hot poker or torch lily, does not have to produce red flowers. *Kniphofia* 'Bees' Lemon' is an upright-growing plant reaching 1m (3 feet) high with a spread of 45cm (18 inches), producing lemon-yellow flowers in late summer. The serrated leaves are adept at catching fallen leaves in autumn, and if they are not removed the crown of the plant is liable to rot. Clearing debris from inside the crown of leaves and from around the plant is a pleasing job to do on a misty morning in autumn. If you like and want a red, grow *K. uvaria* 'Nobilis'. It grows to 2m (6 feet) high, and has strappy leaves and torch-like blooms in bright red.

◆ *Crocosmia* 'Zeal Tan' is dotted among the border to link the colour scheme. It is a compact variety, reaching around 45cm (18 inches) and produces large, dark red flowers. The sword-like foliage is dark green. All crocosmia require a sunny position and must not sit in waterlogged soil. It is best to divide established clumps in spring. Lift them with a garden fork, ease the congested clump apart and replant immediately in well-prepared soil. *C.* 'Lucifer' is the best-known variety and unfailingly sets the benchmark in late July for brilliant, red-hot flowers, while the large, upright, sword-shaped leaves add a valuable structural element to the border. *C.* 'Emily McKenzie' is more modest in growth, with bronze leaves and orange flowers that last well into autumn. A star plant.

◆ *Canna*: for a long while I found cannas too flashy and fleshy to incorporate easily into a mixed border. But I am discovering that they can be dramatic and even beautiful. At Berryfields we have planted them at the hot end, as much for their foliage as their startlingly bright flowers. *Canna* 'Striata', sometimes incorrectly named 'Pretoria', has large green leaves with yellow veins and pink stems. It has large orange flowers, which are produced in midsummer. *C.* 'Durban' is a stunner that also has large orange flowers that make a startling contrast to its rich purple – almost chocolate – foliage. *C.* 'Musifolia' grows to a whopping 3m (10 feet) and rarely flowers, but the banana-like foliage certainly makes up for that, the dark, brooding, green leaves with maroon veins adding drama to our long border. Another giant, *C.* × *ehemanii*, produces green leaves and drooping pink flowers and is considered by many to be the hardiest of the cannas. Hardiness is a question that crops up on the *Gardeners' World* website, whenever we hold our roadshows and at the shows we cover throughout the year. Cannas are not hardy. So it is best to lift them after the first frost or the beginning of November – whichever comes first – and store them like dahlias in a frost-free place over winter. Bring them back into growth in early spring by potting up, putting the pots in a warmer place in the greenhouse and watering. They can be safely planted out after the last frost.

◆ *Achillea* 'Fanal' is one of the final plants before the brick path and hot end of the long borders. The ferny foliage is soft grey and the bright red flowers are produced in large heads from mid to late summer. Flower colour fades from red to yellow with age, but they still manage to attract hoverflies until well into autumn, which is wonderful for the garden because, of course, hoverfly larvae feed on aphids. It grows 1m (3 feet) tall and thrives in sunny positions and in well-drained soil. It does have a habit of sprawling – especially after the tail of Hurricane Alex passed through in early August 2004 – and we support it with garden twine tensioned between two stout canes.

◆ *Dahlia* 'Grenadier' and *D.* 'Bishop of Llandaff' grow at the end of the central section, just by the brick path that crosses the borders (and runs from the potting shed down to the greenhouse). Both give us a constant supply of flowers with crimson petals and yellow bosses from July through till November, although 'Grenadier' is double and the 'Bishop' single. As with cannas, we lift our dahlias in autumn and store them in the greenhouse, but they should always be left in the ground right up until frost has blackened off the topgrowth, as the tubers go on growing vigorously up until that point. As with all dahlias, it is essential to deadhead the spent blooms every few days to ensure repeat flowering.

THE HOT END

The path separates the two 'hot' borders from the main borders, but from the outset the plan was to integrate the planting so that the colour changes developed seamlessly. This was done by duplicating some of the plants on either side of the path. So the dahlias leap the

the long borders

path and cannas were used in both the warm end and the hot end. Meanwhile, one of the grasses used in the temperate part of the borders, *Pennisetum glaucum* 'Purple Majesty', is also used in the hot end of the borders. The deep scarlet leaf colour is perfect.

The hot end beds measure 4m (13 feet) in length by 3m (10 feet) in depth, and this was the last section to be planted up – in fact we did not begin it until a full year after we began down at the other end with the cool beds. Well, it is a long border and it is not a makeover!

Berryfields is in the Midlands and winters can be cold. Anything that is of borderline hardiness is planted out in midsummer, and even planted in pots that can be lifted and rehoused in the cold part of the greenhouse until the following late spring or early summer.

◆ *Leonotis leonurus* is a plant I have been using for many years to zizz up the late summer borders. The square-shaped stems will reach over 3m (10 feet) by autumn and have bright orange flowers, produced in compact clusters in whorls along the flower stalk. Tall, dramatic and orange – what more could a hot border want? It is a perennial but is not hardy, so it is best treated as a half-hardy annual, with seed sown in spring and the plants put out after the last frost.
◆ *Tithonia rotundifolia* has bright orange, velvety flowers with yellow centres drawn with a child-like simplicity, sitting on a long, slightly funnelled, hollow stem, which has an extraordinarily velvety

texture. It can grow to a sprawly 2m (6 feet) – although mine are much smaller this year because I did not plant them soon enough – and will go on flowering until frost destroys it. 'Torch' is a very good variety but a little smaller – perhaps 1.2m (4 feet) – and 'Goldfinger' is smaller yet, keeping to 1m (3 feet) tall.
◆ *Cosmos atrosanguineus*, or chocolate cosmos, settled in quickly in the hot end of the long borders and soon formed bushy plants. Its deep maroon – almost brown – flowers are carried on long, delicate stems and smell deliciously of chocolate: hence the name. It needs a sunny position and isn't too fussy about soil, but it has to be well drained. It's rather like a dahlia – in mild areas the tubers can be left in the soil, but in colder areas the tubers need to be lifted in late autumn and stored in a cold greenhouse over winter, before planting out in late spring. When planting tubers it is best to plant them at least 15cm (6 inches) deep in well-drained soil.
◆ *Gazania*: gazanias are jolly – it is hard not to be cheered by them – as long as it is sunny, because they need sunshine for the daisy-like flowers to open and reveal a central dark ring surrounding the dark disc. The petals are available in a number of colours and all are best grown in well-drained soil and full sun. Seeds can be sown in February in a heated propagator and planted out after the last frost. Always nip off the flowers as they fade, which stops the plant from putting all its energy into seed production and neglecting the next flush of bloom. Plants grow to around 25cm (10 inches) tall and are best treated as

OPPOSITE The chocolate cosmos, *Cosmos atrosanguineus*, has velvety, deep-claret coloured flowers that are both delicate and strong, with their extraordinary chocolate fragrance. As with dahlias, if they are deadheaded regularly, they will continue until the first frosts.

annuals, as the first frost will destroy them.

◆ *Tropaeolum speciosum*, or flame flower, is usually grown either as a climber or scrambling through hedgerows. In the hot end of the long border it's being trialled as a ground-cover plant (which, after all, is only a climber without a support). Once established it should both cover the soil and feel its way through upright shrubs. It needs a sunny position, moist soil and a couple of years to become established. The wiry stems are clothed by five-lobed leaves and the scarlet-red flowers are produced in late summer and early autumn. Stems will reach 3m (10 feet).

◆ *Helenium*: heleniums come from damp meadows in America and have done very well in the long borders. They add a special burnt caramel hue to the late summer border. This is because each individual flower can have three or four different shades of red and orange. *Helenium* 'Moerheim Beauty' is one of the best, with dark, copper-red, daisy-like flowers. 'Rauchtopas' is a new variety that Chris planted in August 2004, with golden uppers and a rich brown reverse to its petals. 'Sahin's Early Flowerer' has big yellow and bronze flowers washed with red. As its name suggests it flowers in June, but if cut back or regularly deadheaded will repeat through the summer. Heleniums attract bees and last for ages as cut flowers. Plants grow to a height of 1m (3 feet) with a spread of 60cm (2 feet). On established plants, and this can be within a couple of years in the correct growing conditions, it is best to place stakes around the plant and

support with garden twine. The flower stems are easily broken when in full flower and under the weight of a summer storm.

◆ *Rudbeckia* 'Herbstsonne' is one of the American coneflowers that are so good in late summer. There was some debate about the role of this yellow giant (was it too yellow for the hot border? Too tall and dominant?), but I love it. It will reach 2m (6 feet) and need some staking, but the big yellow daisies with their green central cone are pretty robust. One way of limiting its height is to lift and replant it each spring. This breaks the roots and acts as a curb on its growth.

BULBS

The long borders are mixed, which means that we happily include every type of plant, and bulbs of all kinds are an important part of our planting scheme, from the tulips and daffodils of spring to the dahlias, crocosmias, cosmos and gladioli of late summer. The beauty of bulbs in a mixed border is that they provide colour when herbaceous plants are either dormant or only just starting to grow, but their dying foliage is in turn hidden by the emerging growth around them.

You buy a bulb and everything is self-contained. They are nature's perfectly packaged product, with an embryonic flower bud and immature leaves, all carefully wrapped inside a papery covering. All gardeners have to do is plant them. The rule of thumb is to plant bulbs in deep holes three times their height, and if in doubt you can never do harm by planting too deeply, especially in

a border where you do not want to disturb them.

Berryfields had a scattering of daffodils in flower when filming started in April 2003, and since then the collection has been added to, plus a few other types of bulbs.

◆ *Narcissus*, or daffodils, are best planted in late summer and early autumn. Plant in drifts and plant the same variety in clumps. It looks less busy than mixing a few different varieties together. The choice is immense, but *N.* 'King Alfred' (yellow trumpets), *N.* 'Mount Hood' (white trumpets) and *N.* 'Golden Harvest' are traditional and popular. Never cut the leaves back, but allow them to die down naturally once flowering is over. This feeds the bulbs for next year's flowers. Try not to grow them in a shady position, or where exuberant herbaceous growth will completely smother them before the leaves have done their essential work.

Tulips

Tulips are special. Their flowering is an event on a par with the best of roses. Whereas the progression through snowdrops and crocuses to daffodils is one of tentative hope that spring is on its way, tulips make a festival of colour at exactly that moment in the year when spring is assured and confident. They announce – with a shout of satiny colour – that we have all arrived at exactly the place where we want to be.

We have incorporated most of our tulips at Berryfields into the long borders rather than displaying them in beds of their own. I think that they work best in this way, as part of the unfolding pageant of colour that will hopefully reveal itself ceaselessly from April right through to November.

It is worth remembering where tulips come from, so that the ground can be properly prepared. They mainly originate from an area that now occupies Turkey, Iraq, Iran and Armenia, where they grow on shale slopes. This means that they are often snow-covered in winter – which protects them from much of the cold – and have very sharp drainage so that they never sit in the wet. In the summer months they are baked by a burning sun. Your back garden may not be able to match this, but you can give them as much sun as you have and – most important – do whatever you can to improve the drainage.

Many tulips do not make it through to the following season, and if they do the flowers will inevitably be smaller, although probably more numerous. So I find it best to top up those that you particularly like and add new types where the previous spring had shown a lack. With any luck these tulips will arrive in time to plant them some time from the middle of October onwards, although there is no pressing hurry in this. I have often planted tulips in January without any ill effects other than delaying flowering by a few days. When ordering tulips there are only two considerations that really need dealing with. The first is colour and the second is timing. Each tulip will stay in flower for approximately two weeks, although it can vary by as much as a fortnight from year to year. Tulips are catergorized into fifteen divisions, roughly grouped into times of flowering, with bulbs of each group sharing recognizable characteristics. So, for example, after the species tulips, the first to flower at Berryfields are from the Triumph Group (Division 3), which was bred about a hundred years ago specifically for bedding and cutting. Consequently they all have long, strong stems and clear colours. In addition to *Tulipa* 'Negrita', at the end of whose long stems is poised a plum-purple flower with single, satin petals, we have 'Abu Hassan' and 'Prinses Irene'. 'Abu Hassan' follows about a week after 'Negrita' and has the most extraordinary burnished copper colour at the base of its petals, lightening to a rim of orange as they fold inwards at their edges. The result is a flower that looks as though it has been cast in bronze and yet is lit from within. It is one of my favourites. 'Prinses Irene' has a chocolate stem and orange petals flushed with pink and streaked with plum and a touch of green.

If you want one spectacular display, then it makes sense to choose tulips from the same group that will all flower together. But if you want a longer, changing display, then a wide spread is sensible. So we also have very similar-shaped but later flowers such as the intensely dark 'Queen of Night' and 'Recreado', which Sarah Raven used in her cutting bed and which is plum with a violet flame. Both come from the single late group (Division 5), which means they are the

last tulips to flower in late spring. They are usually tall, bearing single flowers on long flower stalks.

Although I love almost every tulip I have seen, some I love more than others. My fancy is fickle and I am quite capable of swearing undying favouritism for ten different cultivars on ten consecutive days. But two of the groups consistently entrance me. The first is the lily-flowered group (Division 6), which are, I think, the most graceful of all tulips. They all have long, narrow flowers with pointed petals that bend outwards. In sunshine they open out completely. We have a number of these in the garden at Berryfields. 'West Point' is primrose yellow and surely one of the most elegant flowers on this earth. It will tolerate light shade and is very good rising above the blue mist of forget-me-nots. We also have the pure white 'White Triumphator', which is very long-lasting although it fades more messily than 'West Point'. 'Queen of Sheba' is early and has a lovely, curvy swell to its hips, with the burnt orange petals arching outwards, making each flower look like a cock pheasant in full mating rig frozen in display. 'Ballerina' will come a couple of weeks later, also with orange petals, but it holds itself with great poise and grace, despite its party clothes.

Then there are the 'parrots'. To me, a parrot tulip often looks as though it has just been hit by a bullet, the petals flayed and ripped on the exit but otherwise scarcely touched. We have 'Blue Parrot', which is not blue at all but the colour of

the long borders

red paint water with a blue brush dipped in, and 'Black Parrot', which is, you guessed it, not black but instead, and the better for it, the richest, deepest shade of burgundy. Opened out, it is like a frosted port-wine stain on a window. We also have 'Rococo', which is a brilliant vermilion corrupted by a puckered scar of greeny blue and which opens out flat in the sunshine. It is earlier than the other parrots. Finally, 'Flaming Parrot' has pale yellow flowers flamed garishly with a raspberry streak that is not for the faint-hearted – but then in truth no tulip is. They are flowers that exuberantly celebrate the arrival of spring and I love them for that.

Tulip Fire

This year at Berryfields we had the first indications of tulip fire on our tulips. Tulip fire is caused by a fungus, *Botrytis tulipae*, and initially manifests itself with small pinprick-sized holes and lumps on the petals and some visible grey mould on the leaves. The holes are caused by spores being exposed to sunlight, and the leafmould is a sign of the rot that can totally destroy the tulip. There are two courses you can take. The first is to dig up all the tulips, burn them and not replant more in the same area for at least three years. The second, less drastic approach is to lift all the bulbs after flowering and store them carefully. Then, before replanting, inspect each bulb for the tiny black sclerotia that the fungae over-winter in, and manually rub them all off before replanting. We have chosen the latter course of action but shall be watching them carefully to see if it

returns next year. If it does, then there will be nothing for it but to burn the bulbs and leave the long borders tulipless for a few years.

◆ *Fritillaria*: there are many fritillarias to choose from, with *Fritillaria meleagris* (snake's head fritillary) being a popular choice. The chequered flowers in purple and white are delightful in woodland settings, but in the long borders something more substantial is required. *F. persica* produces impressive spikes of deep purple flowers, each spike carrying around 15 blooms. It grows to around 1.5m (5 feet) and when in full flower is a stunning sight. Crown imperial (*F. imperalis*) grows to an equally imposing 1.5m (5 feet), producing five widely bell-shaped flowers crowned by a tuft of leaf bracts. Orange, red and yellow varieties are available and all are solid additions to a sunny border. Fritillaria bulbs dry out quickly, so only

OPPOSITE The crown imperial fritillary is one of the oddest and most dramatic of all spring bulbs. It can reach a height of 1.5m (5 feet) on a chocolate stem, with a display of orange ('Rubra') and yellow ('Lutea') flowers, which is as gorgeous as an exotic headdress. It also has the added distinction of smelling of rancid tomcat.

buy bulbs that have been packed or stored in compost or sawdust. Handle the bulbs carefully, as the soft scales are easily damaged. Larger bulbs can rot in wet winter soil, so it is a good idea to place some coarse sand in the planting hole and plant the bulbs on their sides. This prevents water from accumulating around the bulb. Plant bulbs in early autumn for flowering the following spring and early summer.

◆ *Crocus*: crocuses have been planted around the Berryfields garden and are among the first bulbs to flower in spring. The corms are planted in autumn. There are many species and varieties to choose from, but *Crocus tommasinianus* is one of the best. Blooms in varying shades of

lilac, white, red and purple are produced in spring.

◆ *Eucomis comosa* 'Sparkling Burgundy' has been a great success as part of our summer display. It is best planted in a container, plunged into a long border and lifted in mid autumn. Keep in a greenhouse over winter, after which it can be started into growth in March. Its common name is pineapple lily, and when it flowers in midsummer it is easy to see why. Rosettes of leaves part to allow the pineapple-shaped flower cluster to emerge. 'Sparkling Burgundy' has the added beauty of deep red leaves – perfect when a potful is plunged into the hot end of the long border. Plants can be expensive to buy, but propagating a few

for free once you have a plant is easy. Cut a strong, young leaf from the plant. Cut into 5cm (2-inch) sections, making sure the sections stay the right way up (a slanted cut makes this easy). Insert the cuttings into gritty compost, water and place in a greenhouse or on a bright windowsill. Roots will be produced after three months, and then small bulbils appear on the surface of the compost, connected to the leaf. Pot the cuttings and bulbils into larger pots and in five years' time you will have many new flowering plants.

YEW HEDGING

Common or English yew, *Taxus baccata*, was the first plant I planted at Berryfields. Young plants were spaced 45cm (18 inches) apart along the length of the long borders. When planting any hedge it is always better to plant small, healthy plants that will establish and grow fast than to 'cheat' the hedge with larger plants that grow much more slowly and are much more likely to die back. 'Plant small and grow fast' is the motto. Yew is the ideal hedging plant when used as a backdrop for planting of any kind. It is evergreen, dense and once clipped will look tidy for eight months of the year and can be clipped right back to the bare wood and will soon form new shoots. The secret to successful yews is drainage. If the roots become waterlogged, they turn bronze and eventually rot. Add plenty of organic material and horticultural grit to the soil and to the planting hole at planting time. Good drainage doesn't equate to tolerance of drought, and the plants will

need lots of water. At Berryfields the hazel hurdle helped in this, giving protection from wind as the plants developed, thus reducing evaporation.

It is a myth that yew is a slow-growing plant. Young plants can put on 30cm (12 inches) of new growth a year for at least the first ten years, and a solid 2m (6-foot) hedge can be established inside ten years from 30cm (12-inch) plants. For this plants need soil that is well drained and high in organic matter. They also need a sunny position and should never run dry of water. If left to its own devices, a yew will reach around 15m (50 feet). As the yews age, growth does slow down, but this is compensated by the fact they can live for an astonishing four *thousand* years.

It's strange that the only edible part of a yew plant is the bright, warning-red flesh around the seed produced by female plants, called the aril. Every other part of the plant is poisonous.

BORDER EXTENSION

The back of one of the long borders adjoins the garden known as Rachel's garden. It was designed and planted by Rachel de Thame for an hour-long programme, and was a blank canvas when it was presented to her with the brief of creating a flower garden. The area is 10m x 8m (33 feet x 26 feet), and perfect for a colourful display, but in keeping with the rest of the garden it needed to be interesting for twelve months of the year. Drawing on the inspiration gained from many garden visits, Rachel has created a garden packed with flowers.

OPPOSITE This clipped, mature, yew hedging shows how it makes the ideal formal backdrop to any kind of border, as well as making the best permanent structure within a garden.

TOP The mauve and
violet heads of *Allium
sphaerocephalon* rising
above the bleached grass
inflorescences, perfectly
illustrate the colour theme
of pink through to deep
burgundy, with touches
of white.

MIDDLE The gravel paths
in this part of the garden
are designed as sinuous
curves and are edged
with brick.

BELOW Ivory-coloured
Helleborus orientalis
flowering in early spring
under the beech tree.
By early summer this area
of Rachel's garden is in
deep shade.

Outline

The shade cast by established trees and
the south-facing aspect mean that a
variety of plants can be grown
successfully in this garden. The soil was
tested, as all soil should be before you
contemplate drawing up a plant list, and
found to be slightly alkaline. Sowing
seeds or planting into unsuitable soil is
both wasteful and costly. The conditions
in this part of Berryfields rule out lime-
hating plants, unless the pH is lowered
significantly. This is of course possible,
but it seems strange to make a drastic
alteration to one particular asset of the
garden. In any case the pH will revert to
type over time. If it isn't natural to grow
ericaceous plants in the garden soil, then
so be it.

Looking at a garden from a fixed
viewpoint is fine, but an area this large
has to be explored, and that means you
have to be able to get in among the
plants. A gently curved path would be
ideal and was easily constructed. The
path is both wide enough to allow
enjoyment of the surrounding plants
and, just as important, will take a fully
laden wheelbarrow. The path takes you
to the brick wall of a neighbouring
building, and then off again through the
planting. This path demands a leisurely
stroll, which in turn calls for a peaceful
resting area. For this practical purpose,
and to serve as a focal point, Rachel's
garden has a bench ideally placed against
the brick wall.

Star Plants

A plant wish list can be endless. Where do you stop when planning and planting a flower garden? The main colour scheme for the garden is dark, sultry colours. This can be beguiling, but *en masse* it can also be a bit morbid, so Rachel wanted acid greens, silvers and the occasional blue to break up the image, giving accent and focal points to the garden. The rose of the year 2003 was the super Rhapsody in Blue, whose blooms are hybrid tea and an intriguing mix of velvety purple and red. The result is a beautiful rose that fades through to a blue hue. Originally bred by a keen enthusiast, Rhapsody in Blue looks set to stand the test of time. Far from being a one-year wonder, it's destined for great things. Simple box balls, *Buxus sempervirens*, are superb punctuation marks in the bed, with the fresh green growth lifting the colour scheme.

◆ *Lilium longiflorum* 'White Elegance' is a lovely new trumpet lily, growing to 1m (3 feet) tall and producing elegant white blooms in summer. Bulbs were planted in pots during April and flowered in July.
◆ *Pittosporum tobira*, or Japanese pittosporum, is an evergreen shrub with a bushy habit. Leaves are oval, glossy and dark green, but it's the flowers that are delightful. Produced in late spring, the creamy white blooms are richly fragrant. The shrub will grow to 4m (13 feet) high.
◆ *Heuchera* 'Plum Pudding' is an adaptable plant but happiest in the shade. The stunning leaves are deep red and the flowers are tiny, maroon and green. Plants grow to around 45cm (18 inches) high.

LONG-BORDER BASICS
◆ Make a plan but be prepared to be flexible.
◆ Get the soil right before planting. It is your last chance to improve the soil without disturbing plants, and your plants are only as good as your soil.
◆ Place plants on the soil and leave for a day or two. Evaluate and only plant when happy. Place twice, plant once.
◆ Make a note of what has worked and not worked. Move plants that do not work.
◆ Don't forget to use height in long borders. Use wigwams of beansticks, canes or shop-bought structures.
◆ Don't forget to underplant with bulbs for easy colour.
◆ Keep deadheading – it can double the flowering life of many plants.
◆ Be prepared for a long haul – getting borders absolutely right does not happen overnight. It is a long-term and constantly evolving project.

◆ *Hosta* 'Halcyon' is a popular hosta with heart-shaped, tapering leaves that are greyish-blue. Clusters of violet blooms open above the leaves in summer. Plants grow to around 30cm (12 inches) and form clumps 1m (3 feet) across.
◆ *Lythrum salicaria* 'Robert' is a clump-forming perennial that produces clear pink flowers from mid to late summer. The mid green leaves fit the colour scheme perfectly. Plants grow to around 75cm (2½ feet) high.
◆ *Astelia chathamica* is a striking, evergreen perennial with arching leaves covered in silvery scales. It grows to around 1.5m (5 feet) high, forming a clump 60cm (2 feet) wide.

A YEAR IN THE LONG BORDERS

SPRING
◆ Plant pot-grown shrubs.
◆ Protect newly planted hedges from wind.
◆ Water newly planted shrubs in dry weather.
◆ Weed.
◆ Sow annuals to fill gaps and for colour the same summer.
◆ Harden off tender plants in a greenhouse or cold frame.
◆ Stake plants before they need staking. Growth is fast and will soon cover supports.
◆ Take photographs and make notes on the borders. Make a note of successes and failures.

SUMMER
◆ Weed.
◆ Water in dry weather.
◆ Deadhead herbaceous plants to encourage more flower production.
◆ Check for pests and diseases and sort them out before they become a major problem.
◆ Check that stakes are adequate now that growth is strong.
◆ Trim yew hedges.
◆ Take photographs and make notes on the borders. Make a note of successes and failures.

AUTUMN

◆ Plant spring-flowering bulbs. Tulip planting can be delayed.

◆ Plant shrubs and herbaceous plants.

◆ Move any plants growing in the wrong positions.

◆ Weed.

◆ Take photographs and make notes on the borders. Make a note of successes and failures.

WINTER

◆ Plant tulip bulbs if this was not done in late autumn.

◆ Double dig vacant soil if it is compacted.

◆ Add organic matter to all soils wherever possible.

◆ Take photographs and make notes on the borders. Make a note of successes and failures and plan for the following year.

ABOVE We used woven hazel hurdles throughout the garden to provide shelter, until the hedging plants grew large enough to do the job, and to provide instant visual structure for the garden. This is a shot looking through the spring garden across the long borders.

OPPOSITE A view across the pale end of the long borders to Rachel's garden in early May.

'I *love* this kind of challenge, not least because I am **much happier** growing my plants from seed than spending huge amounts of money buying them from a garden centre. I suppose I am just mean, but *why spend a fortune* when a single packet of seed will provide **dozens** of lovely plants?'

the £20 border

IT'S INEVITABLE THAT ANY TELEVISION PROGRAMME IS
going to be accused of spending far more than the average
gardener simply to achieve maximum dramatic effect for a
particular programme. It is a fair criticism – and one that
could easily be levelled at *Gardeners' World* from time to time.
But then we are making a programme that we hope is both
entertaining and informative. It is carefully constructed,
filmed and edited and, believe you me, not even so-called
'reality' television is like real life. So sometimes we cheat a
little and buy three plants to cover one pruning shot, or plant
bigger, more expensive specimens than we need to, simply
because they make a better picture. However, we decided to
make a border for strictly £20.

The £20 border is an area 5m x 4m (16 feet x 13 feet) tucked between the back of the long borders and the house. The target was to make a border that would look good by the end of its first summer and yet have the staying power to continue for years. This would mean growing perennials as well as annuals. The only way that we could possibly afford to do this was by growing everything from seed. So in February I was handed a £20 note and told to get on with it!

I love this kind of challenge, not least because I am much happier growing my plants from seed than spending huge amounts of money buying them from a garden centre. I suppose I am just mean, but why spend a fortune when a single packet of seed will provide dozens of lovely plants?

£20 – THE BUDGET
◆ All seed costs are included in the £20 limit.
◆ The manure used when the soil was prepared is not included in the price, as Berryfields is lucky enough to be near a farm, and the farmer was more than pleased to reduce his mounds of muck. Local newspapers often advertise free manure, but be prepared to collect.
◆ Bamboo canes and other supports were already in the garden and are not included in the £20 budget.
◆ Propagators and compost used initially to raise the seedlings are not costed into the budget, as they have been at Berryfields for over a year and have been used for many other projects.

◆ Any paving materials have been strictly recycled within the garden and are therefore not included in the £20 budget.
◆ Plants that drift on the wind, or arrive on muddy boots, into the £20 garden from elsewhere at Berryfields are priceless. Aquilegias will probably arrive from the cottage garden, and I am sure that forget-me-nots will make an appearance sooner or later. These are also not included in the £20 budget.

Timings
Most of our seeds were sown in heated propagators in the greenhouse during February and March. Hardy annuals were sown directly in the soil at intervals between the end of March and mid April. It is wrong to assume that early sowings of annuals will result in earlier flowers, as the chances are that the seeds will rot in cold soil. It's worth waiting until the soil is warm enough, when the seeds soon catch up. I always use the elbow test – which is just like testing a baby's bathwater: you roll up your sleeve and feel the soil with your elbow. If it is at all cold to touch, wait a little longer – regardless of what the weather or calendar are up to. Sow seed directly only when the soil is warm to touch.

ANNUALS AND PERENNIALS
Perennials
The backbone of the £20 garden is made up of herbaceous perennials. A perennial is any plant that lives and flowers for more than two years. Perennials protect themselves by dying down in winter, but the roots remain healthy below the

PREVIOUS PAGE, LEFT Iceland poppies, *Papaver nudicaule* 'Meadow Pastels', which we grew in the £20 border. These are annuals, although they may flower again in their second year if the soil is exceptionally well drained – which is certainly not the case with the heavy clay at Berryfields.

PREVIOUS PAGE, RIGHT It is amazing what results can be achieved from a handful of seed packets.

OPPOSITE The site of the £20 border, prepared and ready for sowing. Note the very wide paths laid around it especially to accommodate the film crew.

ground and in spring new growth appears. Although none lives for ever, many will live for a number of years, and self-sown seedlings often appear around the parent plant, going on to grow and flower, and the clump or population soon increases. If sown early enough, many perennials have enough vigour to grow to flowering size in the same year. Some perennials are monocarpic, which means that they die down as soon as they flower, and it often takes these plants several seasons to build up the necessary strength to produce flowers.

Annuals

The definition of an annual is a plant that germinates, grows, flowers and sets seed within the space of one growing season. This 'season' may extend across a calendar year, but most annuals germinate as the soil warms up in spring and by the end of summer have flowered and died down. So-called 'half-hardy' annuals germinate in hot, moist conditions and flower in late summer and autumn. They mainly originate from subtropical areas and are killed by the first hard frosts. Examples include cosmos, nicotiana and salvias. In this country it is easiest to raise these under cover and plant them out after the last frosts have passed in spring. But 'hardy' annuals, such as alyssum, nigella and poppies, can be sown directly in the soil in the position where they are going to flower. No amount of bad weather will deter hardy annuals, and nothing can be easier than sowing a pinch of seed into prepared soil for a fabulous display later on in the year. Tender annuals need

protection all the year round, and are not included in the £20 border.

Biennials germinate in spring or summer, grow through one summer, over-winter in a semi-dormant state, and then grow again and flower the following spring and summer before dying. Well-known biennials include wallflowers, foxgloves, cotton thistle, sweet William and Honesty (*Lunaria*).

DOUBLE DIGGING CASE STUDY

The garden was cleared of all plants, weeded and double dug in November. I remember that this evoked a mixed response from *Gardeners' World* viewers, and is still a hotly debated subject. Areas of the Berryfields garden

haven't been cultivated for many years, and the site of the £20 border was horribly wet and compacted. I have no doubt about this at all. If you wish to prepare a compacted piece of ground for best results – whether for edible or decorative plants – there is no substitute for double digging if it can be done. Single digging will turn the top 15cm (6 inches) of soil, but below that remains a solid pan of clay. This clay will stop water from draining and will stop roots from growing into the lower soil. Double digging helps to aerate the soil and is the one chance to improve the structure to a good depth of soil by incorporating organic matter. It certainly is brutally hard work, but much more useful than going to a gym, and cheaper too, and I confess that I thoroughly enjoy it.

◆ Mark off a trench 60cm (2 feet) wide and remove the soil to one spade's depth, often called a spit.
◆ Remove the soil to just beyond the far end of the plot.
◆ Dig or fork over the bottom of the trench.
◆ Add home-made compost or manure to the bottom of the forked trench.

◆ Dig out the next 60cm (2 foot) trench, putting the soil from that trench into the dug and manured first trench.
◆ Then it's a case of repeating the procedure along the whole length of the border.
◆ Fill the last trench with the soil you removed from the first. Now the border is fully double dug.

Frost will do the hard work for you. If you break the clods up youself before the onset of winter, rain can cause the small particles to form a hard surface, which will need breaking up in the spring. Make it easy on yourself and leave the clods large.

Take your time when double digging and never rush. Start with twenty minutes a day and take plenty of rests. Use a good spade and keep it upright at all times – this will avert most back problems. Never dig if the soil is wet enough to stick to your boots. Not only is wet soil heavier, but you will also damage the very structure you are trying to improve. When performed correctly and thoroughly, double digging need be done only once in about twenty years. Adding a good mulch of organic matter to the surface, or digging this into the first spit, will be enough to keep the soil in good heart for many years. Finally, when double digging make sure you remove all traces of weed roots as you go.

SOWING PERENNIALS

Perennials are best started off early indoors. Basic propagators are useful but are governed by the temperature of the room in which they are placed. Heated propagators open up a whole new world of seed germination, as you control the temperature and therefore the success of the seed. If your budget can stretch to it, a thermostatically controlled propagator is best; failing that, a heated propagating mat is an investment I heartily recommend. Both will pay for themselves very quickly in saved plant costs. Most of the perennials in the £20 garden need a temperature of 15–20°C (59–68°F) to get growing. Sow the seed at the depth indicated on the seed packet, and cover it with a layer of vermiculite. The fine nature of vermiculite will not impair the seedlings as they develop and will help drainage around developing seedlings.

◆ Sow perennials early to ensure flowering in the first year of growth.
◆ Remove propagator covers and wipe away condensation to reduce fungal infection.
◆ Ensure that seedlings gain as much light as possible, but avoid direct sunlight.
◆ Move or prick out seedlings to individual pots once a true pair of leaves has developed.
◆ Acclimatize seedlings to the outdoors before planting. This hardening-off process should start around April, and the seedlings should live outside in their pots for at least ten days before planting out.
◆ Developing seedlings must never get frosted, so protect them at night with horticultural fleece if necessary.

SOWING ANNUALS

Annuals are wonderfully easy. After double digging and letting the winter weather break the soil down, rake over and remove any stones, roots and weeds. You should then have a fine tilth, and can simply sow the seed on to the soil. This can be done in a broadcast way, where seed is scattered randomly around your garden, or in a controlled fashion. Whichever method you choose, seedlings will appear in around ten days and will soon develop into strong plants. Cover broadcast-sown seed by raking over gently. Do this in opposite directions to ensure good coverage and distribution.

◆ Annuals sown in rows can look regimented. Mark out areas with sand and sow into these allotted areas.
◆ Alternatively, sow seeds in an X or O formation. Once the seedlings are up and thinned out, the X shape disappears and the final look is fantastic. The X shape also enables you to weed out the inevitable mass of weed seedlings that will appear – which will initially look very similar to your annuals.
◆ Whether sowing in rows, areas, Xs or Os, cover seeds with a peat-free

MONTY'S TIP
Each time you sow a packet of annuals directly into the soil, keep a pinch back and sow it in a small pot of peat-free compost. Water and label it clearly and place it in a greenhouse or on a windowsill. These protected seeds will germinate more quickly than the rest of the packet sown outside, and it is a good way of identifying your annuals among the weed seedlings.

LEFT Hollyhock seedlings in individual biodegradable pots, ready for planting out.

OPPOSITE Seed sowing is one of my favourite gardening jobs, because it promises so much for the months to come.

TOP Sowing large seeds into individual biodegradable pots.

MIDDLE Covering seeds with a thin layer of vermiculate to stop capping.

BELOW Healthy verbascum seedlings.

multipurpose compost or sand. This will be different in colour from the soil and will indicate where your seedlings should appear. Also label very clearly.

Always check for 'sow by' dates or 'packed in' dates. With fresh seed and good growing techniques the majority of seed will grow, and you then have a choice – either plant all your seedlings into the garden, or swap any spares with gardening neighbours.

COMPOST AND CONTAINERS

I make my own compost based on coir. Seed can be sown into pure coir, but I mix sieved garden compost, sharp sand, coir and soil from molehills for potting (when I showed this on *Gardeners' World* a well-known newspaper ran a headline saying 'Monty's Molehills Madness'). If you don't make your own, then always use a peat-free compost. Bark-based composts are good, but sieve out any large clods before use.

◆ COIR 7s are compressed discs of coir which, when soaked in water, swell into cylinders of growing medium perfect for seed sowing. Dab a couple of seeds into the top of each cylinder and place them side by side in a seed tray. They are easy to use, but remember to keep them moist.
◆ ROOTRAINERS are useful for most seeds but perfect for the sweet peas in the £20 garden. Sweet peas, and all legumes, need long root runs, and Rootrainers provide this. Clip the base together, fill with compost and sow your seeds as indicated on the packet. Stacked

OPPOSITE Four of the perennials grown in the £20 border. They all flowered in their first year, just months after sowing.

TOP LEFT The mallow, *Malva moschata f. alba*.
TOP RIGHT *Nepeta × faassenii*.
BELOW LEFT *Gaillardia* Goblin.
BELOW RIGHT *Verbascum phoeniceum*.

in the frame, the Rootrainers support each other. When transplanting the seedlings into the garden, simply unclip the base to reveal healthy roots supporting sturdy plants. Although each Rootrainer has a small surface area, they hold a lot of root and a lot of compost, so remember to water them adequately.

SEED CHOICE

Choosing the seeds to be sown and grown in the £20 border was tricky but fun. The hard part was not deciding what to have but what to leave out. The budget of £20 was strict and non-negotiable, and most single varieties of seeds capable of producing flower from an early sowing cost under £2 a packet. Annual seeds tend to be cheaper and are sown later in the year when conditions are good enough for seeds to germinate directly in the soil.

Perennial Flowers

Some of the single varieties of perennials at Berryfields:

◆ *Agastache rupestris*: each plant has warm, apricot-orange flowers contrasting purple calyces and fine, blue-green leaves. The bonus is that the foliage is aniseed-scented. Plants grow to around 60cm (2 feet) tall.
◆ *Linum perenne* 'Blau Saphir': gorgeous blue flowers are produced on lax stems that hopefully will wave in gentle summer breezes. No doubt about the plant, which grows to 30cm (12 inches) high, but who can honestly guarantee the weather?
◆ *Gaura lindheimeri* 'The Bride': this was the undisputed revelation of the

herbaceous borders at Berryfields last year. Planted as rootbound plug plants, it flowered all summer and well into winter. It has a dark green rosette of foliage and tall, delicate, white flowers tinged with pink. It is a rather tender perennial but well worth growing if treated as an annual.

◆ *Penstemon heterophyllus*: it produces electric blue trumpet blooms all summer long. The plants grow to 45cm (18 inches) and start to flower in June from an early sowing.

◆ *Salvia nemorosa* Select Rose: compact plants growing to 50cm (20 inches), and producing elegant spikes of deep lavender and pale rose-coloured flowers. A classic of any border, garden or container.

◆ *Dicentra scandens* 'Golden Tears': a superb climber that produced its first flowers late in summer but will get better each year. Growing up bamboo canes

MONTY'S CONFESSION
We originally planned sweet peas to give height in the centre of the border. The seeds were sown in spring and were being hardened off in the cold frames when mice got in and ate the lot. However, there was just enough money left in the £20 budget to cover this situation, and morning glory (*Ipomoea* 'Purple Haze') seeds were bought, sown, protected against mice and hardened off before replacing the sweet peas in the centre of the border. And guess what? The plants never really got growing and only one survived a cold spell in June 2004. As a result the bamboo canes looked quite naked during the revelation of the £20 border.

that were already in the garden, or costing a few pence, it will eventually make a stunning annual display of golden-yellow flowers.

◆ Lupin Gallery Dwarf Mixed: a reliable mix of colours on plants growing to 50cm (20 inches). The flower spikes are densely packed and the stature of the plants lends itself to strong impact statements in the £20 garden, or in any exposed position where taller lupins will be blown to pieces.

Annual Flowers
Used around stands and drifts of the perennials, a couple of packets of annual seeds finished off the garden design. Sweet peas produce wonderful scented flowers when grown up bamboo or spare split hazel posts, and larkspur makes graceful spires up to around 1.2m (4 feet) wherever height is required. Candytuft can extend the flowering season deep into autumn, and nigella will add a delicate, lacy touch to the planting plan. An alternative to carefully planning colours and sizes is to buy a mixed packet, or for £20 a few mixed packets, of annual seeds and rake them into well-prepared soil.

Mixed Packets
Packets of seeds containing a mix of either annual or perennial seeds are a good way to get a variety of plants for little outlay. Sow the contents of the pack on to moist compost in a seed tray placed in a propagator set at 15°C (59°F). The seedlings should be pricked out into individual pots or larger trays once they are large enough to handle. Although the

small print says that contents of the packs may vary, it is safe to assume that you will have seeds of delphiniums, lupins, achillea and dianthus in the mix.

Selection Packs

These are larger packs containing individual sachets of seed. The idea is that you pay for only one expensively coloured printed piece of packaging while buying, in some cases, six types of seed. One such collection used at Berryfields contained:

◆ *Achillea* Summer Pastels: oranges, reds and yellows all jostle for attention in this popular choice of seed. Plants grow to 60cm (2 feet) and flowers start to appear in July.

◆ *Gaillardia* Goblin: a bold perennial whose daisy-like blooms have a strong central red colour, radiating through to yellow petal tips. Plants grow to 40cm (1 foot 4 inches) and start flowering in June.

◆ *Malva moschata* f. *alba*: pretty white flowers with delicate pink stamens that will cool down any colour scheme. Plants grow to 70cm (2 feet 4 inches) and flowers are produced from June until October.

◆ *Nepeta* × *faassenii*: sprays of lavender-blue flowers add a gentle touch to the £20 border. Plants grow to 40cm (1 foot 4 inches) and flowers start to appear in June and last until autumn.

◆ Poppy Meadow Pastels: lending a loose touch to the border, the simple flowers in shades of orange, yellow and white are produced all summer long. Plants grow to 60cm (2 feet).

£20-BORDER BASICS

◆ Come up with a budget and stick to it.
◆ Shop around for better-value seeds – consider mixed packets.
◆ Prepare the soil before sowing or planting.
◆ Regularly weed the border.
◆ Mix annuals and perennials for short- and long-term displays.
◆ Allow plants to self-seed to save even more money next year.

LEFT It is vital to label seeds and seedlings clearly with the full name and date of sowing. We have a policy at Berryfields of writing a label for every container.

◆ *Verbascum phoeniceum* Mixed: the tallest of the plants in this collection, its spires of blood-red, pink and white flowers will add drama to the garden. Growing to 1m (3 feet), flowers appear from June until late summer.

Planting Out

Once the seeds have been pricked out and acclimatized to outdoor conditions, they should be planted into well-prepared soil. We spaced the perennials about 25cm (10 inches) apart, but these may have to be thinned a little as they mature. To add colour, freshness and a carefree texture to the border, annual flowers can be sown directly into the soil in the spaces between perennials each year.

A YEAR IN THE £20 BORDER

SPRING

◆ Sow first-year perennial seeds early in the spring. Sow indoors or in a greenhouse, following seed-packet instructions regarding heat requirements.

◆ Prick out perennial seedlings into individual pots to ensure unrestricted development of roots and plants.

◆ Harden off in late spring in readiness for planting out.

◆ In late spring, or when soil temperature allows, sow annual seeds directly into the soil.

◆ In late spring plant out hardened-off perennials.

SUMMER

◆ Make sure the plants do not dry out.

◆ Regularly weed to ensure plants get all the nutrients in the soil.

◆ Feed with seaweed extract – either as light dusting or a spray.

◆ Check for insect infestations and rub out small colonies before they become destructive.

◆ Enjoy the first flowers of the display.

AUTUMN

◆ Enjoy the display of perennials.

◆ Deadhead annuals to ensure a continuity of flowers through to the first frosts.

◆ Remove dead plants to the compost heap or

◆ Allow seed heads to mature and self-seed in the border.

WINTER

◆ Double dig the soil, incorporating heaps of organic matter.

◆ Remove all weed roots.

◆ Allow soil to settle and be broken down by winter rain and frosts.

◆ Place an early order for your seeds.

ABOVE The £20 border in July, with the pale end of the long borders behind, where the onopordums are at their dramatic best. The £20 border had not yet got into its flowering stride.

OPPOSITE The *Achillea* Summer Pastels Group planted at Berryfields were one of the undoubted successes of the £20 border, flowering over a long period and making loads of very healthy, strong plants from our one packet of seed.

'We have chosen to grow a mixture of *bedding plants, tender exotics* that can stay outside only between May and September before going back into the shelter of the greenhouse, and *hanging baskets.*'

the courtyard garden

THE BERRYFIELDS COURTYARD IS HIDDEN AWAY AT THE side of the house. It measures 6m x 3m (20 feet x 10 feet), and although it is shaded by the building in the early morning, in summer it is in sun from mid morning until evening. On three sides are white-painted walls, one of which is covered by a large climbing rose, while the fourth side is the house. The floor is cobbled and sloping and has great character. Because it is tucked away around a corner it probably gets shown less than we would like and less than it should — after all, there must be many people with a similar back yard, half shaded but filled with potential.

Ours has no borders, because the floor is stone, but we have many containers in there with a wide range of plants. We have chosen to grow a mixture of bedding plants, tender exotics that can stay outside only between May and September before going back into the shelter of the greenhouse, and hanging baskets. The truth is that if a container is large enough and is cared for with regular watering, a good potting mix and perhaps the occasional feed, then you can grow almost anything in this kind of yard.

THE EAST-FACING WALL

One of the most dramatic plants growing in the Berryfields courtyard is *Brugmansia arborea* 'Knightii'. You might also know this as datura or angel's trumpets. It can grow 3m (10 feet) tall and wide, forming a strong skeleton for the large, very dramatic, trumpet-shaped flowers. It is one of our tender plants and has to be taken to the greenhouse in early autumn, re-emerging in late spring when all risk of frost has passed. It is a member of the potato or Solanaceae family, but unlike potatoes and tomatoes, every part of brugmansia is poisonous. Even the perfume is said to be intoxicating. It's certainly strong and I think delicious, with one plant filling the courtyard with sweet scent on warm summers' evenings.

Brugmansia are native to South America, particularly the Andes. They can be grown outside on the Isles of Scilly and in some parts of the south-west, but not, alas, in the Midlands where Berryfields is situated. They are generally very vigorous plants and the container needs to be large to accommodate strong root growth. The compost has to be well drained and rich because they are greedy feeders, and when planting up plants we used a mix of equal parts of organic potting compost, sieved garden compost and horticultural grit. Watering and feeding are the keys to success, as the large leaves result in high water loss. Plants can recover once wilted, but flowers are often aborted if plants are allowed to dry out. On the other hand, plants should never become waterlogged. Once the flower buds are forming, and this can be as early as May, help the plants with a weekly feed of dilute seaweed extract.

Brugmansia takes very easily from cuttings, and the best time to do this is when you take the plant indoors in early autumn. Shoots suitable for cuttings are this year's growth. Cut 15cm (6-inch) lengths, stripping off the lower leaves, and insert into a cutting compost that is at least 50% grit or perlite. Water, label and place a plastic bag over the pot. Put the pot on a warm windowsill. Alternatively, place the pot in a heated propagator set at 18°C (65°F). Cuttings will quickly root and need to be potted the following spring. Plants in greenhouses or conservatories can be hard pruned in spring, which will stimulate vigorous new growth. This is also another opportunity to take cuttings.

Lonicera hildebrandiana, or giant honeysuckle, is aptly named. It produces the largest plants, leaves, flowers and

PREVIOUS PAGE, LEFT The courtyard in late August. Judging by the direction of the shadows, this was taken in the late afternoon.

PREVIOUS PAGE, RIGHT *Pelargonium* 'Decora Lilas'.

OPPOSITE *Brugmansia arborea* 'Knightii' showing its deliciously fragrant, white flower trumpet.

fruit of all the honeysuckles. It is native to Thailand and south-west China, growing in forests and reaching the tops of the tallest trees. Grown in a conservatory, it can soon take over, but grown in the Berryfields courtyard and brought under protection from mid autumn to late spring, it reaches a controllable 2m (6 feet). It is evergreen, and its leaves are broadly oval and up to 15cm (6 inches) long. Flowers appear in terminal leaf axils from June to August and are white, changing to rich yellow and sometimes flushed orange. Young plants do not flower well, but once they are established and more than four years old, you can expect flowers every year followed by red-black berries 3cm (1¼ inches) long. It is best grown in a sunny position and in a well-drained compost. Even though the weather and container will severely limit its growth, be sure that the supports are robust as the weight of the plant when growing is considerable.

Trachelospermum jasminoides, or star jasmine, is a slow-growing climber but given time is capable of reaching 9m (30 feet). The leaves are narrow, shiny and dark green, and the highly scented flowers are white and produced in summer. It is native to central and south China, and is frost-hardy when grown in well-drained soil and either a sunny or semi-shaded position. It stays outdoors all winter at Berryfields, because it is growing against the end wall in the courtyard garden, which provides protection and radiates back heat on sunny days. In colder areas it is wise to provide some winter protection.

Camellias

There are over two hundred species of camellia, most of which originate from China and South-east Asia. While a majority will grow in the UK, camellias need either neutral or acid conditions, and at Berryfields the only site where the soil is naturally acidic – and then only slightly so – is in the woodland. In general my gardening philosophy is to grow only plants that naturally thrive in the conditions available and to make the most of the plants that are at home in your garden. Luckily, however, camellias can be grown in containers, using a neutral or acidic compost. There are three main ways to create appropriate compost conditions when growing camellias in containers:

◆ Use peat. There are no circumstances in which we would use peat at Berryfields, as to do so is to deplete a precious natural resource and to encourage further stripping of rare wetlands. It is against all the principles used at Berryfields and not recommended by the RHS, the National Trust or any responsible growers.
◆ Use sulphur chips, which will temporarily lower the pH. This is allowed if one is gardening organically, but it is a short-term solution and not one I favour. If you do use sulphur chips, always use in accordance with the manufacturer's instructions.
◆ Use composts with a low pH from sources other than peat. Composted bracken will provide this, as will compost with a high proportion of pine needles.

MONTY'S CONFESSION

It is impossible to feel the same level of affection for all plants. Some you like more than others; and some, I find, I can never grow to like at all. Camellias fall into this category for me. I can see why other people get pleasure from them, and on a big scale, as woodland planting, they are very impressive, but I have a problem with the uneasy relationship between the texture of the flowers and those glossy, hard, green leaves. It doesn't work for me.

The last course of action, using a non-peat neutral compost, is the best solution if you must grow plants that are not naturally at home in your non-acidic soil. Many camellias are perfectly happy with a pH of 6–6.5.

Camellias need a cool root run and plenty of moisture, but never allow them to become waterlogged. A woodland site is ideal, but any overhead shade is good. Plants often flower more freely when exposed to full sun, but more care and attention has to be paid to watering and mulching. Bright, direct morning sun can damage flowers and buds if following on from a frosty night, as the speed at which the water in the plants melts causes the cell walls to rupture. A north- or west-facing position is best if this looks like being a problem. Camellia care is simple. Prune out straggly branches in April and, if you have a young plant, two to three years old, have horticultural fleece handy in the coldest spells of winter.

Shy-flowering camellias are a common problem. There are three main reasons:

◆ Flower buds start to form in late summer to early autumn for the following spring. Any spell of drought during this period may interrupt bud formation. The effect is seen only the following spring, when it is too late to do anything about it. Always make sure your camellias are well watered during this critical time. It's also a good idea to mulch with leafmould, which retains moisture in the container.

◆ Plants that are over-fed will put on leaf growth at the expense of buds and flowers. Never feed a camellia after July, and feed in April only if leaves are looking yellow and blotched.

◆ Some varieties shed flower buds. This happens if plenty of buds have formed, when smaller, immature buds are easily lost. There should be enough buds left on the plant to produce a good show.

When all the cultivars are taken into account, there are thousands of camellias to choose from. Most of the popular ones, and indeed most of the Berryfields plants, belong to one of two groups:

◆ *Camellia japonica*. Originally introduced in 1739 from China, the common camellia is large and evergreen with highly polished leaves. Flowers are produced any time from February to the end of May, depending on variety and local growing conditions. *C. japonica* 'Adolphe Audusson' produces large, semi-double, blood-red flowers. It's a vigorous yet compact plant. *C. japonica* 'Apollo' produces rose-red flowers that are sometimes splashed white. Leaves are pointed and twisted at their tips.

OPPOSITE Camellias are not my favourite flowers, yet they are undeniably striking and provide colour very early in the year, especially in a sheltered spot like our courtyard garden. Here are four camellias that we grow in pots.

TOP LEFT The double flowers of *Camellia × williamsii* 'Donation', perhaps the most popular of all camellias.
TOP RIGHT The blood red *Camellia japonica* 'Adolphe Audusson'.
BELOW LEFT The compact *Camellia × williamsii* 'Jury's Yellow'.
BELOW RIGHT *Camellia saluenensis*.

C. japonica 'Mathotiana Alba' produces pure white flowers, occasionally blushed pink. Flowers are double.

◆ *Camellia × williamsii*. This is a hybrid between *C. japonica*, giving the plant large glossy leaves, and *C. saluenensis*, which gives it the capacity to produce plenty of flowers. Cultivars are extremely free-flowering, some starting in November and others finishing in late May. Most important, these flowers do not fade on the tree as many camellias do, but fall when finished, thus avoiding the effect of used tissues that disfigures so many otherwise good camellias.

C. × williamsii 'Anticipation' has an upright habit and produces large, deep rose flowers. Perhaps the most popular camellia is *C. × williamsii* 'Donation', with its large, candy-pink flowers and vigorous growth. *C. × williamsii* 'Jury's Yellow' produces flowers in a mix of white and yellow. Growth is compact and upright.

HANGING BASKETS

We have a row of hanging baskets in the courtyard and they look good for a remarkably long season – in fact a well-grown and regularly tended hanging basket will add colour to a wall for months. The keys to success are:

◆ If you have a greenhouse, start early in the year. February is a good time to take cuttings, either from plants over-wintered from last year's baskets, or from established parent plants. This can be done only in heated conditions – a heated greenhouse is ideal.

◆ Grow cuttings on and plant up at the beginning of April. This is when the first hanging-basket plants start to appear at garden centres and it is a good time to buy and plant the basket up for hanging out later in the year. Choose the largest basket your wall or budget will allow. It will dry out slowly and hold more plants. Unclip one or two of the hangers to allow easy access to the basket. Stand it on an upturned pot to make working easier.

◆ Prepare to plant a basket up by lining it with a hanging-basket liner. There is a choice of liners – empty compost bags turned inside out with slits in are a good way to recycle unwanted bags; coconut-fibre mats are good; foam and plastic-lined foam are both now readily available; compressed fibres are useful.

◆ Place a small saucer in the base of the basket. This will act as a reservoir for water. Remember that there will be a lot of root in a relatively small amount of compost competing for water and nutrients.

◆ Place a layer of compost in the base of the basket and gently firm. The best mix is a peat-free multipurpose potting compost mixed with about 20% perlite. This gives the plants a good start of nutrients and a weight of compost slower to dry out than 100% peat-free multipurpose compost.

◆ A good tip is to wrap the leaves and shoots of trailing plants in newspaper. This will help when you are easing them through the slits and gaps in the liner and basket and makes the plants less prone to damage. Ensure that the small rootballs are in contact with the compost, add more compost around the rootballs and gently firm. Continue doing this until the basket is completely planted.

the courtyard garden

Avoid the temptation to over-feed containers or hanging baskets. This will only produce lush stems and foliage that attracts pests and potential diseases, and not the extra flowers that you really want. It is better to mix a rich, well-drained compost by adding sieved garden compost to a peat-free potting compost as well as sieved leafmould, if you have any, in equal proportions. This will provide steady nourishment for even greedy plants throughout a long season. If you do feed, use a dilute seaweed or comfrey liquid, which will primarily encourage healthy roots and flowers.

Plant upright-growing plants in the top of the basket. There should be a 3cm (1¼-inch) gap at the top of the basket. This is the watering space. It allows water to soak into the compost as opposed to running out down your arms and over your feet.

◆ When the weather is right – no frosts, warm day and night temperatures – your basket can be put outside. The earliest a basket should be hung outside is late May. Until then it should be hanging in a warm greenhouse or standing on an upturned pot in a conservatory or porch. Make sure the bracket is strong, as a developed basket is heavy.

◆ To ensure that your basket looks good from every angle, attach the swivelling section of a dog lead chain to the bracket and hang the basket on this. It allows 360 degrees of movement without any twisting of the chains.

◆ Water the basket every day. Do this in the evening and early morning, which gives the plants time to take up water before the sun begins to dry out the plants and compost. In hot, dry weather the basket may need watering twice a day. Water slowly to allow the compost to soak water up and to prevent too much run-off.

◆ At every watering remove all fading or dead flowers to encourage more flower production. The swivelling dog-lead chain makes deadheading around the basket easier.

◆ At the end of the season cut off all flowering shoots, put the basket in a warm greenhouse over the winter, allowing the plants to grow, and then use them as parent plants for fresh cuttings the following spring.

Hanging-basket Plants at Berryfields

◆ *Dichondra micrantha* 'Silver Falls' is a silver-leafed trailing plant with furry, silver leaves produced along strings around 1.5m (5 feet) long. It prefers full sun but will tolerate partial shade. Keep it moist but do not over-water. Seeds can be sown in March to produce large plants by May. They are becoming popular and are now available as small pot-grown plants in spring.

◆ *Lobelia* is very common but still one of the best hanging-basket plants and will grow in any situation. Choose the trailing types for baskets – look out for any name with 'fountain' in – Blue Fountain, Lilac Fountain, Rose Fountain and White Fountain – and Sapphire is a popular choice for dark blue flowers with a white eye. Trim off the end 5cm (2 inches) of growth once flowering fades, to encourage strong growth and more flowers.

◆ *Brachyscome*, or Swan River daisy, is a native of Australia with ferny foliage topped by a cushion of daisy-like flowers. White, lilac, pink or blue flowers are available, all with a central yellow eye. Sow seeds in March in a heated propagator, prick out into individual pots in April and plant out after the last frost in June. It needs high nutrient levels in the compost (sieved garden compost will provide this very adequately) and must never become waterlogged. A sunny position out of drying winds is best.

◆ *Nasturtium* is a rampant plant capable of growing in most conditions, although the best flowers are produced in poor soil or crowded conditions in full sun. There are many varieties to choose from, including 'Double Gleam Mixed', which has semi-double, scented flowers in a mix of yellow, oranges and reds, and 'Jewel of Africa', with its cream-striped leaves and a mix of red, orange and yellow flowers. Seeds can be sown directly into baskets when they are made up or sown individually into peat-free compost and added later in the year.

◆ Nolana, or Chilean bellflower, needs sun and a well-drained compost to produce its frilly-edged, blue flowers. It does not require as much water as other basket plants and is best when grown in a single-flower basket. The flowers are blue with white throats and yellow eyes and appear in June. Sow the seeds in a heated propagator in March, prick out, harden off and plant out in June.

◆ *Sanvitalia*, or creeping zinnia, is a good performer regardless of the summer conditions, but it thrives in a sunny position and requires well-drained compost. The yellow flowers with black centres are produced from July to early autumn. Sow seeds during March in a heated propagator and plant out after the last frost.

◆ Trailing pelargoniums are my favourite hanging-basket plant and always look good in any situation. They are also the easiest of all plants to grow, as they are happy in both sun and partial shade and the only consideration is to be careful not to over-water. Remove flower stalks as the blooms fade to encourage more flower production. Before the first frost, remove plants from the basket and pot up individually into potting compost mixed half and half with grit or perlite. Over-winter in a frost-free position (a cool greenhouse or cold frame is ideal) and water only when the leaves start to wilt. Repot in spring, replant the basket and hang out after the last frost.

DRY CONTAINERS – SUCCULENTS

Not all container-grown plants need a daily watering in summer. Succulents have adaptations that allow water to be stored and then used in times of drought. They are also suited to low levels of nutrients in the soil or compost. Containers, including hanging baskets, can be made up using just succulent plants. Well-drained compost is essential. Add horticultural grit in equal measure to any peat-free multipurpose compost. When watering it is important not to allow water to accumulate around the necks of plants, as this will cause rotting. It is also better not to splash the leaves of succulent plants with water, as drops can settle on the waxy or woolly leaves and

OPPOSITE *Echeveria lindsayana* forming an almost surreal mound of foliage and flower in a terracotta pot. It comes from Chihuahua in Mexico and was only discovered in 1972. We give ours very good drainage by mixing our potting compost with the same volume of grit. We also bring it into the greenhouse where it can rest protected from frost.

act as magnifying glasses in the sun, and then holes are easily burnt in leaves. Use echeveria, sempervivum, aporocactus or rat's tail cactus, epiphyllums and sedums to create exotic baskets and containers. Hang out only when frosts have finished.

WET CONTAINERS

More containers are now being offered without drainage holes. This saves the manufacturers time and money, but creates extra work for gardeners if drainage is required. But it is an ill wind that blows no one any good, and to those wanting to create mini wet or bog gardens these undrilled containers are a boon. Choose glazed terracotta or another material that is non-porous. Part fill the container with an aquatic compost. This is low in nutrients and more suited to bog conditions. Mix a handful of crushed charcoal into the compost. Any excess gases produced in the anaerobic conditions adhere to the charcoal, ensuring healthy root growth. Plant up, top-dress with gravel or pebbles to prevent water evaporation from the compost surface, and water well. Place in a partially shaded place. The courtyard at Berryfields has one wall that is shaded for most of the day, and we put our mini bog garden against this. Don't neglect to top up the water throughout the summer. Many bog plants are frost-tender, so containers need to be carried under protection for winter. The following plants are suited to a bog garden in a container:

◆ *Zantedeschia aethiopica* is a summer-flowering plant with funnel-shaped spathes and available in red, orange, yellow or white. A popular choice is *Z. aethiopica* 'Crowborough', with white spathes and yellow, club-shaped spadix.

◆ *Houttuynia cordata* 'Chameleon' is safer in a container where it cannot escape into the rest of the garden. If you can provide moist conditions it will appear everywhere, so do not set it loose in a pond. In a container the red, green and cream leaves and tiny white flowers need a semi-shaded position and plenty of water. The colour in the leaves is enhanced by sun, so do not plant in full shade. It is hardy and deciduous.

◆ *Equisetum scirpoides* is a low-growing member of the horsetail family with twisted, dark green stems with black tips. The plant has developed specialized aerenchyma cells, rather like straws, that transport oxygen from the leaves and stems to the roots growing in airless conditions.

◆ *Geum rivale*, or water avens, grows 50cm (20 inches) tall and produces dark red and pink, nodding, bell-shaped flowers from May to September.

BEDDING PLANTS

The courtyard at Berryfields provides ideal growing conditions for bedding plants – it is warm, sunny, enclosed by walls providing protection from wind, and in need of colour in summer. We also used bedding plants in other parts of the garden, and they are always useful as 'dot' plants, filling gaps throughout the year.

Spring Bedding

At Berryfields wallflowers dominated the spring bedding plant displays. As they

belong to the brassica family they shouldn't be planted in the same soil as other brassicas – cabbages, cauliflowers, broccoli, radishes, turnips – for three years. This prevents a build-up of parasites and a depletion of nutrients in the soil. Wallflowers, 'Blood Red', were planted in both the cottage garden and the courtyard garden to add spring colour. Wallflowers are biennials, and plants can be easily raised from seed. They can be sown in May and June in seed trays under cover or in drills in any spare soil. When they are a few inches tall, plant them out at 7–10 cm (3–4 inches) spacing into a spare piece of soil (the vegetable patch is usually the best place for this) and grow them on, pinching out the growing tip to encourage well branched plants, then lift them in early autumn and replant them in their flowering positions. If you have acidic soil, add a small amount of lime to the water when you water them into position to avoid club root. Wallflowers should be planted at the level of their first branches and planted firmly.

Summer Bedding

These are plants raised from seed, or bought as seedlings or plug plants in spring, grown on, hardened off and planted out either into display beds or into containers.

◆ *Cosmos bipinnatus* has fern-like foliage and a capacity to flower all through the summer, which makes it a popular choice. Single colours in pink, red or white are available, as are mixed plants. It is not hardy, so cannot be planted out until after the last frost. Cosmos does

RIGHT *Nemesia* is a good bedding annual but needs to be kept moist if it is to flower continuously. To help this, when growing them in a container, add extra organic material, such as sieved garden compost. This variety is 'Honey Girl'.

best in rich, well-drained soil in a sunny position. Grow your own by sowing seeds in March and planting out in June. Deadhead often to maintain constant flowering into autumn.

◆ *Lobelia* is an accommodating plant and isn't fussy about soil type or position. Its only requirement is water. Plants should never dry out. Blue flowers are the popular choice, with the variety 'Cambridge Blue' producing light-blue flowers and 'Crystal Palace' producing dark blue flowers and dark foliage. Sow seeds in February, prick out and then plant out in May and June.

◆ French marigolds grow best in a sunny position but will adapt to partial shade. Plants produce lots of flowers in a range of yellow, orange and red. Flowers can be either single or double. 'La Bamba' produces single flowers with gold and orange stripes, 'Durango Red' produces double, anemone-like flowers in mahogany red, and one of the popular French marigolds is 'Naughty Marietta' with its golden-yellow blooms with a maroon blotch.

◆ *Nemesia* is easy to grow but will stop flowering if allowed to dry out. Plenty of

moisture and organic matter in the soil or compost will stop this from happening. Once you have planted it in the soil, pinch out the growing tips to encourage bushy plants. When the first flush of blooms has faded, cut the plants back to 10cm (4 inches) to encourage fresh growth and new flowers. *Nemesia* is not fussy about sun or partial shade. There is a growing number of varieties available, and popular choices include 'KLM' with its blue and white flowers, 'Orange Prince' with its vivid orange flowers and 'Tapestry' with its mix of yellow, blue, white and orange flowers. Sow seeds in April on a sunny windowsill and plant out in June.

◆ *Nicotiana*, or tobacco plant, is one of my favourite bedding plants. 'Lime Green' produces blooms in that colour that are unaffected by rainy summers, while 'Domino Series' produces flowers that open all day and are fragrant (some varieties are not). Without doubt the most striking tobacco plant is *Nicotiana sylvestris*. It produces candelabras of white flowers that will fill a corner of the garden with a muskily fragrant scent, on plants growing up to 1.5m (5 feet) high. They are easy to raise from the tiny seed, which should be sown in March. If you already have plants, collect seed from the sticky seed pods, sow in late summer or early autumn and over-winter in a greenhouse. Plants will be vigorous and will produce flowers in June and July. It is a perennial and will withstand mild winters outdoors, but in cold areas is best treated as an annual. It will self-seed if the ground is left undisturbed.

◆ *Petunia* thrives best in hot, dry summers. Almost every colour of flower

is available – 'Prism Sunshine' is yellow, 'Plum Purple' is plum purple and 'Pink Lady' is pink, resistant to rainy weather and produces enough blooms to cover plants. Seed is slow and erratic to germinate, requiring very high temperatures (24°C/75°F). If growing from seed, sow in January and prick out when plants are large enough to handle. Otherwise buy the plug plants (see opposite) available in spring. A sunny site is essential, and well-drained soil best. Container-grown plants grow well in an equal mix of peat-free potting compost and horticultural grit or perlite. Pinch out the tips of growing plants when they reach 10cm (4 inches) high to encourage branching and compact, bushy growth. Remove flowers as they fade.

RIGHT Petunias are ideal for containers or hanging baskets because they love dry conditions, especially if they are in full sun. These are *Petunia* 'Prism Sunshine'.

Autumn and Winter Bedding
Not many bedding plants flower in the winter months. However, winter-flowering pansies do an excellent job of

MONTY'S TIP
Hardening off plants is vital if they are to grow unchecked. Take a plant straight from the cosy shelter of a greenhouse to a container or border and they will react exactly as you would if you were taken from a warm bed to a cold bath. Do it by degrees. Start by putting plants in a cold frame for a fortnight before planting out, shutting the frame every evening to prevent cold night temperatures damaging plants. If you don't have a cold frame, simply put plants outdoors during the day and bring them back under cover in the evening. After a fortnight, and only when the outdoor conditions are suitable, place the plants in a sheltered spot for at least ten days, covering them with fleece at night if there is a cold snap. Only then, a full three weeks after they left the greenhouse, plant out your hardened-off bedding. There will be no check to growth and plants will perform better all summer.

filling this gap. Buy only plants that are already showing colour in their flower buds, as green plants will not actively produce buds in winter, and always remove flowers as they fade. If any flower is allowed to set seed, the plant will stop producing flowers until the seed is actually shed from the plant. When you buy plants in flower, remove all blooms immediately after planting. This may seem a bit drastic, but they soon grow back and it ensures healthy root growth and longer and more vigorous flowering throughout the winter. Once plants have exhausted themselves, cut them back to within 2.5cm (1 inch) of the soil and replant in a quiet, shadier spot in the garden.

Polyanthus will also hold flower buds in a dormant state before flowering in warmer spells during winter, although the main display is in early spring. Remember to water polyanthus, as they require moist soil. This also applies when the compost is frozen, as plants are still actively growing yet the roots cannot get water from the compost. Take containers into a warmer area to defrost and water thoroughly.

A main feature of the winter display at Berryfields is ornamental cabbage. The leaves are brightly coloured – you can have green, white, pink and purple on the same leaf – and the colours intensify as the temperatures fall. The leaves are edible but extremely bitter. Plants grow to around 30cm (12 inches) high.

Bellis daisies can be grown either in single colours or as a mix. Red, pink and white single or double daisies are all available from garden centres from autumn for immediate planting. They are frost-hardy and will hold their blooms throughout winter. Most gardeners grow *Bellis perennis* as a biennial, discarding plants once they have flowered, but if replanted in a shady part of the garden and watered throughout summer, the plants will flower again. The main flowering period is between March and July, but plants can be bought in autumn already in flower.

If you haven't the room to raise your own bedding plants from seed, there are other ways to obtain bedding plants.

◆ Seedlings are usually the first to arrive in nurseries and garden centres. Check that seedlings aren't etiolated, stretched and yellowing. Make sure the seedlings look healthy and haven't been exposed to cold. Seedlings need to be pricked out as soon as possible into pots of peat-free multipurpose compost. Carefully ease the seedlings out of the compost and lift individual plants by a pair of true leaves. Never handle the thin seedling stems. Gently firm and water. Place in a sunny position out of direct sunlight.

◆ Plug plants are young plants growing in plugs of soil. They are sold as trays and are generally good value for money. When buying trays of plugs look for healthy roots growing from beneath the tray. Never buy plants with yellowing leaves or damaged stems. Pot up plug plants into individual pots as soon as possible.

◆ Pots and modules (plastic trays moulded into small pot shapes) contain plants that are partially developed and have been growing in the containers for a few weeks. They are ready to be hardened off and planted in their final positions. Garden centres and nurseries often sell pots with open or slatted sides. Within each pot is one plant, often from a cutting. Roots are exposed and such plants need to be planted immediately. Do not remove the pot, as roots will grow out of the open sides and into the surrounding soil or compost. Removing the pot is not only unnecessary but would also damage the delicate roots. With modules, simply ease the pots out of their moulds and plant.

A YEAR IN THE COURTYARD GARDEN

SPRING

◆ Sow many bedding plants under protection. Provide heat from heated propagators.

◆ Plant up hanging baskets early on.

◆ Buy plug plants early when there is plenty of choice.

◆ Warm up compost before potting up tender bedding. Place compost in a greenhouse for a couple of days before using it.

◆ Keep tender plants under cover.

◆ Begin to harden off a fortnight before planting out.

SUMMER

◆ Plant out tender plants only when all frosts have finished.

◆ Continue sowing nasturtiums for continuous displays of flowers.

◆ Deadhead all flowers as they fade.

◆ Water hanging baskets and containers every day if the weather is dry.

◆ Even when it has rained, water hanging baskets, as walls can shield the basket from rain.

◆ Feed all container plants with seaweed extract to encourage flowering and strong growth.

◆ Top-dress established plants growing in large containers if the roots are exposed.

AUTUMN

◆ Lift tender plants under cover.

◆ Lift pelargoniums before the first frost and repot individually. Reduce watering.

◆ Collect seed wherever possible and either sow (for example, *Nicotiana sylvestris*) or store in airtight containers for sowing in spring. Don't forget to label the containers.

WINTER

◆ Order seeds when catalogues become available.

◆ Clean all empty containers and store.

◆ Ensure that propagators are in working order and are clean.

◆ Wrap containers with bubble plastic if the weather is extremely cold and likely to cause damage.

ABOVE Ornamental cabbages thrive in temperatures that would destroy most of our other plants in containers in the courtyard garden, and provide winter and spring colour.

OPPOSITE *Cosmos bipinnatus* 'Dazzler'. If the spent flower heads are pinched out almost daily, this will flower in a mass of colour, backed by its delicate foliage, well into the autumn.

'Cottage gardens are not the place for exotica. They should have the *comfort* and *familiarity* of a much-loved armchair. Free-flowering abundance is more important than a *rare* or *difficult* plant that displays your horticultural skills.'

the cottage garden

THE PHRASE COTTAGE GARDEN EVOKES A LOOSE,
informal style of gardening, with roses scrambling around
the windows and the path to the front door flanked by pinks,
sweet William, snapdragons, hollyhocks, delphiniums, lupins
and phlox. It is a style that has become identified with rural
charm, innocence and a sense of harmonious abandonment.
In fact the cottage garden evolved out of harsh necessity and
always included a mixture of decorative and edible plants.
The result was a utilitarian jumble with a heavy stress on
fruit, herbs and vegetables, and the only grass was on narrow
paths between the beds.

The nearest modern equivalent to this is to be found on any allotment site, where rows of beans or cabbages grow cheek by jowl with sunflowers, sweet peas or antirrhinums. But at Berryfields, where we already have a big, productive vegetable garden, I wanted to capture the spirit of the cottage garden while at the same time making an entirely decorative, floral place.

One of the features of cottage gardens is that they were never planned or designed. It seems to me that this is the most useful inheritance for the modern gardener from this tradition. If you can let the garden grow up around you, then you will tap into a much looser, freer kind of creativity. You simply plant according to the dictates of surrounding plants and your own intuition, mixing shrubs, flowers, herbs, fruit and vegetables in an entirely unstructured way. This takes quite a lot of confidence and courage, but the results are both modern and much more like old-fashioned cottage gardening. It is also in line with modern organic theory. By planting the garden as a happy jumble you are avoiding a concentration of pests and diseases that monoculture encourages.

SITE
At Berryfields the cottage garden is situated at the back of the house, the other side of the wall from the long borders and straddling the path. The total area is 7m x 10m (23 feet x 33 feet). The peachy-coloured brick of the house on one side and the lovely little barn building on the other set the tone as well

as the dominant colour scheme. This is a domestic garden and I wanted to relate to the house in every way.

We inherited what amounted to two very large borders, with the one furthest from the house built up into two tiers by a low stone wall. The soil, like most of Berryfields, was heavy and compacted, with much buried rubble from the old farmyard.

HARD LANDSCAPING
The low wall dividing the upper and lower sections of the cottage garden was tumbledown but added to the charm of the garden. We thought of rebuilding it, but decided that its slight wonkiness suited the style of the planting much better than a neatly repaired construction such as we made for the dry garden. However, we needed a basic path to the upper level, where a small seating area was planned. A formal paved area wouldn't look comfortable in this garden, so the remains of paving, bricks and walling used in other projects were retrieved from the rest of Berryfields and a small diamond-shaped area was laid, keeping to courses but mixing the materials.

The plan was always to leave planting areas between the bricks and off-cuts on the floor, but that didn't mean the construction of the flooring could be compromised. Wobbly stones and bricks are deeply irritating and invariably mean wobbly chairs and table. However, laying the paving was very straightforward:

the cottage garden

◆ Soil was removed from the top area of the cottage garden where the seating area was planned. This was done to a depth of 10cm (4 inches).

◆ A 5cm (2-inch) layer of broken bricks and hardcore was placed on the soil and tamped firmly down.

◆ A 5cm (2-inch) layer of sharp sand was then placed on the hardcore and tamped down. This formed a firm base.

◆ Because the paving slabs and bricks were of uneven depth, levelling pegs weren't used. If all the slabs were of equal thickness, pegs would be driven to the sand and hardcore and levelled against each other to ensure a flat foundation ready for slabs.

◆ A mortar consisting of six parts cement to one part building sand was mixed, and small beds were put on the sand and hardcore base. The brick or broken slab was then firmed into the mortar. This was done over the whole of the seating area, each piece of slab being levelled with the next. The area was out of bounds for a couple of days while the mortar set.

◆ It was a quick and easy flooring project, as we wanted large gaps between some of the bricks and broken slabs for planting. It was therefore unnecessary to point or fill in the gaps between the bricks and paving slabs.

PREPARATION AND PRUNING

There was not much in the borders that we wanted to keep. (Actually, as with the long borders, by the time we had removed the ancient hybrid tea roses and discounted the forget-me-nots and daffodils, there was not much there at all.)

There was, however, a very overgrown lavatera, or mallow, that would suit our purposes well, and a ribes and a forsythia, which also fitted the scheme. So these were kept, although severely pruned. The theory was to rejuvenate the plants, encouraging new growth on which, in the case of forsythia and ribes, flowers would form next spring, while the lavatera would produce a few flowers this year but, more important, a strong framework of branches full of energy. It worked. The lavatera almost immediately began to shoot from the base, with dormant buds along the stump breaking and forming new shoots. The new growth of the ribes and forsythia quickly formed, and the inherited backbone of cottage garden

shrubs was brought to life. The area hadn't been cultivated for many years and the soil was heavy and compacted. It was also riddled with bindweed. Then we double dug the ground over, getting rid of the compaction, weeding carefully as we went and adding plenty of muck.

PLANTS

We have tried to create a relaxed planting style in these cottage garden borders at Berryfields. The great joy of cottage gardening is that everything and anything can be added to the mix. We have not included vegetables or fruit in our borders, but the spirit of that eclectic planting is there with the easy jumble of plants. There are no rules other than to listen to your own instincts and give the plants the conditions in which they will thrive. Cottage gardens are not the place for exotica. They should have the comfort and familiarity of a much-loved armchair. Free-flowering abundance is more important than a rare or difficult plant that displays your horticultural skills.

Pink is an important colour in any soft, gentle planting scheme like this – after all, this should be pretty rather than dramatic and certainly never hard-edged. The combination of white and red will, of course, provide scores of different variations, but on the whole we have gone for the paler end of the pink scale, although a note of blue adds depth without being garish. So we are planting columbine (*Aquilegia*), bleeding hearts (*Dicentra spectabilis*) and lupins (*Lupinus polyphyllus*), which have been bred from their original purplish blue introduction from America in 1826. If you prefer single colours there are many varieties to choose from, including a number of good pinks. We have planted the pink cranesbills *Geranium endressii*, *G.* × *riversleaianum* 'Russell Prichard' and *G.* × *oxonianum* 'Claridge Druce'

MONTY'S TIP
Many of the plants in the cottage garden flowered almost immediately after planting. That was great for the camera but not the best practice for the garden. To make the most of the plants, especially the perennials such as delphiniums and lupins, it is a good idea to pinch out these first flowers that appear on young plants. This might seem impossibly harsh, but cottage gardening is not a quick fix and the plants then put all their energies into bulking up, forming compact, bushy specimens, and next year's display will be better.

and pink peonies and oriental poppies – all archetypal cottage garden plants.

Mix blue with pink and let the spectrum between them of mauves and lilacs have full rein, and you cannot help but capture the true cottage garden spirit. Bellflowers (*Campanula*), knapweed (*Centaurea nigra*), catmint (*Nepeta*) and *Anchusa* 'Loddon Royalist' are all good blue perennials. A good blue clematis like 'Perle d'Azur' can be allowed to scramble through a rose or other shrub and then be pruned back hard each spring. If the site is well drained and sunny, then the bearded iris, *Iris germanica*, is a true cottage plant. If the ground is heavy and wet, then *Iris sibirica* will grow in a border even though it is usually thought of as a bog plant.

Annuals and biennials have an important part to play. They can be allowed to self-seed freely as part of the general air of carefree enjoyment of all that is soft and sensual in the garden. Certainly a cottage garden is no place for gardeners who

wish to control every leaf and twig of their garden. So all the annual poppies, from the yellow *Meconopsis cambrica* to Shirley poppies and the magnificent opium poppy, *Papaver somniferum*, have been included. I would like to include the fabulous blue Himalayan poppy, *Meconopsis betonicifolia*, but I suspect that conditions would not be ideal for it. But it might be worth a try. Snapdragons (*Antirrhinum*), cornflowers (*Centaurea cyanus*), sweet peas, sunflowers, annual mallows (*Lavatera*) and love-in-a-mist (*Nigella damascena*) are all hardy annuals that can weave among more permanent planting, while half-hardy annuals like cosmos, tobacco plants and annual pinks (*Dianthus*) are all appropriate.

Biennials seem to me to be right at the heart of cottage garden philosophy. They are tough, quick but not flashy, and tend to seed themselves with abandon. We include forget-me-nots, wallflowers, sweet William (*Dianthus barbatus*), Canterbury bells (*Campanula grandiflora*), foxgloves – both white and purple, Honesty (*Lunaria*), Brompton stocks, pansies, and sweet rocket (*Hesperis matronalis*), which has been growing in cottage gardens for the past 600 years.

Bulbs such as snowdrops, crocus, hyacinths, fritillaries, Solomon's seal, snowflakes (*Leucojum*), daffodils, tulips and alliums are essential right in and through the borders, and later in the year lilies (especially the madonna lily, *Lilium candidum*), crocosmia, gladioli and dahlias are all an important part of the planting balance.

LEFT Cottage garden plants are suffused with romance and colour.

TOP Lupins are stalwarts that immediately add unselfconscious colour and gaiety to a border. This is *Lupinus* 'The Governor'.

MIDDLE One of the things I love about cottage garden plants is that so many have beautiful names and love-in-a-mist (*Nigella damascena*) is almost as beautiful as the flower itself. It is an annual that will self-seed happily from year to year.

BELOW The Himalayan poppy, *Meconopsis betonicifolia*, has perhaps the most brilliant blue flowers of any in the plant world. It can be tricky to grow unless you have slightly acidic soil and mild conditions with moist air. However, it is worth trying just for the sake of that astonishing azure blue.

Lupins: Large spires of colour are an essential ingredient of cottage gardens. The soil must not be acidic and lupins do best in a well-drained soil and a sunny or partially shaded site. If growing from seed it is best to sow fresh seed, and germination will be within the week. For the first year they will slowly establish themselves and it is a good idea to nip out early flowers to help the plants establish. *Lupinus* 'Chandelier' is yellow, *L.* 'The Governor' is blue and white, *L.* 'My Castle' is red and *L.* 'Noble Maiden' is creamy white.

Delphiniums: These are a must, and the *elatum* hybrids are perhaps easiest to grow. They have a good range of soft colours, although my own personal prejudice is that delphiniums lose part of their essence if they are not blue. Of the *Delphinium elatum* hybrids, the King Arthur Group, 'Nimrod', 'Nobility' and the Black Knight Group will all give you rich, dark blues. 'Fenella', 'Blue Tit' and 'Blue Nile' are lighter, clearer tones. My other prejudice is that delphiniums must be tall. This is not the place for dwarf hybrids, even in a small garden. Let them grow proud and tall – and blue. Delphiniums grow best in a well-drained soil. Add plenty of well-rotted manure at planting time. A sunny but sheltered position is best, and they will need staking. Take precautions against slug and snail attack – growing plants under cover until they are larger will help. Pinching out the growing tips when plants reach 45cm (18 inches) high will help produce stocky plants. Cut back the flowering stems in July to encourage another flush

of bloom. It's best to lift clumps every three years, divide into smaller plants and replant. The best time to do this is in early spring, just as you see new growth appear.

Delphinium cuttings can be taken from the first new shoots in spring.

◆ Remove strong shoots, 10cm (4 inches) long, from parent plants.
◆ Remove lower leaves.
◆ Push the cuttings into pots of gritty compost (add horticultural grit to peat-free multipurpose compost).
◆ Water, drain, label and cover the pots with a clear plastic bag.
◆ Place the pots in a warm, bright position out of direct sunlight.
◆ Remove the bags and pot up when roots are seen growing through the base of the pots.

Verbascum: Most verbascum originate in Turkey and western Asia, where they grow in sun-baked, impoverished soil, and they like a sunny site with well-drained soil. Many verbascum are biennials, producing their distinct rosette of leaves in the first growing year, flowering and setting seed (which can become invasive) in the second, and then dying. Even perennial verbascum can die after three or four years. *Verbascum chaixii* is a perennial, growing and flowering year on year, growing to 1m (3 feet) high and producing spires of yellow flowers. *V. chaixii* 'Gainsborough' produces creamy-yellow flowers and is also long-lived. *V.* 'Helen Johnson' appeared as a chance seedling in Kew

Gardens and is now a firm favourite. The spires of buff copper-pink flowers have appeared in most show gardens and domestic gardens since its discovery twenty years go. It's also in the cottage garden at Berryfields. There are other flower colour choices: *V.* 'Clementine' produces pale orange flowers with a violet eye, whereas *V.* 'Virginia' produces multiple stems of white flowers with purple centres.

Hybrid verbascum are sterile. Vegetative propagation is the only way to increase the number of plants for free. Taking root cuttings is the easiest and most successful way. It can be done at any time of the year, but autumn creates less disturbance to the parent plant.

- Cut a pencil-thick root into 5cm (2-inch) lengths.
- Lay the cuttings on the surface of peat-free multipurpose compost in a full-size seed tray.
- Cover with a 1cm (½-inch) layer of vermiculite.
- Water and allow to drain.
- Label and place in a greenhouse or on a windowsill out of direct sunlight.
- Shoots will appear through the vermiculite along the length of the cuttings. Shoots appear before roots are formed, so wait a few weeks before potting up.
- When roots appear through the drainage holes in the seed tray, pot the plants up into individual pots of peat-free multipurpose compost.
- Never allow cuttings or plants to dry out.

MONTY'S TIP
Whenever planting plants to climb up canes or supports, plant them on the inside of the supports. This protects them and stops any accidental nicking with the hoe when weeding. The everlasting sweet peas in the cottage garden were planted like this and developed into strong plants.

Honeysuckle: These evergreen, semi-evergreen or deciduous, woody stemmed, twining climbers often produce deliciously fragrant flowers in summer. This scent is stronger at night, and the flowers are pollinated by hawk moths and bees. All honeysuckle grows best in fertile soil in sun or partial shade. *Lonicera henryi* is a vigorous evergreen honeysuckle with downy shoots and yellow flowers stained red. Blue-black berries are formed in early autumn. *L. japonica* 'Halliana' produces very fragrant, white flowers that fade to yellow, and *L. × brownii* 'Dropmore Scarlet' produces clusters of bright scarlet, tubular flowers from July through to early autumn. In the cottage garden at Berryfields fragrance was top priority and *L. periclymenum* 'Graham Thomas', which was originally found growing in a Worcestershire hedgerow in the early 1960s, is one of the best for fragrance, its white flowers changing to yellow with age, and each producing a strong perfume. Two were planted to grow up a wigwam of hazel poles in the lower section of the cottage garden.

Roses: We removed the existing roses because they were old and tired rather than because they were necessarily

unsuitable. In fact, a cottage garden has to have roses, although I think that the shrub varieties are closer to the spirit than most hybrid teas. So we have chosen a range of blowsy, soft shrub roses, including 'Königin von Dänemark', an alba whose ruffled pink petals are highly scented; 'Charles de Mills', one of my favourite roses of all, a gallica with flowers whose rich crimson massed petals look as though they have been sliced off with a sharp knife; the bourbon 'Madame Knorr' (previously 'Comte de Chambord'), which is a compact shrub but has large pink flowers that are produced all summer long; and the modern Cottage Rose, which has old-fashioned, cupped, pink flowers. Bare-rooted plants were bought at the end of winter just before growth appeared but well before the cottage garden was ready for planting up. It's an economic way to buy roses – lifted from the nursery without soil – but they must be either potted up or planted out.

Potting up is easy. Choose a large container with drainage holes and spread the roots out on a layer of peat-free multipurpose compost. Fill around the roots with more compost, firm in, water and put in a sunny position until it is ready for planting out. With the Berryfields cottage garden there was a gap of two months between potting up the bare-root roses and the final planting out. When planting any rose, dig a large planting hole and add plenty of organic matter to the soil. Water the potted rose well before planting. When taking out of the pot, try to keep the rootball together,

although with freshly potted roses this is difficult. Ensure that the grafting point – the bulge on the stem where the chosen 'top' variety has been grafted on to the lower rootstock – is at least 2.5cm (1 inch) below the soil level. This stops the plant from rocking around, reduces sucker formation and prevents this potentially weak spot from being nicked by an over-enthusiastic hoe. Refill with a soil and organic matter mix, firm in, water well and label clearly.

Foxgloves: These have a happy tendency to arrive in most cottage gardens on their own. Some are biennial and others are perennial. The biennials – such as the familiar *Digitalis purpurea* – self-seed freely all over the garden. Foxgloves do best in semi-shade and moist, well-drained soil, but will grow virtually anywhere. *D. purpurea* is a short-lived perennial growing 1.5m (5 feet) high, producing a rosette of green, oval leaves and tall spikes of purple, white or pink-spotted flower spikes in summer. *D.* × *mertonensis* forms clumps of leaves and coppery-mauve flowers on spikes 75cm (2½ feet) tall. Once plants have become established it is best to divide them into smaller ones immediately after flowering. Ease the plants out of the soil and gently pull apart new plants, complete with roots. These are then replanted elsewhere in the garden. This technique ensures that all plants retain their enthusiasm for flowering.

Aquilegias: One of the nice things about cottage gardens is that they encourage use of the old-fashioned plant names, and none is nicer than the columbines,

or granny's bonnets. They are short-lived perennials, native to Britain, and are one of the oldest of British garden flowers. Aquilegias thrive in sunny positions and well-drained soil. They invariably cross-pollinate freely, so special varieties must be kept well apart if they are not gradually to become a muddy mixture – although I am rather fond of the general random colours that are produced as a result. I always cut back the whole plant after flowering to encourage new growth, which often produces a fresh batch of flowers.

Corsican mint, or *Mentha requienii*, was planted in the larger cracks on the flooring. We filled the cracks with an equal mix of peat-free multipurpose compost and horticultural grit and planted into this. Clumps can be pulled apart to form smaller plants to fit smaller spaces. It grows low, reaching 4cm (1½ inches), and can produce light purple or white flowers. The leaves are highly aromatic when crushed – in this case by our feet. Corsican mint will also grow quite happily in the shade.

Geraniums: The hardy geranium is a good old-fashioned plant and, unlike the scented-leafed pelargoniums grown in pots and placed in the Berryfields cottage garden, is as tough as old boots and will stand any amount of cold. *Geranium cinereum* 'Rothbury Gem' is a dwarf geranium growing to 15cm x 25cm (6 inches x 10 inches). It needs a sunny position to produce masses of mid pink, darkly veined flowers with raspberry-red eyes. Cut the whole plant back hard to encourage vigorous regrowth with a fresh batch of flowers. It requires a moist, free-draining soil.

Everlasting/perennial sweet peas need lots of organic matter in the soil, and the soil needs to be moist yet well-drained. Plants will produce masses of flower from summer through to autumn and can reach 3m (10 feet) in a season. Cut them down in mid to late autumn and the plants reappear in the following spring. The flowers are unscented but are available in a choice of colours. *Lathyrus latifolius* 'Red Pearl' is red, *L. latifolius* 'Rosa Perle' is rose-pink and *L. latifolius* 'White Pearl' is, would you believe, white.

Scented-leafed Pelargoniums in Pots

Scented-leafed pelargoniums are not hardy and need to be taken under protection in autumn. They can be grown as houseplants, greenhouse plants or, best of all, outdoors in the cottage garden throughout summer. Terracotta pots are best, as they keep roots cool and retain water better than small plastic pots – and they look much nicer! Use a well-drained compost, consisting of peat-free multipurpose compost mixed 50:50 with horticultural grit. Drainage and sun are the two vital elements to success with scented-leafed pelargoniums. Although many gardeners (myself included) have neglected their pelargoniums and still achieved good results, a fortnightly feed

RIGHT We are growing a number of scented-leafed pelargoniums in pots to keep in tune with the gentle, fragrant prettiness of the cottage garden. This is *Pelargonium crispum* 'Variegatum'.

with seaweed extract will create an even better display. Once planted, our pots were placed on the wall dividing the upper and lower areas of the cottage garden, where they look great and enjoy a full day's sunshine.

There are many varieties to choose from, with the following all being grown at Berryfields:

◆ *Pelargonium* 'Atomic Snowflake': pungent, tri-lobed leaves blotched and striped white, bright mauve flowers.
◆ *Pelargonium* 'Lara Jester': deeply cut leaf, lemon-rose scent, cerise-pink flowers with white eye.
◆ *Pelargonium* Fragrans Group: grey-green foliage with pine scent, white flowers.
◆ *Pelargonium* 'Mabel Grey': rough, deeply cut leaf with strong lemon scent, mauve flowers.
◆ *Pelargonium crispum* 'Variegatum': attractive cream-and-green-variegated leaf with lemon scent, pale mauve flowers, upright growth.
◆ *Pelargonium* 'Pink Capricorn': mauve-pink flowers with a white eye, shallow, tri-lobed leaves with lemon-rose scent.
◆ Pelargonium 'Old Spice': white, round leaf with spicy scent.
◆ *Pelargonium* 'Royal Oak': dark mauve, dark green, oak-leaf-shaped leaf with central dark blotch.
◆ *Pelargonium* 'Lady Scarborough': sweet lemon-rose scent, pink flowers veined purple.
◆ *Pelargonium odoratissimum*: apple-scented leaves, white flowers.

Lilies in Pots

Lilies are easy to grow in pots and *Lilium regale*, or the regal lily, is one of the best. Planted in long-tom pots (these are taller than usual pots and were originally used for growing tomatoes) in the Berryfields greenhouse in early spring, plants were in full flower by early summer. They are then easily placed in the cottage garden to add their delicious, heady scent. Always use well-drained compost for lilies – a peat-free potting compost mixed 50:50 with leafmould is ideal; failing leafmould, add grit to your potting compost. When planting lilies in pots, point the noses of the bulbs towards the edges of the pots. When the shoots begin to grow they reach the edge of the pot and grow upwards, following the pot line. This results in a balanced pot and an even display of shoots. Use a deep or tall pot as many lilies (including *L. regale*) are stem rooting, with roots formed on the shoots as they grow. These roots are vital to anchorage of plants in the compost or soil. Once growing, the bulbs should never dry out, nor should they become waterlogged. Many lilies are tall-growing – *L. regale* grows to over 1m (3 feet) – and should be staked to avoid breakages. A bamboo cane pushed into the pot and a loop of twine will keep everything in its rightful place – but be careful not to spear the bulbs when pushing the cane into the compost!

Lilies need a sunny position, although ideally their base is in shade. If bulbs are planted in the soil it is best to leave them undisturbed as bulbs are easily damaged. To ensure that bulbs are growing in well-

On the day that we filmed the planting-up of the cottage garden it poured with rain. All day. But the soil was in good condition and the plants went in. However, it takes a lot of rain to show up on camera – which is why films use huge rain machines – and nobody really noticed. Except that the grass path between the two cottage borders making up the cottage garden was churned into mud. Remember, it's not just the presenter who tramples around the garden but also the team of camera men, sound recordist, director, researcher, assistants, runners, producers, Uncle Tom Cobley and all. However, the grass recovered remarkably well. It was hosed down to remove the larger clods of soil, swept and left to its own devices for a week. The following week, when the cameras returned, the quagmire had returned to a semblance of a grass path.

drained soil, plant on a small mound of grit placed in the bottom of the planting hole. If you are worried about cold, wet winters (and just writing that certainly worries me) and your soil is on the heavy side, plant the bulbs in pots, and then plunge the whole thing into the soil and lift them in autumn. This is also a good way of avoiding slug and snail damage, as both are attracted to the young, emerging shoots in spring. Pots can be over-wintered in a greenhouse and plunged again when the shoots are taller and less attractive to slugs and snails.

BINDWEED CASE STUDY

Field bindweed (*Convolvulus arvensis*) was growing throughout the cottage garden. Its twining stems and pink and/or white flowers were growing through established plants. This is one of the worst garden weeds as it grows very strongly, wrapping itself round and eventually smothering even large plants. It is hard to get rid of, because it will reproduce from every tiny section of its roots. To make life even harder, these roots are extremely brittle and will easily snap as you try to dig them out. Leave the tiniest section behind and your border will soon fill up again with bindweed. Roots can grow as deep as 15m (50 feet) and one plant has the capability of spreading for 30 square metres (323 square feet) in one year. It can arrive in a garden from neighbouring land, on plants or in manures. Bindweed doesn't like disturbance and areas where little or no cultivation is done are where it is most prevalent.

TWO MAIN TYPES OF BINDWEED

FIELD BINDWEED CONVOLVULUS ARVENSIS	HEDGE BINDWEED CALYSTEGIA SEPIUM
Smaller shield-shaped leaves	Larger heart-shaped leaves
Flowers 2cm (¾ inch) across	Flowers can reach 3cm (1¼ inches) across
White/pink flowers	White flowers, often tinged pink
Deep-rooting	Shallow-rooting
Creeping roots	Fleshy roots

If your neighbours have a problem with bindweed it is a good idea to put a vertical barrier in the soil to prevent the roots from creeping into your garden. Even a concrete slab sunk vertically will stop some roots from entering your garden. Persistent hoeing and digging will weaken the plant, but remember that any piece of root left behind in the soil is capable of producing a new plant. The only solution is carefully to dig out every scrap of root, including those entangled in the roots of plants that you wish to keep. Double digging results in you seeing more of your soil and potentially having the chance of removing more bindweed roots. If, unlike us at Berryfields, you garden with chemicals, there are herbicides, but they are non-selective, killing every plant they come into contact with. Also residues from these chemicals, glyphosate and dichlobenil, may be left in the soil.

An alternative to removal is smothering. This is done with a permeable membrane that allows water to pass through but stops weed growth from growing up. It is only really practical where a piece of land has been cleared, or is in need of total clearance. The membrane is placed on the soil, and an organic mulch is placed on top to keep the membrane in place and improve its appearance. Planting is done by cutting crosses in the membrane and planting into the soil below, after which the flaps of the membrane are then folded back close to the stem. Even doing this it is important to weed around plants, as bindweed will see the chink of light and

COTTAGE-GARDEN BASICS
◆ Do not draw up a plan.
◆ Let your gardening instinct dictate what is planted.
◆ Mix species and colours of plants.
◆ Make room and time to sit in the cottage garden.
◆ Prepare the soil before planting and sowing.

LEFT The opium poppy, *Papaver somniferum*, produces both a beautiful flower and a seed head that is perfect sculpture. Like aquilegias it seeds promiscuously and you never know what each opening flower – which only lasts for a day – will be like. But I have yet to find one I did not like.

grow towards it. An alternative to synthetic permeable membrane is a thick layer of newspaper topped with shredded bark or leafmould. The idea with all mulches is to stop the light from reaching the plants.

A YEAR IN THE COTTAGE GARDEN

SPRING

◆ Sow annual seeds when the soil is warm. Weed-seed growth is a good indication that temperatures are high enough for annual germination.

◆ Keep weeding. A little every day is better than blitzing the garden every fortnight.

◆ Plant young plants, nipping out any early flowers to encourage bushy plants.

◆ Watch out for young colonies of aphids and squash them before they do lasting damage.

SUMMER

◆ Sow fast-maturing annuals in any gaps.

◆ Ensure that plants do not suffer from water stress. Water in dry weather.

◆ Nip off flowers as they fade if you want more flowers later and want to prevent self-seeding. If you want self-seeded plants, leave flowers to mature seed.

◆ Keep the hoe moving to prevent weed seeds – especially important if the ground has been double dug, as this exposes weed seeds to light and many will germinate.

AUTUMN

◆ Leave late flowers on the plants to self-seed or feed the birds.

◆ Take scented-leafed pelargoniums indoors or into a greenhouse for protection from frosts.

◆ Lift lily pots if plunged in the ground and take under protection or place near a wall. This will prevent waterlogging.

◆ Clear away all leaves from the soil to prevent disease.

WINTER

◆ If preparing a cottage garden on virgin soil, double dig the soil, removing all weed roots and incorporating organic matter.

◆ Order seeds and plants.

ABOVE The cottage garden in midsummer, just a few months after planting, with the path leading through the gates to the long borders. The small round table is an ideal place to retreat from the hustle and bustle of filming.

OPPOSITE Snapdragons are another of the familiar, old-fashioned flowers that look completely at home in a cottage garden.

'The whole point of a dry garden is that it is designed to **look good** even in times of drought. It is *never watered*, relying solely on rainfall for its irrigation. It is by no means the *biggest* or most *ambitious* project that we have undertaken so far, but I believe that it has been one of **the most successful.**'

the dry garden

THERE IS NO DOUBT THAT OUR CLIMATE IS CHANGING AS A result of global warming caused by our consumption of fossil fuels over the past hundred years. Our winters are becoming wetter and warmer and our summers hotter and drier. It is also certain that this trend will continue. The effect on our gardens has been profound and complicated, altering the life cycle of many insects and fungi and changing the flowering patterns of many plants, especially in early spring. But the most dramatic effect has been on the water supply to summer plants – especially from midsummer through to autumn.

Research findings from the Met Office's climate prediction model suggest that within the next seventy years winter rainfall will increase by 30%, but summers will be up to 50% drier. As always, the clever gardener works with nature rather than trying to fight it. So, to keep our gardens looking vibrant and healthy throughout the year, we must start to choose plants that are adapted to cope with periods of drought as well as create soil conditions that will avoid winter waterlogging.

The dry garden at Berryfields is situated behind the house and faces east, back towards the building. It is backed by a wall and has the gable end of another building on its south side, so is very sheltered and gets lots of sunshine except in the late evening. When we took the garden over it was a muddle, with some crazy paving, a small pond and an island bed. None of it worked together. So we took the whole lot out, kept the stone to make the retaining walls of the beds and used the site to create the dry garden.

The whole point of a dry garden is that it is designed to look good even in times of drought. It is never watered, relying solely on rainfall for its irrigation. It is by no means the biggest or most ambitious project that we have undertaken so far, but I believe that it has been one of the most successful. From the first day it has looked good, caused us no problems at all and shows that change – even unwanted change – can often provide the best opportunities.

In its own modest way, the dry garden at Berryfields is a really good example of working with nature. The Royal Horticultural Society has calculated that a well-stocked back garden, 35m x 9m (115 feet x 30 feet) needs an average of 19,550 litres (4300 gallons) of water to survive. In an ideal world that water would all fall as rain, preferably at night, just when the garden needed it. But global warming means that the majority of rainfall occurs in winter – when plants need it least – and most of that moisture will have gone by high summer when the demand for moisture is greatest and the rain most scarce. But our dry garden is designed not to require any artificial irrigation at all – and its success depends on creating the right conditions and choosing the right plants.

PLANT ADAPTATIONS

Choosing the right plants for the conditions you either already have or create is crucial to the success of the garden, because a plant forced into the wrong conditions will soon suffer. The plants chosen for the dry garden are all suited to well-drained, impoverished soil and are quite happy not to be artificially watered. The fact that they are suited to such conditions is no surprise when you look at how the plants are made up.

Plants take up water from the soil by osmosis via the roots and then lose water by transpiration through small holes or stomata in the leaves. So it is helpful to look at both the root and leaf adaptations that plants make to cope with periods of drought.

Leaf Adaptations

When selecting plants for a dry garden, the following adaptations may give clues to their suitability for the conditions:

◆ Plants suited to dry conditions often have small leaves. Larger leaves lose more water than smaller leaves.

◆ Leaves that grow close to the ground are less likely to be damaged by drying winds.

◆ Silver-coloured leaves reflect sunlight, reducing the heat stress on the plant and therefore reducing water loss. The same principle applies to white or grey leaves.

◆ Being hairy is a huge advantage in drought conditions. Hairs on leaves trap available water in the atmosphere, such as morning dew, and then channel this free water down to the stem, which in turn funnels it down to the roots. Hairs also capture water in the immediate layer of air surrounding the leaf surface, which increases the immediate humidity of the air and reduces water loss from the leaf as well as creating a tiny windbreak around plants. If that were not enough, hairs also reflect light.

◆ Leaves with waxy surfaces retain more water within the plant than non-waxed or naked leaves.

◆ Fleshy leaves are capable of storing water and releasing it only in times of need.

◆ Reducing leaves to prickly spines is the ultimate in leaf adaptation, but filling the dry garden with cacti wasn't an option at Berryfields. Warwickshire winters and springs are just too cold.

◆ The stomata of many dry garden plants are sunk below the surface of the leaf. It therefore takes longer for water to be lost by the leaf, as it has further to travel than in leaves where the stomata are at the surface.

◆ Some plants have leaves that may roll themselves up when under drought stress, such as some rhododendrons. This hides away the stomata and reduces wind over the undersurface of the leaf where most of the stomata are situated.

Root Adaptations

Roots are harder to inspect when choosing a plant, but the fact that they go largely unnoticed doesn't mean they lack adaptations.

◆ A large tap root on a plant suggests an ability to search deep for water. Research

hard cap of soil forming, which can prevent water from soaking into the soil. The plants were then watered in for the first and last time.

PLANTS

◆ *Artemisia schmidtiana* 'Nana' is a prostrate plant growing to 10cm (4 inches) tall with a similar spread. The fern-like silver foliage is silky-soft to the touch. Yellow daisy flowers are produced in late summer and it is ideal for growing either in walls or over the edges of walls. In the Berryfields dry garden it has been planted to grow over the edge of a wall. It is adapted to dry conditions by growing low to the soil and producing grey foliage.

◆ *Cistus* × *crispatus* 'Warley Rose' grows

to 40cm (16 inches) high with a 75cm (2½-foot) spread. This low ground-cover plant is suited to windy, exposed positions. I think that the pink blooms are softer and less harsh than some other cistus. They do not like being moved once they are planted.

◆ *Jasione laevis* 'Blaulicht' has narrow, hairy, grey-green leaves and blue, ball-shaped flowers on erect stems in summer. Plants grow 30cm (12 inches) high with a 15cm (6-inch) spread. Once the seed heads have ripened and shed their seed, remove flower-heads. They are prone to rotting in wet winters, so must have really good drainage. Hairy, grey-green leaves lessen the effects of scorching sun and reduce water loss.

◆ *Knautia macedonica* produces lax, wiry stems and globular flowers in shades of crimson in summer. Plants grow 75cm (2½ feet) high with a spread of 60cm (2 feet). Deadheading the flowers as soon as they start to fade encourages more flowering over a longer period. The roots form a fine network, enabling the plant to take up most of the available water in the soil.

◆ *Lavandula angustifolia* 'Munstead' produces blue flowers on dense, bushy spikes around midsummer. Plants grow 75cm (2½ feet) high with a similar spread. It's best to prune the plants, cutting off the flower spikes and a third of the growth, but without cutting back into old wood, to help maintain compact plants. The best time to do this is as soon as flowering has finished. Left unpruned, plants will develop bare, woody bases. The grey foliage and stems contain high concentrations of oil, which

reduces water loss from the plant.

◆ *Origanum* 'Thundercloud' grows to around 35cm (14 inches) tall with a spread of 50cm (20 inches). Masses of small, purple flowers are produced from early spring in warmer areas, through to midsummer. At other times of the year the bronze-coloured leaves are the main attraction. Cut back hard after flowering to retain a compact plant, although it is ideal for draping over and softening the edge of a wall. Release of oil from the leaves in times of water stress, making them aromatic, helps reduce water loss.

◆ *Salvia nemorosa* 'Rose Queen' is a naturally neat and compact plant. Plants grow to 1m (3 feet) high with a 45cm (18-inch) spread, and the deep rose-pink flowers are produced from late spring through to midsummer. To maintain a compact look to the plant it is best to lift and divide it every two years. Do this in spring, splitting plants so that each new individual has plenty of healthy shoots with a root system.

◆ *Scabiosa atropurpurea* 'Chile Black' is a fast-growing plant, growing to 1m (3 feet) high with a 50cm (20-inch) spread. Each plant produces wiry flower stems throughout summer and early autumn. The deep purple, almost black flowers are scented. A spadeful of home-made compost in the impoverished, dry garden soil will improve it, but go steady because too much organic matter will encourage lush foliage growth at the expense of flower production. Scabious can produce thickened roots capable of storing water for use in periods of drought.

◆ *Sedum* 'Purple Emperor' grows to 45cm (18 inches) tall with a similar spread. The fleshy leaves are waxy and crimson-purple. It is happy in very poor soil. When flowering in summer the yellow blooms attract butterflies. The thick leaves store water and have a waxy surface or cuticle, reducing water loss.

◆ *Teucrium* × *lucidrys* grows 2m (6 feet) high with a similar spread, and is planted near to the back of the dry garden's raised beds. It has hairy leaves and intense blue flowers that are produced from midsummer through to early autumn. It is easy to grow and take semi-ripe cuttings in summer from non-flowering shoots and it can happily take being cut back to size. Its hairy leaves help trap water in the immediate vicinity of the leaf, increasing humidity and therefore reducing water loss.

ALLIUMS CASE STUDY

Alliums are ideal flowering bulbs for any dry garden. Requiring well-drained soil and an open, sunny position, bulbs planted in the autumn will start to flower in the following summer. Planting allium bulbs in autumn is both easy and enjoyable. Planting holes can be scooped by hand out of freshly prepared raised beds and the bulbs dropped in, pointed end uppermost, and backfilled with soil. The only other rule worth observing is to plant bulbs to a depth of twice their diameter – not that I ever measure this, especially when planting hundreds of bulbs, but it pays to go as deep as possible. Alliums will look good drifting through a border, but plant them in clumps for a natural look and avoid spacing bulbs apart too much.

Most alliums will produce plenty of viable seed and are not shy about shedding it all around the garden. The wispy, grass-like seedlings will grow almost anywhere, and after three or four years of bulking up will eventually produce some flowers. The flower colour will be variable. It's a choice between leaving them to develop and having a naturalistic display, or ruthlessly removing them and maintaining order.

The dry garden at Berryfields has clusters of three different ornamental onions:

◆ *Allium hollandicum* 'Purple Sensation' is one of the earliest-flowering alliums, with the deep purple balls of flower held on stems 1m (3 feet) tall appearing in early May and lasting well into June. Once flowering is over, the drying seed heads turn the colour of straw. Along with most alliums, it's best to plant bulbs where the foliage will be hidden for most of the summer, as leaves turn straggly from midsummer onwards.

◆ *Allium karataviense* 'Ivory Queen' produces globes of white flowers on spikes 50cm (20 inches) high. The foliage is glaucous with a metallic sheen. Although the textbook descriptions always state that white flowers will be produced, don't be surprised to see occasional pink tinges to some blooms.

◆ *Allium sphaerocephalon* may have a tricky name but it has a lovely flower, produced after midsummer – later than most alliums – and is tolerant of most conditions. The flower spikes are 90cm (3 feet) tall crowned with small bell-shaped flower-heads that open green,

LEFT Alliums love well-drained soil and baking in the summer sun. We grow three varieties in the dry garden.

TOP *Allium karataviense* has two broad leaves with a purple streak.

MIDDLE *Allium hollandicum* 'Purple Sensation' is deservedly very popular, with long-lasting rich drumsticks of flowers.

BELOW *Allium sphaerocephalon* is a two-tone egg-shaped onion, with a burgundy top and a green and mauve bottom half. The result is a tapestry of flowers, produced much later in the summer than other alliums.

then take on a deep clover-red coloration. Individual bulbs soon develop into clumps and will need dividing to reduce competition for water, light and air. Divide in autumn when the leaves have died down, lifting clumps with a hand fork and splitting off individual plants, complete with roots, and replanting them elsewhere in suitable conditions.

TULIPS FOR DRY GARDENS

Tulips, as we have seen, all prefer growing in well-drained soil in a sunny position. We have kept the taller-growing hybrids to the long borders and containers. The smaller tulips – especially the species ones – are ideal as spring flowers in the dry garden, where we have five different tulips.

◆ *Tulipa* 'Little Princess' has tangerine-orange petals that flare in the spring sun to expose a cornflower-blue centre. It naturalizes well and can be left in the soil for years. Flower spikes grow to 30cm (12 inches) and plants spread to around 20cm (8 inches). It belongs to that catch-all division of tulips named Miscellaneous.

◆ *Tulipa humilis* 'Eastern Star' is another member of the Miscellaneous division, producing magenta-rose petals with a bronze-green flame and canary-yellow base. Flower spikes grow to 15cm (6 inches) high and bulbs should be spaced 10cm (4 inches) apart. Its narrow leaves are often edged with red.

◆ *Tulipa linifolia* has sickle-shaped, hairless leaves and bowl-shaped, red flowers. The rounded flower bases are often darker. It is a native of Uzbekistan

MONTY'S CONFESSION

It's always better to plant small as opposed to large plants. Small plants grow away quickly, often catching up on the larger specimens within a year or two. Unfortunately a television garden needs plants that the cameras can see. Sometimes, and the dry garden is a good example of this, larger plants are planted more closely together than they really should be to give an immediate strong visual effect for the camera. But plants can be moved once they become overcrowded, and we have already started to thin them.

and northern Iran. The leaves are 8cm (3 inches) long and the flowers are held 20cm (8 inches) high. This is another member of the Miscellaneous division.

◆ *Tulipa* 'Red Riding Hood' is a popular choice for its black-based, scarlet flowers amid dark green leaves that are often mottled purplish-maroon. It belongs in Division 14 of tulips – Greigii hybrids known for their single flowers and their wavy-edged, mottled and sometimes striped leaves. The flowers are held 30cm (12 inches) high and plants can spread to 20cm (8 inches).

◆ *Tulipa clusiana* var. *chrysantha* produces flowers that are yellow, and flushed red or brown inside with yellow stamens. The flower spikes are 20cm (8 inches) tall and plants spread to around 15cm (6 inches). It is another Miscellaneous division member. Many textbooks say that tulips have to be planted in late October into November. But I have often left my tulip planting to January without any ill effects, as a

OPPOSITE The yellow heart of the species tulip *Tulipa humilis* 'Eastern Star' is in fact the base colour, which is overlaid by the more dominant pink.

shortened but fast-growing season isn't a problem for tulips.

There are two choices when considering tulip planting. The first is to plant and forget about the bulbs. This is fine in the well-drained soil of a dry garden, but the quality of flowers may diminish over a period of five years. There is also an increased threat from tulip fire (see page 35). An option is to plant bulbs in aquatic baskets. These baskets have slatted sides that allow water to pass freely in and out of them. Bulbs are planted in a gritty compost in the basket, and then plunged into the beds so that the top of the basket is a few centimetres below soil level, are easy to find when the leaves have died

down and are therefore simple to lift and dry in a potting shed. Dried bulbs are then ready for planting the following autumn or winter. Individual bulbs should be spaced around 4cm (1½ inches) apart, and can be packed close together, although you should avoid having individual bulbs touching each other.

FINISHING TOUCHES

The dry garden was completed by spreading a 3cm (1¼-inch) layer of gravel over the soil around the raised beds and by planting up containers. Bare soil can be covered with a semi-permeable planting membrane, which will stop weed growth while allowing water to pass through. However, this would also stop self-sown seedlings from rooting, and we want the alliums and any other dry garden plant to self-seed in the gravel around the raised beds, so no planting membrane was used. The gravel mulch gives a bright appearance to the area, keeps the necks of the plants well drained and stops the soil from turning to mud.

Containers are useful when introducing tender plants to the area. The pink tinges to the fern-like leaves of *Acacia baileyana* 'Purpurea' and the white flowers of *Agapanthus* 'Snowy Owl' both complement the planting. Although cold weather does intensify the coloration of *Acacia baileyana* 'Purpurea', it is prone to frost damage, and the safest option is to carry the container and plant into the greenhouse at the end of autumn. *Agapanthus* 'Snowy Owl' can also be damaged by cold and wet, so that too is brought in for winter. It is planted in a tall container of well-drained John Innes No. 2 compost. To ensure a large number of flowers from agapanthus, it is best to cram as many plants into the container as possible. The root restriction stresses the plant and its response is to flower. The only time an agapanthus needs repotting is when the pot is on the point of cracking. Even then pot it up only one size, using a free-draining peat-free potting compost with extra grit.

We put two plants of the prostrate rosemary, *Rosmarinus officinalis* Prostratus Group, into containers and placed them either side of the bench between the two raised dry garden beds. These will grow 15cm (6 inches) high and spread 45cm (18 inches) and will cover the tops of the containers within two years. It is the least hardy of all rosemary and needs hot, dry, sunny conditions. As with all rosemary, old plants can be cut hard back to encourage new shoots.

Not all of the gaps between the stones in the raised beds' walls were filled with mortar and this gave us an opportunity to plant in these pockets. Thyme, lewisia and sedums will all grow in walls if their roots are in contact with soil. For larger plants, ease the roots into the soil behind the stone, and for smaller plants, or when sowing seed into planting pockets, push a handful of soil into the hole and carefully plant or sow directly into this.

DRY-GARDEN BASICS

◆ Raised beds help drainage.

◆ Make walls stable enough to sit or walk on. This helps when weeding near the back of the beds.

◆ No matter how poor or impoverished the soil appears, do not add fertilizer.

◆ Take time improving drainage: add grit, fork over subsoil and add home-made compost to the topsoil.

◆ Soak the rootballs of plants thoroughly before planting.

◆ Plant high, with 2cm (¾ inch) of the rootball exposed.

◆ Mulch to the top of the rootball with grit or stone chippings immediately after planting.

◆ Water the plants in with a good drenching.

◆ Don't water if a plant wilts. It's difficult as a gardener, but if you can resist the temptation it will force the plants into hunting for water.

◆ Top up the grit mulch after heavy rain or winter.

OPPOSITE *Tulipa linifolia*. We only grow species tulips in the dry garden.

LEFT The flowers of agapanthus are only produced if the roots are tightly restricted, so we grow ours in pots, which we bring into the greenhouse in the winter to protect against frost.

A YEAR IN THE DRY GARDEN

SPRING
◆ Plan and create your dry garden. The Berryfields dry garden took a week of construction from start to finish.

◆ Plan your plants carefully. The right plant will last for years, but it's all too easy to waste your cash through impulse buying.

◆ Pinch out the growing tips of fast-growing plants to encourage compact growth.

SUMMER
◆ Sit and enjoy the garden. Many of the plants are attractive to wildlife.

◆ Remove flowers as they fade, to encourage new blooms to appear.

◆ Take semi-ripe cuttings from non-flowering shoots.

◆ Cut back lavenders when they have finished flowering. A second flush of flowers is possible later in the year.

◆ Lift tulips growing in baskets once the leaves have died down. Dry in a greenhouse or shed.

AUTUMN

◆ Look out for self-sown seedlings in the grit mulch and gravel floor. Either leave them to develop or carefully transplant them elsewhere in the garden.

◆ Plant bulbs such as alliums where space allows.

◆ Clear away dead leaves as they may encourage fungal diseases in winter.

◆ Leave seed heads intact as the ripening seeds will be irresistible to birds.

◆ Take semi-ripe cuttings from many dry garden plants once flowering has peaked.

WINTER

◆ Take plants growing in containers under cover if frost is likely to cause damage.

◆ After a frosty period check that plants haven't been lifted from the soil. Firm any loose plants into the soil and top up with grit.

◆ Check that the soil level and mulch haven't sunk, exposing the rootball. Always have grit handy to act as a top-up.

◆ Mound grit over plants that have lost all their leaves. It will protect the crowns of plants from severe frost.

◆ Plant tulips either directly in the ground or in aquatic baskets plunged in the ground.

ABOVE The dry garden in May, looking across the cottage-garden borders soon after they had been planted, with the *Clematis montana* flowering on the south-facing wall that encloses this part of Berryfields.

OPPOSITE By grouping pots together you can create a strong display, as well as provide protection from cold winds.

'Nowadays most people are unlikely to treat themselves **extensively** from the herb garden, but I believe that a supply of *fresh herbs* grown *specifically* for the kitchen is essential. I think of it as an **outdoor store cupboard**, *miraculously fresh and alive* and yet no more trouble than unscrewing a jar.'

the herb garden

the herb garden

UNTIL RELATIVELY RECENTLY A HOUSEHOLD LIKE
Berryfields would have used scores of different herbs as part
of their diet, their medicines and their beauty treatments.
It is one of the sad reductions of modern life that herbs have
come to mean a tiny handful of garnishes to a meal. Parsley,
mint, garlic, rosemary, sage and thyme are pretty generally
grown and used, and perhaps some basil in a pot, but that is
about the extent of it for many people. This is just a fraction
of the herbs available, and for centuries herbs covered a wide
range of plants that helped our health, whether by
nourishing, healing or preventing illness. Going back a little
further, 'herbs' also included what we now call salad plants.
So the division between plants for food and plants for health
was not there.

Nowadays most people are unlikely to treat themselves extensively from the herb garden, but I believe that a supply of fresh herbs grown specifically for the kitchen is essential. I think of it as an outdoor store cupboard, miraculously fresh and alive and yet no more trouble than unscrewing a jar.

ORIGINAL HERB GARDEN

One of the first things that we did when we took over the garden at Berryfields was to make a small herb garden. The concept was ideal: six small, symmetrical beds just outside the back door that looked good and above all were convenient – you could pop out for a handful of herbs in the middle of

PREVIOUS PAGE, LEFT The tiny florets on the flowering umbels of angelica explode out from the centre like a rocket burst of flower.

PREVIOUS PAGE, RIGHT Basil is one of my favourite herbs. It is easy to grow as long as it has heat, rich soil and plenty of moisture – it is one of the first plants to die, however, if there is the slightest hint of frost.

MONTY'S TIP

A generous handful of grit directly at the bottom of the planting hole will ensure that all Mediterranean herbs avoid sitting in a puddle of water in winter – which will kill them more quickly than anything.

preparing a meal. However, as the garden evolved over the past year we realized that it was not right. It sometimes happens – the idea is sound but somehow the execution fails to live up to expectations.

Within the same area at the back of the house we put in the dry garden and the gravel area in front of it, which has created a lovely sunny spot for sitting out; and now the cottage garden is taking shape in the other half of that section of garden. Increasingly the herb garden

seemed out of place in relationship to these new, successful developments and we realized that there was a choice to be made. Either it had to be enlarged to over twice its size or moved to another site.

We went for the latter option, carefully digging up and saving the perennial herbs such as rosemary, hyssop, sage, alecost, fennel, lemon balm and marjoram, and grassing over the beds. The new location chosen for our herb garden was the small town fruit garden. I had originally envisaged that the planting to accompany the fruit would be flowers to attract pollinators, but it dawned on me that herbs would be the ideal companions and would probably attract as many pollinators as any other group of plants. I was also keen to show how a small garden in the middle of the city can grow a wide range of fresh fruit and herbs and still look beautiful, even if it means growing them in containers – for which most herbs are admirably suited.

MOVING PLANTS

◆ All plants were well watered the day before lifting.
◆ Plants were lifted in the early morning before too much water was lost by transpiration.
◆ Plants were either transplanted into large containers containing a peat-free compost or transferred into a holding bay, or else heeled into a nursery bed in the vegetable garden. Plants put into containers were destined for an on-camera move in a fortnight's time.
◆ Plants in containers were put into the shade and watered to reduce stress. The

reduction in light doesn't cause any detrimental effects, as long as the move is temporary.

◆ The day before their final move the plants were watered.

◆ Filming of the move took place late in the afternoon. This allowed plants to be watered on camera, again in the evening, and settled in overnight.

◆ I always think of transplanted specimens as being in intensive care until they show clear signs of fresh growth. However careful you are, there will be dramatic damage to the roots, yet the leaves will still be making demands on them. Cut back the top growth hard – particularly the soft growth – and keep an eye on them, watering daily if need be. Plants in the heeling-in bed were watered after their move. They will grow happily there until ready for moving in autumn.

The list of herbs for the kitchen will depend on what you like to eat, but I regard the following as essential: rosemary, sage, thyme, French tarragon, oregano, marjoram, lovage, bay, fennel, chives, mint, parsley, basil, garlic, coriander and dill. On top of that, plants like lavender, borage, alecost, savory, hyssop, lemon balm, chervil, chamomile and vervain – to name just a handful – are useful and very decorative. If you want to make a herb garden with a good collection then there is a huge range to choose from.

However many herbs you decide to grow, they will almost certainly fall into three clear groups:

LEFT Three slightly unusual views of three very familiar herbs.

TOP Although a woody shrub, the soft new growth of rosemary is delicious to munch.

MIDDLE Chives in flower. The flowers not only look very good, both in the garden and as part of a salad, but taste delicious as well.

BELOW Purple sage adds a rare dash of claret and purple to the herb garden, but is less hardy, and perhaps less tasty, than its green counterpart.

Mediterranean perennials. These grow best in hot, sunny conditions and need very well-drained, poor soil. I cannot overstress the importance of this. Normal, well-dug garden soil is too rich and produces soft, sappy growth that will not survive the winter or produce the rich oils that characterize these herbs. Examples include lavender, rosemary, fennel, thyme and sage.

Shade-tolerant and hardier perennials. There are many herbs that come from cooler climates or have adapted to growing in richer soil and some shade. These herbs include lovage, comfrey, angelica (which is monocarpic, so dies after flowering and is normally biennial), mint, sweet cicely and chives. Remember, however, that very few herbs like deep shade. Site any herb garden in a sunny spot.

Annual herbs. There is a huge number of herbs that can be grown from seed every year. These include garlic (a perennial grown as an annual), parsley, dill, coriander, basil, borage and caraway.

Then you have to ask yourself what herbs are for as part of your daily life. I suspect that the easy answer for most of us is to make our food taste better, but we all have culinary preferences that should be incorporated into the ingredients of the garden as well as the table. All gardens are personal places and should reflect all your own fancies and idiosyncracies – even eccentricities.

Having chosen your herbs to suit yourself, it is important to be generous.

Seed is cheap, and it is much better value to buy a number of small plants than one or two large ones. One of the great luxuries of growing your own herbs for the kitchen is being able to have plenty of them, so that you can use them unselfconsciously. If you are used to buying your herbs from a supermarket, it is a liberation and a luxury to be able to pick great bunches of leaves for months on end for the price of a packet of seed or a tiny, hydroponically grown pot.

There are herbs from just about every corner of the globe, but many of the ones that we are most familiar with – rosemary, sage, thyme, fennel, lavender, dill, coriander and rue – all come from the sun-baked hillsides of the Mediterranean. The best way to ensure a plant's health is to replicate its natural growing conditions, and with Mediterranean plants it is striking just how extreme those conditions are. A dry, sun-baked hillside is a desperately harsh place. Despite their preference for heat, almost all these herbs will cope with a surprising degree of cold weather, and they can survive very wet periods too, but the combination of both will kill them more quickly than anything. They hate sitting in cold, wet ground.

But the gardener has to strike a balance. Anybody with an ounce of sensibility wants rosemary flowering for as long as possible and to be as bushy and fresh-shooted as possible. Everybody wants a lavender bush throwing up floral spikes like a flowering pin-cushion. In other words, we want an unnatural lushness

that comes only from unnaturally mild conditions. But it is terribly easy to err on the side of softness with all the Mediterranean herbs.

A little compost is a good idea to improve drainage and stop slumping if your soil is very light, but go steady with it. You are also going to get the best from these Mediterranean herbs if they are placed so that they can get as much sunshine as possible.

Both lavender and rosemary will grow very well in a pot, but only if they have enough space for a root run. In other words, just because they like poor soil and dry conditions, don't fall into the trap of

MONTY'S TIP
Most people sow their annual herbs like parsley, basil, dill or coriander too close together. If you buy a herb in a pot it is likely to be a cluster of small plants, but they grow much better if properly spaced so that each plant becomes strong and healthy. I recommend a final minimum spacing of 23cm (9 inches) in each direction for all these plants.

letting them get pot-bound. My poor pot-imprisoned plants got by so well only because they made their own way out of the containers. Any plant that has evolved to live in drought will have roots that want to range freely to seek out moisture.

None of the Mediterranean herbs likes shade. Some, like thyme or sage, are very prone to becoming woody and straggly if

they have the tiniest bit of shade, so they need to be at the front of a border or in a very open position. If you are using herbs regularly and have the space, there is a strong argument for growing a separate supply where they can be allowed space to grow without competing for light in a mixed bed of other herbs. For many years I have grown thyme, parsley, coriander, dill, basil, chives and garlic in with my vegetables, where they can be harvested as a crop – although this does not stop them looking terrific!

Narrow-leafed, or Spanish, sage, *Salvia lavandulifolia*, has an excellent flavour. This cannot be grown from seed but takes easily from cuttings. It is essential to be really ruthless with sage by cutting back hard in spring to stop it getting too leggy. Unfortunately this means losing the lovely flowers. The sages I like, apart from the narrow-leafed *S. lavandulifolia* (which I think best for cooking), are the ordinary *S. officinalis* and the purple sage, *S. officinalis* 'Purpurascens'. This is less vigorous and hardy than the other two and might need winter protection.

There are many different types of thyme, and a lot of cooks swear by lemon thyme as the best for chicken and fish, while *Thymus vulgaris*, the common thyme, is excellent with all tomato dishes. Whatever type of thyme you grow, give it really sharp drainage and cut it back hard as soon as it finishes flowering, to encourage the soft new growth that is best for cooking with.

Fennel seeds itself everywhere but is in fact a short-lived perennial. The bronze form looks wonderful in a border, but straight, green *Foeniculum vulgare* is best for the kitchen. In good soil it will become 2m (6 feet) tall with fluffy fronds of leaf. The fresh seeds are an excellent aid to digestion and delicious, especially with roast pork.

Origanum vulgare is called marjoram in the UK and oregano in the Mediterranean. At Berryfields we grow French oregano (*Origanum onites*), which has green leaves, and golden marjoram (*O. vulgare* 'Aureum'). As with thyme, the secret is to keep it unshaded and to keep cutting plants back hard to encourage new leaves.

French tarragon (*Artemisia dracunculus*) is certainly desirable but is best grown in a pot and brought into the greenhouse each winter. It is also best replaced every few years. Do not confuse it with Russian tarragon (*A. d. dracunculoides*), which is very hardy but no good in the kitchen. If uncertain which is which, leave the plant unprotected all winter. If it survives unscathed, it is almost certainly Russian.

Garlic, chives, basil, parsley, lovage, mint, angelica and sorrel are among those that thrive in rich soils, so it is a good idea to plan a herb garden with quite separate sections or beds, so that the soil can be prepared accordingly. Mint is famously invasive, so is best grown in containers, even if you then plunge the pots into the ground so that they become part of a border. Peppermint is best for making mint tea, and I like to use applemint and spearmint for cooking.

Lovage, garlic, parsley and chives all do better in richer soil with some shade. Lovage adds tremendous height and stature to a border, with its flowering stems reaching 3m (10 feet) or more, and the leaves are very good for adding a celery-like flavour to soups and stews. Cut it back hard around midsummer and it will grow a fresh set of leaves. Having two plants means that one can be cut back hard and the other left until replacement leaves arrive a few weeks later. I deal with garlic growing in the kitchen garden chapter (see page 135).

All woody herbs take easily as semi-ripe cuttings, and many perennial herbs grow very easily from seed. This means that you can put together a well-stocked herb garden with hundreds of plants for the price of a modest night out. Some important herbs are annual and *must* be grown from seed. Borage, like fennel, will seed itself and become a welcome invader, while feverfew and comfrey will be even more profligate but perhaps not always so welcome.

Basil is extremely tender – a hint of frost will reduce it to black rags – but grows well wherever tomatoes are happy, which is to say it needs lots of sun, water and a rich soil. The trick is to grow it fast once it has germinated, so it never becomes leathery, and to harvest the leaves regularly or as one crop. It freezes very well. It will always do better inside a greenhouse at the base of tomatoes than outside in the herb garden, but it will grow outside in a sunny, sheltered spot in good soil. But do keep it well watered.

Parsley is probably my favourite herb and, despite a tricky reputation, dead easy to grow. All it requires is warm soil or compost for germination. I grow French, or flat-leaf, varieties. They are easier to grow, last longer and, above all, taste better than the curly-leaf form. When you buy parsley in a pot there will be a number of spindly plants, but when growing it yourself it is much better to raise single plants that are given plenty of space to grow strongly. I always sow it in seed trays or plugs, transplant the seedlings to small pots, and then plant them out 20cm (8 inches) apart. To keep a year-round supply I do three sowings, in February, May and August. I grow coriander the same way, although it is

much more inclined to run to seed – but then the seed is half the harvest. Dill is best sown direct, but I sow a pinch per 8cm (3-inch) pot, thinning to a healthy plant and placing them in the border before the tap root gets too big.

LAVENDER CASE STUDY

Lavender is a native of the Mediterranean region. The Romans first used it as a bath additive – the word is derived from the Latin *lavare*, to wash – and it is still used as a soothing relaxant today. The smell also discourages moths, midges, mosquitoes and even mad dogs and vipers. The oil within the plant, mostly esters, is concentrated in the spikes and flowers. In June the oil is disseminated throughout the plant, but it peaks in the flowers and stalks during July, where on sunny days you can actually see globules of oil oozing from the flowers. Concentrations begin to fall in August.

Lavender needs well-drained, poor soil and will not tolerate sitting in cold, wet soil in winter. Sun is therefore preferable, but lavender is surprisingly tolerant of dappled shade. Dig plenty of grit into the soil before planting and do not add any fertilizer or compost. When planting young plants, it is best to cut the plant down to within 5cm (2 inches) of the soil. This will encourage new shoots, compact plants and better flowering.

With established plants never cut into old wood, as lavender often will not regrow from old wood. The best practice is to cut the flower stalks off once the flowers have faded and then give plants a pruning in March, which can mean removing up to half of the plant. (Don't worry – lavender puts on a lot of growth and cutting half of it away still doesn't touch the old wood. It may sound drastic but be brave.) Otherwise there is little maintenance to be done on lavender. Older plants, perhaps inherited when moving to a new house and garden, may be neglected. Usually this is seen as plants with woody bases and a few flowers perched on top of straggly stems. The best thing to do in such a case is to take cuttings from any non-flowering shoots and discard the plants.

Pests and diseases are few and far between, but cuckoo spit can be a nuisance. It first appears as sticky white froth on flower stalks, usually in May and June. Inside the froth is a light green, sometimes yellow, sap-feeding insect. It is the nymphal stage of a froghopper. Once the nymphs have matured they stop producing the protective froth (birds don't like the stickiness of the froth and leave the bugs alone) and are less noticeable. The nymphs and adults don't cause too much damage and some gardeners see it as a cosmetic nuisance. Spray with a jet of water to dislodge the froth and nymphs or rub them off.

There is a growing problem with a fungus of lavender called lavender shab. Branches die off one by one and whole plants can die. The fungus enters the plants through pruning cuts, and tiny, blackish-brown, raised fruiting bodies appear on the dead leaves and stems. The only treatment is to remove infected branches, cutting back to healthy wood. Clean your secateurs before pruning healthy plants.

HERBS IN POTS

Herbs grow well in pots and can be located next to a kitchen door, where they are readily accessible. Cover the drainage holes with broken pieces of terracotta pots or pebbles to ensure good drainage. Peat-free multipurpose compost mixed with horticultural grit is a good mix for most herbs. Mint is the best herb for growing in a pot because it is so invasive, but almost any herb can be grown in a container. They will need more watering than if they were planted in the ground, and do not make the mistake of thinking that Mediterranean herbs do not need water. Give them a soak once a week – and if the water seems to pour straight through the compost and out of the bottom of the pot then you have probably got the drainage exactly right.

HERBS AND COMPANION PLANTING

If certain plants are put together, each is helped by the natural properties of the other. This can work by:

◆ Attracting insects for pollination.
◆ Attracting insects for predator control.
◆ Giving off scent that repels insects.
◆ Acting as ground cover and thereby suppressing weeds.
◆ Fixing nitrogen in the soil, reducing the need for additional fertilizer.

The principle of companion planting is used throughout Berryfields, and in the fruit gardens, where most of the herbs

OPPOSITE *Lavandula angustifolia* 'Hidcote' is a compact, slow-growing, form of lavender with dark purple flowers. Like all lavenders, it must have very good drainage to thrive.

are grown, there are some great examples of this at work:

◆ The smell of chives leaves, *Allium schoenoprasum*, or any member of the onion family, repels aphids on roses (I always plant a clove of garlic next to a rose for the same reason). It also helps protect against blackspot and mildew on apples. Once the flowers of chives have faded, cut the flowers and stalks and lay them in your strawberry patch. This will help reduce the incidence of botrytis on the developing fruit. Chives grow to 30cm (12 inches) and produce purple flowers and delicious cylindrical leaves throughout summer. Plants are easily grown from seed and can be divided and replanted in spring. They die back in winter but will regrow vigorously in spring. Cut back hard every six weeks or so and new, fresh growth will appear in days.

◆ Lemon balm, *Melissa officinalis*, attracts bees into an area. We planted it in the small town fruit garden, where the bees will help pollinate the apples, plums, cherries and nectarines. Plants grow 75cm (2½ feet) tall with a 45cm (18-inch) spread. The oval leaves are green, slightly crinkled and highly aromatic, and pale yellow flowers are produced in summer. It can grow very vigorously in rich soil and be invasive, so cut back hard after midsummer. The quickest way to propagate lemon balm is by division. Dig up a plant, or a section of a plant, divide the straggly roots and replant each section. Each will produce a new plant. Plants grow in any situation but prefer a sunny spot.

◆ Tansy, *Tanacetum vulgare*, is useful when grown near fruit trees to deter fruit moths. Dry the leaves, crush them and sprinkle them on the ground to deter ants, and hang a bunch of leaves near the door of the house or greenhouse to deter flies. Plants grow up to 1m (3 feet) high with a 60cm (2-foot) spread. The dark green leaves are deeply serrated and highly aromatic, and yellow flowers are produced in late summer. Gold and variegated forms are more controllable. Tansy will grow anywhere except in waterlogged conditions. Cut back after flowering to encourage compact growth of new shoots.

LAVENDER

There is heavy planting of lavender in the small town fruit garden. Marvellous for attracting bees, lavender also attracts lacewings and ladybirds, both predators of aphids. In addition lavender produces root exudates that inhibit the growth of other plants. There is also evidence that root exudates from lavender encourage the micro-organisms in the soil, which is one of the ways that lavender has adapted to grow in harsh conditions and grabs every available nutrient for itself.

A selection of popular varieties was chosen and planted in groups at Berryfields that will melt into each other to form a tapestry of colour in summer:

◆ *Lavandula angustifolia*: Old English Lavender, a robust plant with broad grey leaves and stems 1.2m (4 feet) high. The flowers are lavender-blue and open, like most lavender, in July.

the herb garden

TOP LEFT Apple mint, *Mentha suaveolens*, has a soft, almost furry, texture to its leaves and is, I think, the best mint to accompany new potatoes.
TOP RIGHT When backlit, the leaves of bronze fennel, *Foeniculum vulgare* 'Purpureum', have an orange cast. Although perfectly edible and certainly more decorative than the green form, bronze fennel is not, I think as good, so we relegate it to the flower border.
BELOW LEFT Spearmint (*Mentha spicata*) in flower. Although they are decorative, it is best to pinch off the flower heads as they appear, to stop the mint from becoming bitter.
BELOW RIGHT All mint can become very invasive so it is best grown either in an isolated bed or in a container. Spearmint is a wonderful all-round mint for drinks and sweet and savoury dishes, as well as being the ideal cure for an unsettled stomach.

◆ *Lavandula angustifolia* 'Hidcote': a compact form of English-type lavender with narrow grey-green leaves and stems up to 1m (3 feet) high. The flowers are violet and produced in dense spikes.

◆ *Lavandula angustifolia* 'Munstead': a compact form with narrow leaves and spikes up to 75cm (2½ feet) high. It has lavender-blue flowers.

◆ *Lavandula angustifolia* 'Lavender Lady': compact, growing to around 30cm (12 inches), producing pale lavender flowers in dense heads in July.

◆ *Lavandula angustifolia* 'Lavenite Petite': a compact plant with short spikes of dark blue flowers growing to around 40cm (16 inches).

◆ *Lavandula angustifolia* 'Loddon Pink': grows to around 45cm (18 inches) with short, narrow, grey-green leaves. Pale pink flowers are produced on short spikes in July.

◆ *Lavandula stoechas*: French lavender, dwarf, with narrow, silver-grey, intensely aromatic leaves. Dark purple flowers topped by rose-purple bracts are formed in summer in dense heads.

◆ *Lavandula stoechas* 'Madrid White': semi-hardy lavender producing white flowers of the French lavender type in July. Take under protection of a cold greenhouse in winter.

MINTS

Mint is notorious for its wandering habits. Planted in a border, the runners will run and new plants will pop up all over the garden. It also grows well in sunny or partial shade, but most mints prefer soil that doesn't dry out too quickly. To stop plants from spreading,

MONTY'S CONFESSION

Moving plants is always a tricky manoeuvre and is best done when plants are in a dormant state. Autumn and winter are the traditional times to do this. However, my promise to finish the fruit gardens by the end of last years' series meant that the herbs had to be moved in early summer. Almost all of the plants came through the move, but one particular rosemary plant didn't like it. On the day of filming the star of the herbs had wilted and looked to be struggling. We had a choice – film something else, buy in a replacement and pretend it was our plant, or tell the truth. And of course we ... told the truth and showed the plant looking terrible. The good news is that it recovered and is looking great. And you thought that we would cheat ...

sink a bottomless bucket in the garden, leaving 2cm (¾ inch) of the rim showing above soil level. Fill with soil and plant into the centre. The runners will stop when they reach the sides of the buried bucket and not invade the garden. Pick leaves as and when they are required, but early-morning pickings are tastier than those taken later in the day. Once plants begin to flower the leaves become coarser, so cut plants down to just above ground level to encourage fresh shoots and leaves. In autumn lift a smaller plant, pot up in peat-free multipurpose compost and grow on under protection – a sunny windowsill is good – to produce small amounts of leaves in winter. Early autumn is also a good time to take root cuttings. Mint is embarrassingly easy to propagate – every piece of root with a

visible node will produce new shoots. Pot up sections of roots into individual pots and water. New shoots will soon appear. This can be done at any time of the year.

Plants growing under stress are more susceptible to mint rust. Leaves and stems become flecked with yellow and orange-yellow spots, and badly infected stems become distorted. The fungus responsible, *Puccinia menthae*, survives as dormant spores in the soil and can also infect other herbs. The first thing to do is to remove infected leaves and stems immediately, but the disease is rampant and the best course of action is to remove complete plants and not to replant in the same soil for three years. Moroccan mint,

Mentha spicata var. *crispa* 'Moroccan', does not suffer from mint rust.

There are many species of mint to choose from:

◆ Apple mint, *Mentha suaveolens*, has thick, soft, rounded leaves and is the best mint for new potatoes. Plants grow up to 1m (3 feet) high with a spread that knows no boundaries. Mauve flowers are produced in summer.
◆ Spearmint, *Mentha spicata*, has green, pointed leaves with serrated edges. It's also known as common mint and is the mint found in many gardens. It can be used in all kinds of cooking but is particularly good with puddings and drinks, and is the best mint for mint sauce. Purple flowers are produced in summer. Plants grow 60cm (2 feet) tall and, again, it can spread with wild abandon.
◆ Peppermint, *Mentha × piperita*, has pointed leaves that are dark green with a red tinge and serrated edges, and is the best mint for making mint tea. A pot of peppermint tea will cure almost any minor stomach ailment better than any medicine. Plants grow 60cm (2 feet) tall and will spread if left unrestricted. Pale purple flowers are produced in summer.
◆ Lemon mint, *Mentha × piperita* f. *citrata* 'Lemon', has green serrated leaves with a lemon scent. Plants grow 60cm (2 feet) tall with a wild spread. Purple flowers are produced in summer.
◆ Chocolate mint, *Mentha × piperita* f. *citrata* 'Chocolate', has green, chocolate-scented leaves and grows to 60cm (2 feet) high with the usual minty spread. Blue flowers are produced in summer.

MORE HERBS AT BERRYFIELDS

◆ Silver posie thyme, *Thymus vulgaris* 'Silver Posie', is evergreen, growing to 30cm (12 inches) high with a 20cm (8-inch) spread. The leaves have a silvery-grey variegation, often tinged pink on the undersides. The flowers are lilac or pale pink and produced in summer. As with all thyme, if grown in rich soil the soft growth is prone to aphid attack. Grow plants hard in poor soil.

◆ Bronze fennel, *Foeniculum vulgare* 'Purpureum', has bronze, soft, feathery leaves and grows to 2m (6 feet) tall. Small, yellow flowers are produced in umbels during summer. (Umbels are flower clusters in the form of an umbrella, with the flowers radiating out from a central point.) It likes a sunny site and fertile, well-drained soil. When grown in hot, dry conditions the plant will be sparse, but in a border it can become a magnificent foliage plant as well as producing its characteristic flower-heads and seeds. Like all umbellifers it attracts hoverflies and therefore keeps aphid numbers down.

◆ Lemon verbena, *Aloysia triphylla*, originates in Chile. It grows up to 3m (10 feet), with a spread of 2m (6 feet). The pale green leaves are strongly lemon-scented. Small white flowers, often tinged lilac, are produced in early summer. It has to have a free-draining soil and a sunny position. It is not hardy in most of the UK and needs to be lifted in autumn, potted into peat-free multipurpose compost and housed in a greenhouse until spring. Give plants a prune in spring before planting out in early summer.

HERB-GARDEN BASICS

◆ Ensure your soil is well drained.

◆ Buy in and use grit in the preparation of the soil.

◆ Plant pots of herbs in the ground and lift under cover in autumn if you garden in an extremely cold area.

◆ Match the herbs to your conditions.

◆ Take cuttings from herbs in summer to ensure a good supply of new plants.

◆ Regularly pick culinary herbs to ensure fresh growth.

LEFT Borage, *Borago officinalis*. The flowers are delicious to eat and borage leaves add a cucumber flavour to drinks and are good with soft cheeses. It is an annual that self-sows very freely.

OPPOSITE Caraway, *Carum carvi*, in flower. The leaves, seeds and roots of caraway have been used for millennia as an aid to digestion and as a delicious accompaniment to sweet and savoury dishes all over the world. Caraway is an annual that likes rich soil in full sun.

A YEAR IN THE HERB GARDEN

SPRING

◆ Sow most annual herbs in trays and pots under cover.

◆ Take softwood cuttings from perennial herbs.

◆ Cut lavender hard back but never into old wood.

◆ Trim back strong-growing herbs to retain shape and to produce new shoots.

◆ Divide established plants.

SUMMER

◆ Cut leaves for the kitchen at regular intervals.

◆ Trim off lavender flowers and flower stalks once they have faded.

◆ Trim all herbs once flowering is over.

◆ Take cuttings from non-flowering shoots of all thymes.

AUTUMN

◆ Protect many perennial herbs from hard frost and excessively wet weather.
◆ Lift tender herbs, pot up and take into the greenhouse for winter.

WINTER

◆ Ventilate greenhouses on sunny days.
◆ Lightly spray herbs in greenhouses to prevent red spider mite attacks.
◆ Protect containers outside if excessively cold – bubble-wrap the outside of containers to protect roots.

ABOVE Lemon verbena, *Aloysia triphylla*, is a tender herb whose leaves make a wonderfully refreshing tea. We dig up some plants to overwinter in pots in the greenhouse and mulch others to protect them from frost.

OPPOSITE Comfrey, *Symphytum officinale*, is an essential herb for the organic garden, making liquid fertilizer as well as ideal composting material. It is also good to eat – I love comfrey fritters. It grows best in very rich, moist soil, and can be cut to the ground up to four times a year for a valuable harvest of its goodness.

'Everything that we grow is eaten, and I *love* seeing the crew set off for home at the end of a filming day *clutching bags of vegetables*, because I firmly believe that the journey of those vegetable seed we sowed months before is not complete until the produce has been *eaten – and enjoyed.*'

the kitchen garden

the kitchen garden

I HAVE GROWN VEGETABLES SINCE I WAS A SMALL BOY AND for me a garden without vegetables is like a house without a kitchen. Exclude anything edible from your garden and you exclude a great slice of life itself. All gardeners should judge the food that they grow by the way their palette responds before any received horticultural notions of size, shape or quantity. Yes, homegrown, organic fruit and vegetables are undeniably more healthy than the chemically grown supermarket alternative, and the process of nurturing and growing them creates physical and mental well-being, but the most important fact remains that they taste so much better than any bought alternative.

Much of this is simply due to eating the right thing at the right time. New potatoes, sweetcorn, peas and asparagus start to convert their sugar to starch within hours of being harvested. Anyone who has not tasted a tomato or strawberry with the warmth of the sun still on it simply does not know how these two fruits ought to taste. And this is without beginning the pleasure of exploring all the different varieties and types that give subtle but significant taste variations according to soil, climate and season.

The massive food companies have effectively brainwashed us into believing that we are fortunate to be supplied with every type of food at every hour of every day. But the price for this has been the loss of taste and of association with season. It is the difference between living in a world of 24-hour strip-lighting uniformity and living with the rhythm of light and the seasons, experiencing dawn, bright sunshine and dusk. If you eat food in its own season, when it has been well grown and is ready to be harvested – whether it be a 'King of the Pippins' apple in October, a perfect raspberry in July or a bundle of asparagus taken straight from the garden to the pan on a May evening – then it will always taste as good as it possibly can. Food that is grown slowly, with the emphasis on raising healthy plants, harvested when it is ready and not according to a business plan, and then eaten as soon as possible with minimal cooking or chilling, will always be good. This is where gardeners have a fantastic privilege. All of us, even if we have only

a tiny backyard, can raise some fruit, vegetables and herbs to take us back to the point at which our food really tastes of itself – which is, of course, the minimum that we should be asking of it.

For the first year at Berryfields we concentrated on improving the soil in the vegetable garden. This was quite a job. Apart from a strip down one side – on what amounts to about a third of the current layout – the ground was horribly compacted, heavy and without any structure at all. Digging it was like lifting a concrete floor. So we made raised beds, added lots of muck, laid some hard paths to accommodate the dozens of feet of a film crew and grew what we could.

But once the framework was there I made three rules that seem to me to be essential for any plot of homegrown vegetables. The first was that the vegetable garden should always look good; the second was that everything grown in it should be judged by its taste rather than size, quantity or appearance, and the third was that we should be strictly organic. If you want chemically raised vegetables, any supermarket will supply them at a fraction of the cost of growing them yourself.

What this meant in practice was that we would not let the plot become a scruffy, ugly part of the garden in the name of good veg or organic production, because there is absolutely no need for that, especially when so many vegetables are beautiful in their own right. The second rule meant we would be choosing our varieties carefully for taste and growing them to maximize that virtue above all else.

Everything that we grow is eaten, and I love seeing the crew set off for home at the end of a filming day clutching bags of vegetables, because I firmly believe that the journey of those vegetable seed we sowed months before is not complete until the produce has been eaten – and enjoyed.

LOCATION

The Berryfields kitchen garden is around the same size as an average-sized allotment. It measures 15m × 15m (50 feet × 50 feet). When we came it was exposed on three sides, and one of the first things we did was to have a beautiful fixed hazel fence woven along the long east and west sides and then to plant a hornbeam hedge inside it. The greenhouse was built within this area, running north–south. There is a water tap in the greenhouse, which provides the irrigation for all the vegetables. Half the growing area is made up of two large cultivated beds and the other half of nine raised beds. Hard pathways cross the plot, while the paths between the raised beds are turf.

PLANNING

Vegetables tend to be relegated to the ends of a garden, but it makes much more sense to grow them near to the kitchen. It makes it easier to nip out and pick a few vegetables. At Berryfields our veg are a few paces from the kitchen door, and sweetcorn or asparagus can be in a pan of boiling water within one

minute of picking. Also, if at all possible, think about positioning the plot for convenience of deliveries of manure. It is not something that you want to carry through the house if it can be avoided.

A well-planned kitchen garden is both efficient and fun to work in. A sunny position is best, and the thick boundary hedge that borders one side of the Berryfields garden shades the area from only the earliest of the morning sun. For the rest of the day, summer sun blazes down on the plot.

Pathways are important. Hard paved paths are good as they allow you to work the plot in all weather. Paths should be wide enough to allow you and a fully laden wheelbarrow to pass without treading on surrounding borders or tripping over raised beds. I reckon 1m (3 feet) is the narrowest workable path for a wheelbarrow. If using wood chippings for your paths it is advisable to lay a semi-permeable membrane on the ground before applying the chippings. This allows rainwater to run through to the soil but stops weeds from growing up. Turf pathways are cheap and look good, but they will need mowing and can get muddy in winter. The plan at Berryfields is gradually to replace the turf paths with paving and brick as and when materials become available from other projects. It's a good off-camera winter job.

A vegetable garden must have a water supply, and the Berryfields kitchen garden is lucky in that the greenhouse is the boundary along one side. Water butts collect the rain falling on the roof, and inside the greenhouse there is a tap connected to the mains. The greenhouse also provides wind protection, as do the hazel hurdles and hedge.

When planning the crops you grow, choose ones you like to eat – even if that means ignoring some popular favourites such as peas or cabbages. Everything in this part of the garden is on a journey – and the destination is your stomach. Avoid mass sowings of one particular vegetable as these result only in a glut, and while nothing is truly wasted as all excess can go on the compost heap, smaller sowings spaced regularly over the season ensure that there are always fresh

ABOVE I always use boards to kneel on when sowing, to avoid compacting the soil.

pickings. Use the space between slower-growing crops for fast vegetables, such as radish, rocket and spring onions.

RAISED BEDS

There is much to be said for creating raised beds. They mean much less wasted space, as they focus the cultivation on to areas that are actually going to be used for growing and, in theory, need much less cultivation because they are never trodden upon, so do not become compacted.

Over the years I have tried many different types of raised bed, and the ones that we now have at Berryfields reflect the experience I have gained from this.

◆ You must *comfortably* be able to reach the middle of each bed from the edge. I have found that 1.5m (5 feet) is the maximum for me and 1.2m (4 feet) about the workable minimum.
◆ If the beds are too long, sooner or later you will get fed up with going round them and step over. And if you do this you will inevitably step on them. So I would say that no bed should be longer than 5m (16 feet).
◆ Some kind of edging is necessary for anything other than the very short term. If the beds are simply long, uncontained mounds, the workable area is radically reduced and the sides spill out.
◆ Do not be tempted to squeeze an extra bed in by making the paths too narrow. You need room to harvest and work. I suggest a central path wide enough to take a barrow down comfortably (1m/3 feet) and all others wide enough to kneel on – about

There are two ways to plant leeks. The first is to make a hole with a dibber (I keep broken spade handles for this), drop the bare-rooted seedling into the hole and water. Soil is washed around the leek. The second way is to sow seeds in clumps into cells. When 4cm (1½ inches) or so high, the whole clump is transplanted, undisturbed, into a planting hole, as you would any other seedling. The leeks develop irregularly, but healthily, and each clump is enough for a meal. The shape of the leeks won't win prizes at the local show but the stems are tasty.

60cm (2 feet). Less is seriously restrictive.

◆ I have made raised beds from recycled scaffolding boards, untreated timber and – best, but most expensive, of all – oak boards. Scaffolding boards have real virtues, being exactly 5m (16 feet) long, about 23cm (9 inches) wide and very strong. They need only a good post in each corner to attach to and are then strong enough to walk along – if you have the balance. I sink them 5–8cm (2–3 inches) below the ground, leaving at least 15 cm (6 inches) clear, using a spirit level to keep them true.

◆ Raised beds save much work over the years, but for best results they do need very thorough preparation. Ideally the whole plot should be dug deeply and rotavated. Then mark out the beds with string and throw the top 8 cm (3 inches) of soil from the paths on to the site of the beds. Be warned – this is hard work. Add a good layer of compost over this and rotavate it in well, shovelling up any spillage back on to the marked-out beds.

Only then should you fix the boards, being very careful not to tread on the beds. If you religiously avoid treading on them – and I keep a length of board that spans the beds so I can kneel on it to plant and weed in the middle – you should never need to cultivate them again. They then just need raking over before sowing or planting, which can be done right up to the very edge of the boards.

◆ One final tip – don't over-fill the beds with soil. Leave a generous 5cm (2 inches) below the top of the boards for adding a compost mulch.

CROP ROTATION

Crop rotation is a cropping scheme designed to avoid growing the same type of vegetable in the same place in consecutive years. The reasons for crop rotation are:

◆ Pests and diseases: it reduces the build-up of pests and diseases. Particular pests and diseases do not get a chance to become established.

◆ Nutrients: it stops the soil from becoming depleted in particular nutrients as different crops have different requirements.

◆ Structure: some crops have deep roots, others shallow. Growing different crops year on year results in a better soil structure.

◆ Weeds: leafy crops such as potatoes produce leaves that suppress weed growth.

◆ Soil treatment: different crops require different soil treatments such as manure. Crop rotation allows efficient use of manures, leafmould, lime and green manures.

Vegetables are divided into four groups, each of which occupies one bed or area of the kitchen garden. Each group then moves to the next part of the garden. It works something like this:

GROUP 1: potatoes, tomatoes, all alliums, courgettes. Add manure to the soil before planting. Salad crops can be grown in this group.

GROUP 2: carrots, parsnips, celery, beetroot, spinach. Do not add any manure as it will cause roots to fork or fang.

GROUP 3: all brassicas. Add leafmould or a small amount of garden compost to the soil before planting.

GROUP 4: all peas and beans. Manure new ground the winter before planting or follow heavily manured crops like potatoes or squashes. Pea and bean plants fix nitrogen, making it available to the next crop (and the next crop on the plan opposite is group 3, leafy brassicas that require lots of nitrogen). Salad crops can be grown in this group.

There will also be permanent beds of perennial vegetables, such as asparagus and rhubarb, that do not get involved in crop rotation.

After all that, there has to be some flexibility in the plan. Sometimes a crop has to grow in the same soil as the previous year. Don't worry – if the previous year's crop was healthy then it will probably be just fine. But it should be

RIGHT Crop rotation is essential for raising healthy vegetables. First in any rotation are potatoes (top), which like freshly dug, well-manured soil. Potatoes are excellent for suppressing weeds and 'cleaning' a new piece of ground. These are then followed by legumes, such as broad beans (centre, above) and peas. These like rich soil but also fix nitrogen from the air and leave a residue in the ground for the brassicas, which are next in the rotation and include crops like cabbages (centre, below) and cauliflowers. Finally, without further manure being added, root crops like carrots (below) and parsnips take over, before being followed by potatoes as the rotation starts all over again.

the kitchen garden

If you have a long, thin kitchen garden, year one would look like this:

| Group 1 | Group 2 | Group 3 | Group 4 |

Year two all groups move along the plot:

| Group 4 | Group 1 | Group 2 | Group 3 |

Year three they all move again:

| Group 3 | Group 4 | Group 1 | Group 2 |

Year four they move again:

| Group 2 | Group 3 | Group 4 | Group 1 |

And the following year they are back where they started:

| Group 1 | Group 2 | Group 3 | Group 4 |

the exception rather than the rule. Crop rotation doesn't just apply to large kitchen gardens or allotments. Moving a crop a few metres away from the previous year's position will make a positive difference. If you have the discipline, make records of how the crops perform. It will prove the effectiveness of crop rotation.

SOIL CONDITIONERS

Garden compost is the best source of organic matter for the kitchen garden – and the garden is also a marvellous source of material for organic matter. Well-rotted animal manure is very useful, too, although it is hard to get organic farmyard manure as, in theory, it is all needed on the farm, while manure from non-organic farms may contain traces of hormones, antibiotics and other chemicals. The best bet is to leave it to

rot for six months or to incorporate it into your compost heap, where it will not only rot down faster but also improve the rest of the compost.

The main purpose of organic material is not to improve nutrition – although it does do that – but to improve the soil structure, which enables the roots of each plant to grow freely and access all available nutrients. It also improves drainage in heavy soil and water retention in light soil. Magic stuff.

Spent mushroom compost is an excellent soil conditioner and over the years I have used hundreds of tonnes of it. The great advantage that it has over animal manure is that it is weed-free, whereas farmyard manure will inevitable bring lots of annual weeds with it. These can be pulled up and added to the compost heap, but it is worth watching out for. Mushroom compost is alkaline, so ideal for clay or acid soils but not ideal for limestone. It is best to check the pH of your soil before use. Organic mushroom farms are the best source of the compost, but many use insecticides in crop production. If this is the case, stack the compost to allow chemical residues to leach out and use it when it has reached a rich, crumbly, black condition. Never use spent mushroom compost and animal manures together as soil conditioners. There is a chemical reaction, which can release gases that are harmful to plants.

Green Manure

Green manure saves not just on artificial fertilizers but also on precious garden compost – of which no one ever has enough. It has many virtues and practically no drawbacks, but has never really caught on with the mainstream gardening public, which is a pity. It isn't the green slimy mush the name conjures up, but is a crop in its own right. The principle is that instead of leaving ground bare you sow a 'crop', the primary harvest of which is the enrichment and improvement of the soil.

Green manures work in a number of ways at the same time. They cover the ground and occupy it, which means that weeds have no room or light to get in, which they surely would do otherwise. On that basis alone, the sowing and cutting of a green manure is less work than weeding.

Some green manures – such as grazing rye – are intended for over-wintering and can be in the ground for as long as nine months, whereas others such as phacelia or mustard can do their job of occupying and nourishing a plot in a matter of weeks. It is important to include them as part of your crop rotation (see page 131). Vetches, fenugreek and field beans, for example, are legumes, and mustard is a brassica.

These are some of the benefits provided by green manures:

◆ Deep-rooted green manures extract minerals from lower soil levels and, when the manure is dug in or composted, these minerals are made available to the following vegetable crop.
◆ Their green foliage also photosynthesizes light and takes carbon dioxide from the atmosphere, which it then converts into starches and sugars which, when they are incorporated into the soil, provide food for future crops.
◆ Bare soil is exposed to rain. This can leach nutrients out of the reach of roots. Green manures cover the soil surface over winter, protecting the surface from leaching rain. They also protect against compaction of the soil by heavy rain and careless footfall. It is unlikely you are going to walk over a growing crop, whereas you might take a shortcut over bare soil.
◆ Green manures with fine root systems can open up the structure of heavy soils

or bind together particles in lighter soils. This helps the drainage of heavy soils and the water retention of lighter soils.

◆ Green manures can smother weeds, preventing them from developing flowers and therefore seeds. Weeds soon colonize bare soil.

◆ They provide a large amount of organic material. This can either be cut and added to the compost heap – which is what I do with over-wintering grazing rye, field beans and vetches – or it can be cut and the whole plant dug into the ground for the soil's micro-organisms to work on, which improves the structure of the soil, completely bypassing the whole composting process.

◆ Many predators of garden pests, such as frogs and beetles, can use the cover of green manures for protection and camouflage.

◆ Any growth can be treated as a green manure, including annual weeds, but it is essential to cut and dig them in before any seed are produced, which can be very difficult to time across a different range of weeds.

A final word of caution about green manures. They work extremely well, and if you time them right they can be a sophisticated way of increasing fertility and soil structure as well as keeping weeds down and providing flowers that many useful insects find very attractive. However, they should not be used instead

OPPOSITE Hungarian grazing rye growing in both an open bed and a raised bed behind it.

GREEN MANURE OPTIONS

TYPE OF GREEN MANURE	WHEN TO SOW	HOW LONG TO LEAVE IN SOIL	BEST SOIL TO GROW IN	COMMENTS
Alfalfa *Medicago sativa*	May–July	12 months	Alkaline, dry soil	Fixes nitrogen; deep roots; dig in when green.
Field beans *Vicia faba*	October–November	6 months	Heavy soil	Fixes nitrogen; will regrow after first cutting.
Buckwheat *Fagopyrum esculentum*	May–July	3 months	Poor soil	No nitrogen fixing; quick growth producing lots of foliage.
Mustard *Sinapis alba*	March–August	2 months	All soils	No nitrogen fixing; treat as a brassica in crop rotation plans.
Hungarian grazing rye *Secale cereale*	August–November	6 months	All soils	No nitrogen fixing; dig in deeply; used at Berryfields.
Winter tares *Vicia sativa*	August–November	6 months	Alkaline, moist soil only	Fixes nitrogen; fast-growing, winter-hardy.

of compost or manure, only as part of the range of soil improvers at the organic gardener's disposal and as part of your general rotation of crops.

COMPANION PLANTING

Planting certain plants near to each other often has an advantage for either one of the crops. The usual advantage is to deter pests and diseases. This can occur in a number of ways:

◆ They can produce chemicals that repel pests and diseases.
◆ They can produce chemicals that mask the scent of vulnerable plants from pests.
◆ Their physical presence may hide vulnerable crops.
◆ They attract pests away from the desirable crops – they are sacrificial plants.
◆ They can attract the natural predators of a pest into the area.

The most popular example of companion planting is growing carrots and onions side by side. The theory is that the smell of the onions confuses carrot fly, a major pest of carrots, and the smell of the carrots deters onion fly. Basic research has shown that you need four times as many onions as carrots and that it is effective only when the onions are actively growing. Once the bulbs start to form, the carrot fly moves in. Whatever you are growing, it is good to avoid massed ranks of one type of vegetable. Visually, mixing vegetable types confuses many pests, including aphids. Monoculture is a playground for pests and diseases.

Basil planted with tomatoes repels whitefly, other flies and midges. Garlic deters aphids; mint deters cabbage moths; nasturtiums attract blackfly, thereby protecting other crops. French marigolds repel greenfly and blackfly because they produce a scent that is offensive – to the flies – and volatile root exudates. Asparagus prevents harmful nematodes from attacking tomatoes, and chervil stops aphids attacking lettuce. Coriander repels aphids, and dill attracts hoverflies and predatory wasps. Cabbages underplanted with dwarf French beans are less likely to be attacked by cabbage aphid and cabbage root fly. This is because a cabbage root fly detects chemicals on the leaf using its feet. If a female lands on several plants in succession, she will stop to lay her eggs. Cause a break in that succession and the fly will move off.

At Berryfields the sunflower trial was planted in the kitchen garden. This acted as an aphid magnet, drawing the pests away from nearby beans. As the sunflowers opened, swarms of hoverflies descended, whose larvae hatch within days and devour aphids. Bingo!

ASPARAGUS CASE STUDY

Asparagus is one of the most rewarding vegetables to grow because it tastes so much better when eaten absolutely fresh. This is something that just cannot be bought. Once the spears are cut, the cells continue to metabolize, converting the stored sugars into starch and tough fibre. So the investment of a little trouble and some patience rewards the gardener with a crop precious beyond price.

OPPOSITE Companion planting of French marigolds and tomatoes in the small greenhouse in the soft fruit garden. The marigolds are planted to deter greenfly and blackfly.

Asparagus can be grown from seed but is normally planted as crowns, which are available from nurseries and specialist suppliers at one or two years old. The older the crown, the stronger the plant. A crown is a young plant consisting of straggly roots and a central body, and the edible stems grow from the crown. The three requisites for successful growth are:

◆ A well-drained soil.
◆ A sunny position.
◆ A sheltered site

Preparation of the soil may seem like a lot of work, but it has to be done only once and crowns can live and be productive for over a hundred years.

RIGHT The lovely ferny foliage of asparagus, which we let grow uncut, so that the young plants could develop strong roots for future crops.

The day's work preparing an asparagus bed is a fraction of the time spent sowing and resowing carrots every year over a period of a hundred years.

◆ Weed the ground and measure out beds 1m (3 feet) wide and up to 10m (33 feet) long. Over 10m and the temptation to jump across instead of walking around is too great – with the chance that soil is trodden on or plants are trashed. Leave 1m (3 feet) between beds.
◆ Remove all the topsoil to a depth of 45cm (18 inches), mounding it on the paths between the beds.
◆ Add home-made compost or spent mushroom compost to the base of the bed and fork it in.
◆ Put a 10cm (4-inch) layer of horticultural grit into the bed (or wide, deep trench) and rotavate or dig it in. Do not stint on this as good drainage is essential.
◆ Rake the bottom of the trench level. Make two ridges running along the length of the bed. The tops of the ridges should be just below the top of the sides of the bed.
◆ Drape the crowns over the ridges, spacing them 30cm (12 inches) apart. Crowns should not dry out – keep them either in their packets or in a bucket covered with soil or compost.
◆ Shovel the mounded topsoil back over the crowns, taking care not to dislodge the crowns. Create a raised bed by using all the topsoil. The surface of the bed should be raised in the centre, sloping down to soil level to the sides.
◆ Congratulate yourself on having crafted a lovely thing that will produce luxury for generations and will not need

doing again in your lifetime.

◆ Throughout the year weed and water as required.

When you have made the asparagus bed, a little patience is required. I love this aspect of gardening, which is the absolute opposite of make-overs but, in its own way, just as exciting. In the first year do not pick any spears. Allow the shoots to develop feathery leaves that will feed the growing root systems. When the leaves turn yellow – around the end of October – cut them down to ground level and add them to your compost bin.

The following spring harvest a few of the strongest spears and enjoy eating them. Allow everything else to develop, cutting it down to ground level when it turns yellow. This cutting back should be repeated every autumn. The following spring cut more freely, but stop at the end of May. Then, after three years you will have strong crowns capable of producing a fine crop of spears, which you should eat without restraint until mid June. But stop then, every year, to allow the crowns to rest and produce foliage that will provide the energy for next spring's harvest.

Cut asparagus 2cm (¾ inch) below soil level with a sharp knife. Special asparagus knives are available that have curved blades and a serrated edge used for sawing the spears. This may have to be done every day when the crowns become established. Once all the conditions are right – both air and soil temperature – spears can grow up to

20cm (8 inches) a day. If you can't use asparagus immediately after cutting, stand the spears upright in a jug of water and store in the fridge

The thickness of the spears depends on the planting depth. Shallow-planted crowns produce thinner spears, deeper-planted crowns thicker ones. Thin asparagus is sometimes called sprue. The two varieties of asparagus growing at Berryfields are 'Connover's Colossal', an old variety that is an early, heavy cropper producing tasty, green spears, and 'Franklim', which produces high yields of thick, green spears with purple tips.

BRASSICAS CASE STUDY

Brassicas are not glamorous – we have all travelled on a train past rainy winter allotments dotted with ranks of sprouts and cabbages – but they are delicious, pretty easy to grow and generally very hardy. Members of the brassica family include brussels sprouts, cabbage, calabrese, cauliflower, Chinese cabbage, kohl rabi, pak choi, radish, sprouting broccoli, swede, turnip, mustard, cress, rocket, seakale, kale, mizuna and wallflowers.

All brassicas prefer cool, moist conditions. They also need plenty of nitrogen in the soil. Fertilizers and manure can add nitrogen – dried blood and leafmould are both good examples – but if they follow peas and beans or leguminous green manures in a crop rotation plan, all their nitrogen requirements are catered for.

Brassicas do not do so well on acidic soil,

where they are more likely to get club-root. So if the pH is below 7, add lime and use mushroom compost rather than manure or garden compost. This raises the pH, and makes it more alkaline. The symptoms of club-root in a plant are wilting, even when the soil is moist, with leaves that become yellow and chlorotic, occasionally pink-tinged, and roots that are swollen (like fingers and toes). Brassica weeds such as charlock and shepherd's purse can also carry the disease. When the roots swell and then disintegrate, spores are released into the soil, causing infection to spread to other brassica plants, and the fungus can remain in the soil for up to twenty years even when brassicas are absent. But if you have soil with a natural pH of 6.5 or higher, you are unlikely to experience the disease.

Other pests, diseases and problems lying in wait are:

◆ Cabbage root fly larvae: plants grow slowly, wilting on sunny days even when the soil is moist, and seedlings completely collapse. Female flies lay eggs near the base of seedlings, usually in the small gap between the stem and soil. Firm soil prevents windrock and reduces the chance of this gap appearing, so tread the prepared ground before planting. The eggs hatch out into white, legless maggots that eat the roots. The best defence is to put pieces of carpet, underfelt or even cardboard snugly around seedlings. The fly then lays her eggs on this collar, where they dry up before hatching. A tin-foil collar placed around the stems of seedlings stops the

maggots from burrowing into plant tissue.

◆ Caterpillars: caterpillars eat the leaves and hearts of many brassicas and can (and frequently do) reduce otherwise healthy plants to shreds and tatters. Control is the same for whichever caterpillar your brassicas have – net with a small-gauged netting before the caterpillars are active, which is any time after the end of June. In fact it is a good idea to net straight after planting to stop pigeons attacking the plants.

◆ Cabbage whitefly are white-winged insects, 2mm long, which feed on the undersides of the leaves. You can identify

NITROGEN-FIXING
Nitrogen makes up around 80% of the atmosphere, but it is in a form that isn't easily absorbed by plants. Some bacteria, called rhizobium bacteria, can convert it into a usable form and are called nitrogen-fixing bacteria. It has been estimated that, globally, the amount of nitrogen fixed by such bacteria is 110 million tonnes per year. Fixing nitrogen means splitting nitrogen molecules and using the atoms to build nitrates or ammonia compounds. These can then be used by plants. In return the plant gives the bacteria protection and sugars. When the plant dies down and decomposes, the fixed nitrogen becomes available to them – hence the reason cabbages follow peas and beans in a crop rotation plan. The peas and beans fix the nitrogen, and when the haulms are removed at the end of the growing season the nodules (the protective structure surrounding the bacteria) and fixed nitrogen are left in the soil.

THE THREE MAIN CATERPILLARS FOUND ON BRASSICAS

LARGE CABBAGE WHITE	SMALL CABBAGE WHITE	CABBAGE MOTH
Yellow with black markings	Pale green	Yellowish brown or green
Hairy body	Velvety	Smooth
Up to 40mm (1¼ inches) long	Up to 25mm (1 inch) long	Up to 45mm (1¾ inches) long
Feeds on outer leaves	Feeds on hearts	Eats leaves and hearts

them because the insects fly into the air when disturbed and infestations can result in sooty mould growth on leaves. These moulds feed on the sugary excrement from the whitefly and cause damage to leaves. Light infestations are tolerable, but if moulds are ruining leaves, use an organic soap spray on the undersides of the leaves.

Brassicas are easily grown from seed. I always used to sow them in a seed-bed, but nowadays I sow them under cover, mostly in spring, which enables me to protect them better from slugs. I then grow them on and plant them out after they have been hardened off. Some, such as radish, are best sown where they are going to mature. Radish is a good example of a catch crop. These are crops grown in soil that is around slower-growing crops. Radish can mature within six weeks in summer.

Spring cabbages are planted in autumn to provide an early-spring crop of leaves and mature heads later in the year. They take 35 weeks from sowing to maturity. Spring cabbage with rib of beef and boiled potatoes is one of my favourite meals.

Summer, winter and red cabbage mature in summer from spring plantings. They take around 20 weeks from sowing to maturity. They can be sown outside in drills during April, transplanted in May and cut in August and September. For an earlier crop, sow seed indoors or in a greenhouse in February.

MONTY'S CONFESSION

It has been well documented that I failed with my brassicas at Berryfields. A lot of attention was paid to soil preparation, correct planting and cabbage root fly, but the main pest of brassicas – the pigeon – was ignored. It was disheartening, but a good lesson – I suppose. But we set out to garden realistically and tell the whole truth and nothing but the truth, and as in every garden there are setbacks. It proves that if you don't net brassicas, you don't get brassicas.

Summer cauliflowers are sown in early spring, under cover, and are planted out in May. It takes around 20 weeks from sowing to maturity. Break larger outer leaves over the developing curds to prevent yellowing in the sun.

Purple broccoli is the most popular broccoli to grow, as it is hardy and

capable of producing a crop in most soil conditions. It is a long, slow crop but worth it, because homegrown broccoli is small and tender and quite unlike the bland stuff sold in supermarkets. I take 40 weeks from sowing to picking, but in mild winters you can sow in February. Cut the main spear first. This allows other side spears to develop fully.

LETTUCE CASE STUDY

I adore lettuce and like to eat a big plate of it every day. This is perfectly possible if you chose your varieties carefully and sow a small amount of seed every few weeks between February and September. The secret of good lettuce is to keep it moist and cool (but not cold). The seeds will not germinate if the soil is hot – about 15°C (59°F) is ideal. If growing plants dry out or get too hot, one or two things will happen:

◆ Leaves will taste bitter.
◆ Plants will run prematurely to seed.

The biggest problem when growing lettuce is getting the whole crop maturing at once. If you keep chickens you will know that they love lettuce that has bolted and gone to seed, and it all makes good compost, but it is a pity to waste too many plants. The trick is to sow little and often.

There are two options when sowing seed. The first is to sow directly into well-prepared soil. Germination will occur within ten days. The alternative, and a much better way to start lettuce off if you have problems with slugs and snails, is to sow under cover. I always broadcast the

seed thinly on to a seed tray filled with a pure coir compost. I stand the sown seed tray for ten minutes in a basin of water and never let it dry out again. Most salad seeds germinate fastest at a steady heat of around 15–18°C (59–64°F). As soon as they are large enough to handle I prick them out into plugs filled with a home-made compost made from one part sieved molehills or loam, one part sieved garden compost, two parts coir and one part vermiculite or grit. I happily discard at least half the germinated seeds at this stage – which is no more than I would do if I thinned a row sown directly outside. After a few days back in the greenhouse to get used to their new soil, the plugs spend a week in a cold frame and then sit in a standing-out bay until I plant them out. The critical factor during these stages is that seedlings are kept free of pests and that they are easy to water and monitor.

LEFT The red-leaved lettuce 'Lollo Rosso', sown in individual plugs and raised under cover, ready to be planted out into the garden.

OPPOSITE Broccoli is sold in every supermarket throughout the year. However, in most cases it's actually calabrese, whereas true purple-sprouting broccoli like this is a delicious seasonal treat, only available in late winter and spring and best eaten fresh from the garden.

The ideal conditions for lettuce, whether sown directly into the soil or in containers, are:

◆ Partial shade – definitely shaded from midsummer sun.
◆ Moisture-retentive soil.
◆ Fertile soil.
◆ Plenty of water.
◆ Successional sowings every fortnight.
◆ Sow under cover to produce strong plants for planting out.
◆ Do not feed with fertilizer, as soft growth is prone to fungal attacks.

Lettuce is prone to attack from a number of pests and diseases, but hard-grown, fast-grown, healthily grown plants can withstand problems.

Lettuce grow perfectly well in containers, where the same lettuce-growing rules apply. With smaller containers it is easy to carry them out of the strong midday sun or position in shade. It is also easier to protect developing plants from slug and snail attack. Bands of petroleum jelly smeared around the rim of the pot will deter slugs and snails.

Varieties
Cos varieties have upright leaves that gently curve and are my own favourite. 'Little Gem' is small, fast-growing, crispy and trouble-free. 'Lobjoit's Green' is an old variety with deep green, crispy leaves

RIGHT Generous spacing from the earliest stages, as with these 'Red Oak Leaf' lettuces, leads to strong, healthy plants.

that fold back in on themselves like the hull of a boat. 'Winter Density' is a sweet-tasting Cos lettuce sown in early autumn for a spring picking.

BUTTERHEAD or round lettuces have flat, rounded heads and soft leaves. 'Tom Thumb' is good for smaller plots and containers, is quick to mature and produces tennis-ball-sized heads. 'All the Year Round' is popular because it is easy to grow and can be sown, wait for it, all the year round. It's also slow to run to seed in dry weather.

CRISPHEAD or Iceberg lettuces produce large hearts of curly, crispy – but to my mind fairly tasteless – leaves. 'Webb's Wonderful' is a popular variety producing large, frilly-leaved hearts that succeed in dry weather. 'Avoncrisp' is resistant to mildew and root aphids and is also slow to run to seed.

LOOSE-LEAF varieties do not form hearts but consist of loose leaves that can be picked individually (pick outer leaves if leaving the plant in the ground and allow inner leaves to develop) or by cutting the whole plant. 'Salad Bowl' and 'Red Salad Bowl', 'Green Oak Leaf' and 'Red Oak Leaf' are all good and produce fine, intricately cut, curly leaves. It's important to pick the leaves regularly to ensure continuous production.

WINTER LETTUCE: I grow 'Winter Density', 'Rouge D'Hiver', 'All the Year Round', 'Kendo' and both green and red oakleaf as my main winter lettuces.

LETTUCE PESTS AND DISEASES

SYMPTOMS	PROBLEM	PREVENTION
Yellow patches on leaves. Mouldy patches develop. Worse in cool, wet weather.	Downy mildew.	Avoid overcrowding. Pick off infected leaves.
Yellow mottling on leaves.	Mosaic virus.	Sorry – dig up and burn plants.
Plants produce flower heads from hearts.	Bolting or running to seed.	Growth has stopped at some stage in the plants' life. Dryness? Late planting out – root-bound seedlings? Lift and put on the compost heap.
Severed stems; plants topple over.	Cutworm. Large grey-brown caterpillars in the soil near the plants.	Regularly hoe around plants to bring the caterpillars to the surface for birds or you.
Hearting varieties not hearting up.	Lack of organic matter in the soil; lack of water.	Improve soil for the next crop and never let plants dry out.
Plants suddenly wilt and collapse. When pulled up the roots have a white, powdery coating.	Lettuce root aphid. The white coating is discharged by little yellow aphids (*Pemphigus bursaurius*) that eat the roots.	Lift and burn all plants in the bed and do not replant with lettuce for two years. Made much worse by drought, so keep well watered.

VEGETABLES AT BERRYFIELDS

ARTICHOKES (GLOBE): sow under cover in February and plant out in April, or take offsets in April. Remove all chokes in first year, harvest throughout second and third years, then discard. They need rich soil and a protective mulch in winter.

BROAD BEANS: sow in October for a May crop. Sow in March and April for a summer harvest. Water only if dry weather coincides with swelling pods.

BEETROOT: sow from April to August for cropping from June to the following spring. Sow thinly, as most seed is actually a cluster capable of producing many seedlings. Pick young to avoid woody roots.

CARROTS: sow from March for cropping from June onwards. Select round varieties if your soil is heavy clay. They come after brassicas in rotation, so never add manure to the soil before sowing.

CHARD: Swiss, ruby or rainbow are all delicious. Sow seed in pots indoors from April for harvesting from August. Cut leaves as you need them and they will regrow from the base. Plants will stand over winter. They like really rich soil.

CHICORY: sow April to June, plant out in rows at 30cm (12-inch) spacing and keep weeded. Summer growth of green leaves serves only to mature the root, and winter leaves – often red – are produced from late September through to March. Plants can withstand cold but hate sitting in wet damp soil, so cloches might be necessary in a very wet winter.

MONTY'S TIP

Courgettes are thirsty plants and put most of their rapid growth on during summer. There is never enough time to water during dry periods, so planting courgettes in hollows made into the soil utilizes the rain. Give the planting hole a generous spadeful of home-made compost to improve the soil structure and its capacity to retain water.

COURGETTES: sow in early May and plant out mid June. Plant into enriched soil and water copiously. Space the plants 1m (3 feet) apart as they grow quickly and vigorously. Pick courgettes every day and pick them young.

FRENCH BEANS: sow May–July for late-summer cropping. Shelter from high winds. Add plenty of manure or compost before planting. Water if dry weather coincides with flowering time and pod production.

LEEKS: sow outdoors from April or under glass in February. Leeks prefer a sunny spot and lots of organic matter in the soil. Plant in dibbed holes or in groups of three or four plants. Harvest young for the tastiest leeks.

ONIONS: can be grown from sets or seed. Sets are immature onions and more reliable. Plant them January–March to harvest in July and August. Seeds give greater choice of variety and can be sown indoors from February for planting out in May for a crop in August. Over-wintering onion sets are planted in August and September, producing an early crop in May. Hand weed around

plants as roots are close to the surface.

PARSNIPS: sow in early march for a crop in late October through to March. Parsnips are slow to germinate, so intersow with radish that can be harvested before the parsnips compete for space. Thin to 5–8cm (2–3-inch) spacing. Parsnips are part of the same rotation as carrots, so never manure the site. Parsnips taste much better after a frost has intensified the sugars.

PEAS: add plenty of organic matter to the soil before planting. Do not water until flowers appear and then do not allow the plants to dry out. Regularly pick pods and eat within hours. Sugars start to turn to starch as soon as the pods are picked. Sow throughout spring for crops from midsummer onwards.

POTATOES: buy only certified virus-free seed potatoes. Start into growth (chit) in egg boxes in a cool greenhouse or on a bright windowsill. Plant out in drills from the end of March to June (traditionally Easter was the time that potatoes were planted). When green growth appears above the ridges, earth up. Assuming steady growth, first early varieties are harvested after 90 days, second early varieties after 100 days and maincrop varieties after 120 days, although all can stay in the ground for quite a bit longer than this. Water well when plants flower. Dry conditions will result in a low yield.

PUMPKINS: sow in mid April and plant

out in early June when nights have warmed up. They like very rich soil and lots of water. Harvest before the first frosts and expose plants to sunshine to harden the skins for longer storage.

RUNNER BEANS: delay sowing outdoors until the frosts have finished. Sow back-up seeds indoors during April. Plant out only hardened-off seedlings. Initially help plants on to supports and tie in. Never allow to dry out.

SHALLOTS: plant out sets from February to April for a crop in July and August. At harvest time loosen soil beneath the bulbs and allow to dry on the soil surface before using and storing.

SPINACH: grow between rows of tall-growing crops. Shade reduces the risk of spinach plants running to seed. Sow summer varieties every fortnight between March and June. Pick outer leaves when they reach a usable size.

SWEET CORN: sow indoors in early May and plant out in early June. Plant in blocks rather than rows as this helps pollination. Mound soil around the base of stems to help anchoring roots develop. Underplant with courgettes. Cobs are ready when the silky tassels turn brown. Have the water boiling before picking to ensure a sweet taste.

KITCHEN-GARDEN BASICS

◆ Grow what you like to eat.
◆ Select a sunny site for your kitchen garden.
◆ Construct raised beds.
◆ Hard pave pathways.
◆ Spend as much time as possible improving the soil with organic matter.
◆ Grow varieties for taste.
◆ Sow little and often to avoid gluts.
◆ Grow in raised beds and containers.
◆ Devise a crop rotation plan.
◆ Grow organically.

LEFT Spinach ready for harvesting, with the leaves still young and tender.

OPPOSITE Collecting our homegrown harvest is one of my greatest pleasures.

A YEAR IN THE KITCHEN GARDEN

SPRING

◆ Sow when the weather conditions are right and the soil warms up.

◆ Weed every day.

◆ Pick early broad beans.

◆ Remove growing tips from broad beans to avoid blackfly infestations.

◆ Plant out many seedlings.

SUMMER

◆ Water crops in dry weather.

◆ Harvest early potatoes to avoid blight problems.

◆ Weed.

◆ Pick crops as they mature.

◆ Sow winter salads and spring cabbage.

AUTUMN

◆ Clear away crops.

◆ Sow green manure.

◆ Sow early broad beans.

◆ Dig ground if it is vacant.

◆ Plant over-wintering onion sets.

WINTER

◆ Dig vacant ground.

◆ Incorporate organic matter into the soil.

◆ Construct raised beds.

◆ Devise crop rotation.

◆ Order seeds, onion sets and seed potatoes.

ABOVE In my element – harvesting in high summer at Berryfields.

OPPOSITE Shallots harvested, dried and ready for storage. In general, shallots keep much better than onions.

'At **Berryfields** there are *borders* down one side of the greenhouse, and a *gravelled area* beneath staging on the other side. Down the centre of the greenhouse is a *hard, paved path*. This enables everyone to use the greenhouse **without damaging** the soil. The central path is *as wide as* a wheelbarrow.'

the greenhouse

WHEN WE TOOK OVER BERRYFIELDS THERE WAS NO greenhouse, so adding one to the garden was among our first priorities. A greenhouse enlarges all the possibilities within any kind of garden. It extends seasons, provides an environment for growing a range of plants that would not otherwise ripen or develop fully, hugely expands the opportunities for propagation, and is a haven for tender plants in winter. It also provides a dry place to film when it is pouring with rain! But with or without a film crew, I cannot recommend too highly the advantages of having a greenhouse in any garden.

GREENHOUSE SELECTION

The Berryfields greenhouse is 3m (10 feet) wide and 10m (33 feet) long, which is clearly enormous and consequentially quite a big investment. We can justify that for the advantages that it brings to the programme, because Berryfields is a big garden, but however big or small your garden and your budget, a greenhouse is going to be a significant investment and needs careful thought.

Before committing yourself to a particular type or size of greenhouse it is important to plan what you are most likely to use it for. For example, headroom is required if you plan to grow tomatoes, whereas plenty of waist-high benching is required if you plan to grow alpines. The ability to split a greenhouse into sections may be required if you plan tropical plants.

Almost everyone with a greenhouse eventually wishes that it were bigger, so buy the biggest greenhouse your garden or your budget will allow. There is a good choice of greenhouses available to gardeners, with the 2.5m × 2m (8 feet × 6 feet) being the number one seller. The first figure refers to the length of the greenhouse and the second the width. It is worth considering buying a wider greenhouse – the door is usually wider, too, giving easier access, and while units are available to enable many greenhouses to be extended in length, it is very tricky to increase the width.

Shape

Straight-sided, rectangular greenhouses are best for gardeners and plants. Canes or strings are easily attached to straight sides and both headroom and growing room is maximized. Octagonal, hexagonal and pentagonal greenhouses are all available but can prove awkward when growing crops such as tomatoes or cucumbers. However, they can be useful for pot plants, alpines and when used as propagation houses.

The pitch or slope of a greenhouse roof is important. A shallow pitch of less than 25 degrees can collect water or snow. This can cause damage through breakages and may encourage moss growth, restricting the amount of light entering the greenhouse. With steeper-pitched roofs, water and snow easily run off.

Frames

Popular greenhouse frames are either wooden or aluminium. Wood can be either softwood or hardwood. Hardwood is more expensive but does last longer, and softwood frames also need regular maintenance. Ensure that all hardwood comes from a managed woodland. (The Forest Stewardship Council (FSC) is an international, non-governmental organization dedicated to promoting responsible management of the world's forests. If you see a label with 'FSC approved' on it, you know the wood is from a reputable source. If in doubt, ask the retailer.)

Aluminium, up to a few years ago, was bright and shiny. Powder coatings have been developed and greenhouses are now available in subtle blues and greens. Both blend well into a garden scheme. Buy only quality aluminium, as it will withstand the considerable forces of a growing year – and the British weather.

Both wood and aluminium have pros and cons. Wooden greenhouses are slower to warm up and cool down – therefore they hold a more constant temperature. Aluminium ones heat up more quickly but also lose more heat. Aluminium ones should last longer and need less maintenance, but wooden ones generally look nicer and are more pleasant to work in. At Berryfields we have a wooden one, but in the end it is a personal choice.

Glazing

There are four main glazing options:

◆ Horticultural glass is the lowest grade of glass available. It is cheap but dangerous – when broken it shatters into large shards.

◆ Toughened, tempered or safety glass is now used as standard in many greenhouses. When broken it shatters into very small pieces – still dangerous, but not as bad as horticultural glass. Buy toughened glass only if it is has the safety kitemark from the British Standards Institute BS6206.

◆ Polycarbonate has many advantages: it does not shatter; its twin-wall-layer construction acts like double-glazing; it doesn't have sharp edges; and it's easy to handle. But it is expensive and the double-glazing effect can result in a hot greenhouse during summer months. In

small greenhouses this effect is intensified.

◆ Acrylic sheets are cheap and lightweight, but can degrade in the sun after a few years, becoming brittle and yellow. All plastics should be UV-inhibited, resulting in clarity for many years. Cheaper greenhouses may not be UV-inhibited.

There are also smaller greenhouses, or grow rooms, that are a simple aluminium or tubular steel frame over which a clear plastic cover is secured. Cheap and easy to assemble, they are similar to a large cold frame or cloche. For their price, they are good at covering trays of tender seedlings, but growing a crop of tomatoes in one is problematical.

If you do buy one, a good tip when erecting it is to lay the plastic cover in the sun to become pliable. The plastic is prone to splitting if forced over the frame straight from the box.

SITING A GREENHOUSE

Ideally, the ridge of the greenhouse should run in an east–west axis to trap as much sunlight as possible without casting shade on itself. However, the advantages are minimal and are important only to commercial growers.

Position a greenhouse as close to the house as possible. This makes it easier to nip out and check, and it will also be cheaper and easier to lay electric cable to it. The main objective when siting a greenhouse is avoidance of overhanging trees. These will cast shadows, shed leaves on to the greenhouse roof and drip water, leading to moss and algae growth. Even a shrub 2m (6 feet) high will cast shadows into the greenhouse when the sun is low in winter. Having said all that, a greenhouse situated away from

MONTY'S TIP

A lot of rain falls on a greenhouse roof and none of it should be wasted. Fix guttering to both sides of the greenhouse and run downpipes into water butts or tanks. Place wire netting over the top of the downpipe to prevent leaves falling into the water and clogging the pipe. Ensure water butts are raised well off the ground – purpose-made stands are available but bricks will do the same job – to allow you to fill your watering-can. Mind you, it is very much quicker to dip a can than to fill it from a tap.

everything, including the home, is not welcoming and may get neglected.

A hedge planted nearby will act as a good wind filter. Stopping the wind completely is not good, as eddy currents are often formed behind such windbreaks that can cause more damage than a simple blast of wind. Filtering the wind is more effective than blocking it and a mixed hedge planted 3m (10 feet) away from the greenhouse will stop any damage. At Berryfields the hazel hurdles filter the wind.

Once the site is selected, it is important that it is level. This is vital if the greenhouse is to survive. On no account should you erect a greenhouse directly on to soil. Soil moves, frames twist and glass breaks. Retailers often sell ready-made bases for their greenhouses. A solid base of paving slabs is good. Even a fully glazed greenhouse is lightweight and a gust of wind through an open door can move a 2.5m × 2m (8 feet × 6 feet) one. Always secure your greenhouse to its base and the base securely to foundations. The Berryfields greenhouse sits on a brick wall, which in turn has been built on top of firm foundations.

If you are planning to grow directly in the soil borders, make sure the soil is in a fit state to support crops, or is at least workable. At Berryfields there are borders down one side of the greenhouse, and a gravelled area beneath staging on the other side. Down the centre of the greenhouse is a hard, paved path. This enables everyone to use the

greenhouse without damaging the soil. The central path is as wide as a wheelbarrow.

EQUIPPING A GREENHOUSE
Water

A dedicated water supply is essential if you are to maintain a well-stocked greenhouse. There are three ways to achieve this. The most basic is a water butt collecting the rainwater from the greenhouse roof. Every greenhouse should have at least one – and preferably two – butts, as a supply of rainwater is essential for some plants. A large container inside the greenhouse (ideally under staging) can be filled by a hosepipe and used for dipping a watering-can. Ideally the container is partially sunk into the ground. This means that the water is at the same ambient temperature as the plants and

avoids giving tender seedlings a shock. But best of all is to have a mains tap fitted inside your greenhouse. At Berryfields we have all three of these water supplies.

Electricity

Electricity adds another dimension to your greenhouse, providing the opportunity for running heaters, propagators, mist units for rooting cuttings, lighting and a radio. But electricity and greenhouses mix only if the electricity is installed by a qualified electrician. Armour cable and waterproof sockets are essential.

Benches and Shelving

Benches and shelving are essential parts of the greenhouse but never seem to be part of the standard package. It's worth bearing this in mind when planning your budget, as benching and shelving can often cost as much again as a cheap greenhouse. Benches, or staging, should be constructed so they are at a comfortable working level, and that depends on your height. Experiment by placing bricks under each leg of the benching to raise the benching until it is at the correct height. Benching should be wide enough to be practical but not so wide that watering or attention to the seedlings at the back of the benching is neglected. In practice it is best to have enough room for at least two seed trays end to end. Whether the benching is made out of wood or aluminium, when loaded it has to take a lot of weight. Make sure the benching is sturdy, adding extra cross pieces if required.

LEFT Any kind of greenhouse hugely increases the range and opportunities for propagating your own seeds and cuttings. These are all seedlings growing for the £20 pound border.

Ventilation

Ventilation is as important as heat in a greenhouse, and as a rule more harm is done by too little ventilation than too much. It helps control the heat and reduce humidity that can encourage fungal and bacterial diseases. The largest ventilator in a greenhouse is the door – and this can be sliding or hinged. Sliding doors don't slam shut, especially on filming days, but the runners can become worn, hindering the opening and closing process. Hinged doors do slam and should open outwards, away from the greenhouse. This increases the usable space inside and it means that wind blows the door against the frame, making a draught-proof seal.

MONTY'S CONFESSION
A large dip tank full of water is a good idea in a greenhouse. It is easier to fill a watering-can by dipping it into a tank than at a tap; the water is at ambient temperature, preventing the shock of cold water on seedlings, and the supply is there, waiting. It's also an accident waiting to happen – if you have a camera crew around. Dipping a watering-can in the dip tank, pulling it out and watering the plants creates a lot of dripping and sloshing. No one has owned up, but resting a camera next to the dip tank between takes, especially when a can is being filled and rushed to the scene of filming is – was – not a good idea. The camera, soaked to the tape, was out of action for three hours. Luckily the tape was blank.

Most greenhouses have at least one vent fitted to the roof as standard, but it is worth asking the greenhouse manufacturer to add another if at all possible. But side vents are equally important. The Berryfields greenhouse has a row of side vents – or windows that open – along both sides, and this encourages good air circulation. For low-level ventilation louvered vents are best, as they open to allow lots of air circulation but will stop any animals entering the greenhouse.

If you are away from the greenhouse during the day it is a wise precaution to fit automatic ventilators. These work by means of a cylinder of wax that expands or contracts according to the temperature. A rise causes expansion, which pushes a piston that in turn pushes the window open, whereas cooling causes a contraction of the wax and the window closes.

Heating

Heating a conservatory is usually done by connecting a radiator to the central heating of the main house. Tubular heaters are often used as they are silent; the even heat is thermostatically controlled; and units can look good.

Two electric fan heaters have been fitted in the Berryfields greenhouse. One is placed in the cool area of the greenhouse and the other is providing the heat to maintain 20°C (68°F) in the partitioned end section of the greenhouse. At Berryfields we have two areas within the greenhouse – one is cool and the other warm. Textbooks and experts all have their differing views on what to call greenhouses when they are heated to a particular temperature. A 'cool' greenhouse is not just a measure of how trendy it is, but describes its temperature range as being kept above 5°C (41°F) – which enables frost-tender plants to be successfully over-wintered. A greenhouse heated to a constant 20°C (68°F) was often called a stove house and more recently a tropical house. The warm part of the Berryfields greenhouse – much valued by the production team as the only warm spot on cold, wet days – is around 18°C (64°F) and capable of supporting year-round growth of house- or conservatory plants.

A cold greenhouse is unheated and is therefore only 3 or 4 degrees above the outside temperature, and in severe weather plants inside the greenhouse will freeze.

Ways to save money on heating bills:

◆ Buy a heater with a thermostatic control. Set the thermostat to the required temperature and the heater will do the rest.
◆ Make sure your heater is serviced and maintained. Trim wicks in paraffin burners to ensure economy and smokeless heat.
◆ Clean dirt off all heating elements.
◆ Block all draughts and ensure doorways are well insulated. Bubble plastic is a good insulator on all glazing

TYPES OF HEATING FOR THE GREENHOUSE

HEAT SOURCE	ADVANTAGES	DISADVANTAGES
Electric fan heater	Readily available No fumes Easy to control Good air circulation Cools air in summer No water vapour output	Expensive to set up. Power cut = no heat; back-up required.
Paraffin	Cheap to buy No installation costs	High water vapour output. Regular refilling. Possible smoke damage to sensitive plants. Low control over heat output.
Gas	Easy to control	High water vapour output. Gas canisters can be cumbersome to handle. Back-up required.

panels and as a draught curtain behind doors, and is easily affixed to both wooden and metal frames. Check that there is a gap between the glass and the plastic, as this is what provides the vital layer of air that heats up in the sun and retains heat in the greenhouse. Some gardeners insulate the whole of their greenhouse, but this can cause condensation problems. Insulating just the roof will save heat and money. Some gardeners leave the insulation in place all year round. In

MONTY'S TIP
Always have a thermometer in the greenhouse and another if it is divided up. Aim for a steady heat of around 15–18°C (59–64°F) rather than huge fluctuations.

summer it acts as shading. However, in spring and early autumn it can filter out too much light and plants can suffer.

◆ Rather than heating the whole greenhouse in winter, condense plants into half of the greenhouse and heat this. It will halve your heating costs. Make sure there is good ventilation to reduce the risk of diseases.

◆ Large greenhouses will be able to accommodate a complete smaller greenhouse inside. This is in effect the ultimate double-glazing.

◆ Use a minimum/maximum thermometer. This thermometer shows what the minimum and maximum temperatures achieved were in the period since resetting. It gives the gardener a precise idea of how well the heating and ventilation are working. It may show that a heater could be turned down. As with all

thermometers, place it out of direct sun in a place where air can circulate around it.

COLD FRAMES

Cold frames are, in my opinion, much underrated. If you do not have room for a greenhouse then you can certainly squeeze a cold frame into the garden, and even if you have dozens of greenhouses, cold frames would still be invaluable. They can be used to over-winter plants, or to grow vegetables directly into the soil, but they are probably most useful for hardening off. Once seedlings have reached the stage prior to planting out, they need to be acclimatized – or hardened off – to outside conditions. Moving many seedlings straight from the greenhouse to the outdoors is like a human going from a hospital ward into icy cold water, and the shock results in stunted growth or even death. Cold frames are therefore a halfway house between the warmth and protection of a greenhouse and the outdoors. Heaters are available for cold frames, but insulation with polystyrene, covered with carpet, rugs, cardboard or newspaper on the coldest of nights, will enable seedlings to survive without extra heat. During all but the coldest of days the tops of cold frames should be opened, so as to allow cooler air in around the seedlings, and then closed before sunset.

EDIBLE GREENHOUSE CROPS
Tomatoes

I sow my seed in two or three batches about two months before planting out, which means from mid February to the end of March. There is no point in

OPPOSITE As well as being the ideal place for raising young plants and growing tender vegetables, the greenhouse provides a warm, light environment in which to overwinter tender plants.

sowing too early if you are growing the plants outside, as they will not grow well until the nights warm up in June. I have tried lots of different sowing methods, but scattering seeds thinly on to a seed tray filled with peat-free compost works as well as anything. Tomatoes need some heat – around 15°C (59°F) – to germinate, so bring them indoors or, as I strongly recommend, invest in a heated propagating mat.

They germinate quickly, and as soon as you can see two 'true' leaves with zigzag edges, carefully pot them on into large plugs with a richer, peat-free compost. I usually pot mine on into 8cm (3-inch) pots once the seedlings are growing strongly. Do not allow plants to be exposed to cold. One cold night where temperatures fall near to freezing will stop your tomato plants from growing. Plants will look purple or blue and they never fully recover. Even when the seedlings are warm and well-watered they will still grow fairly slowly until light levels increase in April.

Tomatoes grow best in soil and under cover, but they will also grow in containers and outside in a bed, although outdoor tomatoes will ripen well only in the hottest of summers and the sunniest of spots.

The choice of location will partly be driven by the way that a particular variety grows. There are two variations, bush and cordon, which you will often see referred to as determinate and indeterminate. Bush tomatoes grow to a

vigorous bushy size, the fruit all ripens more or less at once and is harvested. End of story. Cordon tomatoes will keep growing for as long as the conditions are right, reaching astonishing heights and producing fruit over a long period, although our climate restricts this in most places to between July and October.

Cordon tomatoes are trained up a cane or twine and are pruned by pinching out all the lateral shoots that grow at 45 degrees between the stem and leaves. These shoots are extremely vigorous and take too much energy into plant rather than fruit growth. Bush tomatoes need no pruning at all but take much more space. Always plant tomatoes deeply, so that the stem is buried right up to the first pair of leaves. New roots will grow from the submerged part of the stem that will both anchor it more securely and provide more food and water for the mature plant.

I plant cordons with plants about 45cm (18 inches) apart and 1m (3 feet) between the rows. Although they are so close together there is plenty of room between and around the rows for picking and pinching out and for air to circulate. Stake the cordons very firmly so that even when the plants are 2.5m (8 feet) tall and top heavy with about 45kg (10lb) of fruit, they remain steady.

Allow at least 1m (3 feet) in each direction between bush plants and preferably twice that between rows. Support them with canes and string or wire to stop them flopping over.

If you are growing in containers, a 15-litre pot is about the smallest workable size; 20 litres is much better. Peat-free grow-bags can be much improved by taking a couple of old pots and cutting the bottoms out before fixing them into the bag. Then plant the tomatoes into the pots so the roots grow on down into the bag beneath them.

Tomatoes need plenty of water, especially as they are growing. I water every three or four days in the soil and every day in pots. As the fruits start to ripen this watering regime can be cut back; otherwise the skins may split. Also too much water makes for big, tasteless fruits – and you might as well go to a supermarket for those.

If you have good soil, well enriched with compost, the plants will not need feeding. But container-grown plants do well with a feed once a week. I use liquid seaweed or home-made comfrey fertilizer. Comfrey is very good for tomatoes and the leaves can simply be cut and laid as a mulch around the plants.

Tomatoes are easy to grow but do need regular attention, especially cordon types (which are by far the more common). It is really important to support them well and to keep them tied in. This will have to be done weekly between mid June and August. In an ideal world the sideshoots would be pinched out daily, but this can be done at the same time as the tying in.

LEFT Tomatoes are perhaps the most common crop grown under glass and there are many tried and tested ways of raising them.

TOP Ring culture – a high sleeve is inserted into a growing bag to provide added space and food for the roots.

MIDDLE A young tomato seedling, pricked out in a pot to encourage healthy, strong growth.

BELOW These tomatoes are clearly not as healthy as they could – or should – be. We have our failures at Berryfields too!

Potential Tomato Problems

Although tomatoes like heat and plenty of moisture, many of their problems occur because there is not sufficient air flow around the plants. As the fruits set it is a good idea to remove the lower leaves up to the first truss of fruit. When these have ripened, the next set of leaves can be taken off, and so on until by the end of September the plants are completely leafless. This will also speed up the ripening of green fruits.

BLIGHT. Tomatoes are close cousins to potatoes and suffer the same diseases, especially potato blight. You should not grow outdoor tomatoes in soil that has had potatoes in it for at least two years, and try

MONTY'S TIP

Green tomatoes can be ripened by placing with a ripe banana in a bowl and covering with a cloth. Ethylene from the ripe banana helps ripen the fruit. Whole plants can be pulled out of the soil and hung upside down in a frost-free potting shed. The fruit will develop more flavour if it ripens on the plant.

to keep outdoor tomatoes as far away from your spuds as possible. The blight manifests itself as pale brown blotches on the leaves that will quickly radiate out. The fungus can also get to the fruit, making them inedible. At first signs remove all affected leaves and spray with Bordeaux mixture (an organically acceptable combination of copper sulphate and lime). BLOSSOM END ROT. This shows as a flattened, calloused hard brown disc at the end of the fruit. It is caused by

inadequate water supply which, in turn, stops the plant from taking in enough calcium, so that the cells collapse. Water regularly and, if your soil is naturally very acidic, grow only small-fruited varieties that tend to be less susceptible.

SPLITTING FRUITS AND LEAF CURL. Fruits sometimes split and develop a grey, wispy mould. It is caused by an irregular water supply or big variations in temperature between day and night. Close the greenhouse before the evening cools down and keep it wide open all day. Cold nights will also cause leaves to curl up lengthways and look as though they are about to die. Older leaves are more affected than young ones.

WHITE FLY. The adult lays its eggs on the lower leaves, and after a nymph stage the new adult emerges and feeds on the leaves, sucking sap, spreading viruses and exuding honeydew on which a fungus grows. The flies over-winter, especially on perennial plants, so try not to keep plants like fuchsias over-wintering in a greenhouse that is to grow tomatoes the following summer. At Berryfields we grow basil with our tomatoes as an effective deterrent.

Varieties

There is a vast choice when it comes to tomato varieties, but the following grew well in the Berryfields greenhouse:

◆ 'Shirley': produced heavy crops of medium-sized, red fruits. It has a long fruiting season and is more tolerant to cold than other varieties. The short distance between leaves enables the plant to pack a lot of fruit into the allocated space.

◆ 'Brandywine': very large fruits with very meaty, red flesh. An old Amish variety dating back to 1885 and delicious raw or cooked.

◆ 'Gardener's Delight': one of the tastiest cherry or small-fruiting tomatoes. Each plant produced large trusses of delicious fruit.

◆ 'Sungold': small, yellowy/golden and mouthwateringly delicious. The favourite of the film crew for popping into their mouths when they thought no one was looking …

◆ 'Black Russian': medium-sized fruits with vermilion skin clouding alarmingly to a greeny-chocolate top. It looks as if it is dying, but tastes as if it and you have gone to heaven.

Chillies

Chillies are easy enough to grow, although a greenhouse or at least a cold frame is necessary. They are members of the Solanaceae family, and if you treat a pepper like a tomato you will not go far wrong, although they can be fine-tuned a little to be most productive.

There are five main wild species of chilli: *Capsicum annuum*, that provides all sweet peppers and many of the hot ones including Jalapeno and Bell varieties; *C. frutescens*, most notable for Tabasco; *C. chinense*, which includes the blisteringly hot Habanero and Scotch Bonnet varieties; *C. baccatum*, containing the Aji varieties, and *C. pubescens*, which provides the Rocoto and Manzano varieties.

Chillies, of course, are hot. Heat in chillies is measured in Scoville units. Sweet peppers have none, Jalapenos get measured at 2500–5000 units, the Guajillo are rated at 20,000 and Tabasco at 30,000–50,000. A super Habanero or Scotch Bonnet clocks in at 100,000–350,000 units, although by then taste has become an assault. A few years ago, when *Gardeners' World* was filming at the West Dean chilli fiesta, I tasted a sauce that claimed to be the hottest in the world. It was like eating a swarm of flaming hornets.

While some people take great pride in their ability to withstand such assaults, this has only limited relevence to the gardener. Apart from anything else, individual fruits from the same plant can

LEFT Chillies hanging up to dry in the sun.

vary hugely in heat, and each fruit is always hotter nearer the shoulder than at the tip – so a tentative nibble at the end is likely to give a false sense of security. A chilli is not actually hot, of course. The sensation of heat is caused by an acute reaction to capsaicin, which is primarily found in the pithy white ribs that run down the middle and along the sides of a pepper and which connect the seeds to the flesh. The proximity of the seeds to this pith makes them hot too. The only practical way to eat the very hot chillies is carefully to remove the pith and seeds, wearing disposable gloves or using a knife and fork which are then immediately washed in hot soapy water. There is no connection between colour and heat – plenty of yellow, orange or even purple chillies are hotter than many red ones.

You can increase the amount of capsaicin by making the plant struggle. So the hotter the sun, the poorer the soil and the less water that the pepper gets, the hotter the fruit will be – although the crop will be smaller in yield and individual size. But there is no need to strain after extra capsaicin, as there are plenty of varieties that will blow your head off when grown well.

'Growing well' means sowing the seeds early – in March or even mid February if you have a heated greenhouse – and not letting the temperature drop below 15°C (59°F). Given enough heat, they are fast to germinate but develop slowly as seedlings – in the case of the Habaneros, very slowly indeed. Prick them out into small pots or plugs with a well-drained,

peat-free potting compost (I add extra vermiculite to the mix) before potting them on finally into a 2-litre pot. This can look niggardly for some of the bigger varieties like 'De Arbol', but it is big enough. Growing conditions affect the heat of the fruit. Cooler temperatures, or picking fruit in autumn, will result in less heat. A hot summer combined with picking in midsummer will result in fruit that is really hot. Heat levels also increase with maturity, but may decline in some varieties once the fruit changes colour.

They are best watered every morning and not after about 5 p.m., as they are prone to fungal diseases and should not go into the evening damp. They also need plenty of ventilation for the same reason. (Habeneros are a slight exception to this rule and will grow well under more humid conditions.) A high-potash feed will make a marked difference to flower and fruit production, and I give them a liquid seaweed or comfrey feed once a week. Pinch the tops out around the end of August to encourage them to produce more fruits rather than foliage.

As a rule, the hotter the pepper is, the longer it will take to mature, but the fruits can be picked at any time, although a fully ripe chilli will have more sugars and therefore a richer, more complex taste and will store better. If you keep picking, new flowers and fruits will appear right into autumn. When dried they will keep for literally years in a Kilner jar.

Weight for weight, chillies have 75 times more vitamin C than oranges. They are also packed with beta-carotene and bioflavanoids – both antioxidants – along with vitamins E and B. There's also a soupçon of potassium thrown in for good measure. The shiny green leaves also make chillies attractive plants to grow and display in the house or conservatory.

There are many varieties to choose from, but two stand out from the number grown in the Berryfields greenhouse:

◆ 'Habanero': hot – very hot. Possibly the hottest chilli available, although a variety called 'Tepin' is claimed to be hotter. It will have to be trialled. 'Habanero' grew strongly, producing lantern-shaped fruits that were wrinkled. The salmon-orange colour looked good.
◆ 'Hungarian Hot Wax': has a calmer taste, cropped earlier than 'Habanero' and fruited well. The elongated fruits change colour from light green to yellow, orange and then red.

Cucumbers

Cucumbers (*Cucumis sativus*) are often grown side by side with tomatoes yet they prefer warmer, more humid conditions and are ideal plants for a greenhouse where the temperature never falls below 10°C (50°F).

Sow during March, pushing two seeds on their edge into an 8cm (3-inch) pot filled with peat-free compost. Seed requires 21°C (70°F) to germinate, with seedlings appearing seven days from sowing. Weed out the weaker of the two seedlings, being careful not to disturb the stronger root system. Keep the temperature up

throughout the seedling stage. Pot seedlings on into larger pots until their final growing space of 30–45cm (15–18 inches) in pots, growing bags or border soil. They like very rich soil, so I add plenty of garden compost and water them well every day. Once the first fruits are set, add a small amount of liquid seaweed fertilizer to the watering-can.

Cucumbers can produce both male and female flowers. But if a male flower pollinates the female, the resultant cucumber tastes bitter, so any male flowers on plants should be picked off before they open. Male flowers do not have an embryonic fruit behind the base of the flower, whereas female flowers do, and I am afraid that even varieties marketed as 'all female' can still produce male flowers. Removing the male flowers does not diminish the harvest, because the female fruit does not need to be pollinated to produce a crop. This is a variation on reproduction called parthenocarpy, and also applies to bananas. This is why you seldom find seeds in the final crop – the jelly-like 'seeds' in cucumbers are actually empty ovaries.

Plants can be trained up canes, string, wires or, as at Berryfields, a combination of all three. Whatever you use must be robust, because the weight of half a dozen or more cucumbers is considerable. When the main growing point reaches the top of the support, it needs to be pinched out. Sideshoots are produced prolifically, and ideally each should also be stopped or pinched out. Do this once the sideshoot has produced

a female flower and two pairs of leaves. If a sideshoot doesn't produce a female flower within six pairs of leaves, pinch it out anyway. This will produce a strong framework of leaves for the development of a heavy crop. Cucumbers grow fast, so this is a daily job. However, left to its own devices with no pinching out, a cucumber plant will still produce a good crop of fruit, and I confess that I rarely do it more than once a week.

There are several good varieties to choose from, and the following grew well in the Berryfields greenhouse:

◆ 'Petita': produces smaller fruits but plenty of them. It can tolerate colder conditions than other varieties. Classed as 'all female', it can still produce male flowers.

◆ 'Carmen': spineless skin, seedless fruit that are long, green, tasty and produced in large numbers.
◆ 'Crystal Apple': produces round fruits with large cavities. The ivory-coloured skin changes to yellow on maturity.

Aubergines

Aubergines (*Solanum melongena*) are related to tomatoes but require conditions more like those that suit cucumbers, relishing heat, high humidity and plenty of moisture – although they do need well-drained soil. They should be sown in February with two seeds to an 8cm (3-inch) pot filled with peat-free compost, placed in heated propagator set to 18°C (64°F) and seedlings should appear after ten days. Thin out the weaker seedling and pot the stronger-growing plant into pot sizes one size up. Final potting should be into a 22cm (9-inch) pot, or two plants per growing bag. However, like tomatoes and cucumbers – but unlike chillies – they do best when grown in soil, so a greenhouse bed is ideal.

Once plants have reached 60cm (2 feet), pinch out the growing point to encourage all the plant's energy to be channelled into fruit development. Regular watering is essential and plants should never dry out, but the compost should never become waterlogged. A weekly mist with clear water will reduce the incidence of red spider mite.

It takes around 20 weeks from sowing to picking the fruit. Fruit is ready to be picked when it is firm, with glossy skin,

LEFT Cucumbers grow best with plenty of heat and water. This fruit of the 'Carmen' variety is a beauty.

and does not sound hollow when gently tapped. Good air circulation will prevent any brown marks on the fruit from developing into rot. Avoid splashing the fruit with water, and avoid soil splashes, when watering.

Purple, red, white or mottled fruits are all readily available, and egg shapes (hence the American name 'eggplant') are a diversion from the usual elongated fruit. At Berryfields the variety grown was:

◆ 'Bonica': oval fruits with tender skin and a chewy texture. Each plant can sustain five or six fruits to maturity.

Basil

Basil and tomato make ideal companions on the plate and basil thrives under a tomato-growing regime, so at Berryfields

plants were grown at the foot of the tomatoes directly in the border soil, inside the greenhouse. The key to success with basil plants is not to let their growth be checked by cold or lack of water. They can be grown outside, but the first hint of ground frost will kill the plants completely, reducing them to blackened shreds. Cold nights – dipping below 10°C (50°F) – will make their leaves leathery and bitter, so there is much to be said for growing basil in a greenhouse. Constant growth will produce the tastiest, freshest leaves, so plants should never be left hanging around in pots, seed trays or modules. Sow batches of seed in seed trays in February, April and June for a supply lasting from midsummer through to autumn. Seedlings can then be individually potted into 8cm (3-inch) pots before their final planting place at the base of the tomatoes. They can also be potted into 22cm (9-inch) pots and grown on the greenhouse benching.

Basil is a hungry plant and needs plenty of fertile soil, so add garden compost to your potting mix and to planting holes in borders (this will also benefit the tomatoes). Plants grow to around 60cm (2 feet) and the white flowers appear in summer. It's best to cut the white flowers off the plant as they can spoil the flavour of the leaves, introducing a touch of bitterness. There are many types of basil available – all with different flavours – but the popular sweet basil (*Ocimum basilicum*) is the best, both as a complement to tomato in any guise and as pesto, so that is the choice for the Berryfields greenhouse.

Citrus

Our citrus plants are over-wintered in the greenhouse. Plants are kept ticking over throughout the winter months, with a regular check being made on the condition of the leaves, as even in winter aphids can cause trouble under the protected environment and scale insects are at their worst around the new year. In spring the citrus plants are taken outside and the leaves are washed with clean, tepid water. No additives are put in the water as these can clog the small pores or stomata in the leaves. The top 2.5cm (1 inch) of compost is removed from the surface and replaced with fresh. A weak seaweed extract feed is applied to the compost. Then it really depends on the weather. If a cold spell is forecast, the plants are taken back into the greenhouse until the middle of May. Even when they are placed outside in a warm, sunny position, a blanket of horticultural fleece is kept to hand just in case the temperature drops to freezing. Citrus is surprisingly hardy, but the blossom, which can appear on the plant throughout the year, is vulnerable. Plants are brought back into the greenhouse in October for the winter.

There are two essential factors in growing all citrus fruits. The first is to give them very good drainage – we use a mix of peat-free compost with an equal volume of horticultural grit. The second is not to over-water. Let them completely dry out before giving them a good soak. In summer this means watering at most once every ten days or so, and in winter at most once a month.

GREENHOUSE BASICS

◆ Choose a greenhouse that suits your garden.
◆ Think of what you want to grow and choose accordingly.
◆ Think as big as possible.
◆ Consider the glazing options.
◆ Situate away from overhanging trees to maximize light.
◆ Run power to the greenhouse.
◆ Run water to the greenhouse or have a dip tank inside.
◆ Secure the greenhouse to a solid base.
◆ Ensure you have plenty of automatic ventilation.
◆ Put plenty of sturdy benches into your greenhouse.
◆ Be prepared to move benching out as crops mature.
◆ Heat your greenhouse to extend the seasons.

OPPOSITE Pots planted up with bulbs are forced to grow and flower early by giving them protection from the cold winter in the greenhouse.

LEFT A corner of our hard-working greenhouse, with seedlings pricked out into plugs, orchids in pots and a sticky fly trap. Note the bubble-wrap to provide a steady temperature in winter and spring and to lower light levels in summer.

A YEAR IN THE GREENHOUSE

SPRING
◆ Sow annuals, biennials, perennials and vegetables.
◆ Sow tomatoes, chillies and aubergines.
◆ Check automatic vents are opening and ventilation is good.
◆ Ensure heaters are still in place.
◆ Prepare border soil.
◆ Start to harden off seedlings for planting outdoors later.
◆ Clean and repot houseplants where they have outgrown their pots.
◆ Plant up hanging baskets.

SUMMER
◆ Check ventilation is keeping temperatures under control. Monitor using a maximum/minimum thermometer.
◆ Shade glass if necessary.
◆ Maintain regular watering.
◆ Sow primula seeds.
◆ Regularly train cucumbers and tomatoes to strong supports.
◆ Put hanging baskets outside after hardening off.
◆ Service heaters wherever necessary.
◆ Check for pests and treat with biological controls.
◆ Damp down the greenhouse floor to maintain humidity where required.
◆ Sow cyclamen seeds for flowering plants the following year.
◆ Take cuttings from pelargoniums,

fuchsias, verbenas and penstemons.

◆ Take sideshoots off tomato plants where necessary.

◆ Harvest fruit such as cucumbers when large enough.

AUTUMN

◆ Ventilate to reduce humidity as it may cause fungal problems.

◆ Sow sweet peas.

◆ Stop tomato plants by pinching out the growing tips.

◆ Harvest all mature fruit.

◆ Take care when watering to avoid a cold, damp atmosphere.

◆ Check heaters and position in case of cold nights.

◆ Plant garlic for an early crop.

◆ Plant hippeastrum bulbs for flowers the following spring.

◆ Clean glass – choose a warm day, remove plants and clean the greenhouse inside and out.

◆ Clean and label lifted dahlias.

◆ Put over-wintering pelargoniums in a frost-free part of the greenhouse.

◆ Bring in tender plants such as bananas.

WINTER

◆ Consolidate plants into one area of the greenhouse and insulate this area.

◆ Check heaters are working.

◆ Invest in a paraffin heater as a back-up to electricity or gas.

◆ Ensure ventilators work.

◆ Clean pots and seed trays.

◆ Prune over-wintering fuchsias and pelargoniums.

◆ Sow peas and broad beans.

ABOVE The sheer scale of the Berryfields greenhouse is a constant delight and enables us to use it for a wide range of plants.

OPPOSITE Seedlings ready to plant out, including those sown by Sarah Raven in sections of guttering for her cutting border.

'Then I thought that I would *really like* to make an **ornamental** fruit garden. At the same time I did not want to lose my *no-nonsense soft fruit area* and I was also aware that many people live in *very small* town gardens and I wanted to show that they could grow lots of different fruit in that kind of space as well.'

the fruit garden

the fruit garden

WHEN WE CAME TO BERRYFIELDS WE INHERITED A collection of fruit trees of various sizes and ages. The most notable was the magnificent apple at the end of the long borders, which is worth its place in any garden for its beauty alone – regardless of whether it produces any apples or not. But the rest were a mixed bag. There were various other apples, pears and a plum or two. It was good to have them – mature fruit trees are a bonus in any garden – but all of them were unpruned, straggly and, apart from three or four apples in the area at the end of the long borders that we have now made into the orchard, spread widely apart from each other. There was no sense of the fruit being tended or integrated into the garden.

I think that growing fruit of some kind is an essential part of gardening. It is a very ancient instinct and goes back to the earliest gardens of all, where a collection of fruit trees would be protected by a hedge and the area within tended and enjoyed as a peaceful and safe retreat. From earliest history mankind has treasured the sweet taste of fresh fruit, and we all know how healthy it is for us. But much of the commercially grown supermarket fruit is factory-farmed, smothering miles of beautiful countryside with plastic, drenched in chemicals and relying on gangs of cheap labour living in appalling conditions to gather. The varieties are chosen for their resistance to disease, ability to store a long time and appearance rather than taste. It looks like the real thing but is tasteless, filled with chemical residues and a mockery of what can be so easily grown at home. It is junk fruit.

So, even if we cannot supply ourselves with all of the fruit that we want to eat, we can at least produce some that is grown without chemicals, harvested when properly ripe and eaten completely fresh. On top of that, most fruit looks wonderful too – think of snow-white pear blossom in April, the candy-floss pink of apple blossom in May and the jewel-like fruits on a standard gooseberry. The truth is that if a garden is to be fully fruitful, then it must be full of fruit.

THREE FRUIT GARDENS

It became apparent that our vegetable garden at Berryfields was not large enough to grow a wide selection of veg as well as an equally comprehensive range

of soft fruit, even though we had originally planned to combine the two. So expansion was needed, either for more vegetables or exclusively for soft fruit. I envisaged nothing fancy, just a good, clear area in which to raise a decent cross-section of soft fruit which we could also protect from the birds.

Then I thought that I would really like to make an ornamental fruit garden. At the same time I did not want to lose my no-nonsense soft fruit area and I was also aware that many people live in very small town gardens and I wanted to show that they could grow lots of different fruit in that kind of space as well.

So the idea of three quite different but linked fruit gardens came about. Between them they would give us the

PREVIOUS PAGE, LEFT
Alpine strawberries are ideal for growing in a container and look good, as well as producing delicious little fruit for months.

PREVIOUS PAGE, RIGHT
Ripe redcurrants hang like threads of ruby beads.

RIGHT Strawberries that are available all the year round are not a patch on the warm, delicious fruit eaten straight from your own garden.

OPPOSITE The site of the three fruit gardens after the ground had been levelled and prepared, but before any work was begun above ground.

opportunity to grow almost every type of fruiting plant that would thrive in Berryfields' climate and soil.

The site is to the west of the greenhouse in a space that was dominated by an overgrown hedge when we came to the garden a year ago. It is long and thin – about 22m × 7m (72 feet × 23 feet), although it tapers down a bit at the house end. This means that each of the three areas is pretty much 7m × 7m (23 feet × 23 feet), which is about the size of a small back garden or the area that many people might spare for fruit growing.

Our three fruit gardens now occupy this area with each individual fruit garden being an equal sized square of roughly 7m × 7m (23 feet × 23 feet). The area nearest the hedge is the soft fruit garden (which we also call the allotment), and has its own small greenhouse; in the centre is the ornamental fruit garden, and at the end nearest the house (and spring garden) is the small town fruit garden. Two panels of wooden fencing divide each garden from the next, and the whole area is surrounded by a hazel hurdle and wooden fencing.

SOFT FRUIT GARDEN

The layout is deliberately as simple as possible, with three beds divided by a plain-slabbed path wide enough for a barrow and a film crew. There is also a small polycarbonate greenhouse for propagation, tomatoes and in time, we hope, a vine. This is a wholly practical area with no attempt at decoration other than the beauty of the soft fruit itself.

Within this garden the following fruit will be grown:

Strawberries

No one in their right mind wants Christmas or their birthday every day of the year and it seems equally bonkers to expect strawberries all year round. Strawberries in January spoil the magic of their summer season. It also means that in the search for all-year-round crops, modern strawberry production is fast becoming an industrial nightmare involving thousands of acres of polythene tunnels covering sterilized soil and a regime that is widely at odds with the image of this delicious summer fruit. The answer is to grow some yourself to remind you of

what a sun-warmed, fresh strawberry *really* tastes like. Luckily this is very easy to do even in the smallest garden.

They like well-drained, fertile soil that never becomes dried out and a sunny site. Before planting strawberry plants ensure all weeds are removed, then plant 60cm (2 feet) apart in all directions. A closer planting will not give you any more fruit and will result in less healthy plants. Traditionally strawberries were mulched with straw as soon as the green fruit developed, which kept the berries clean and off the soil, conserved moisture and made them easier to pick. But if you cannot get straw, landscape paper or even cardboard will do the job. Birds love strawberries, so a protective netting is essential. At the end of the growing season cut off all the foliage 5cm (2 inches) above the crown of the plant. Clear away all cut leaves and tidy the plants up in readiness for winter. This reduces the chance of disease infection

RIGHT Tayberries are one of the easier fruits to grow and are delicious to eat, but they are very hard to find in the shops.

and lets light and air get to the growing leaves. Strawberries are short-lived and are best replaced every three years. If plants are grown longer than this, their crop size and quality will diminish and they will be affected by viruses.

SUMMER-FRUITING STRAWBERRIES produce the largest fruits and usually crop between late May and early July. Good varieties include:

◆ 'Cambridge Favourite': reliable crops of medium-sized fruit with good disease resistance.

◆ 'Cambridge Vigour': heavy crops of large fruits are produced, but replace plants every two years to prevent build-up of virus.

◆ 'Silver Jubilee': produces tasty fruits and plants are resistant to many common strawberry diseases.

◆ 'Hapil': good crops of flavoursome fruit, growing well on drier soils.

AUTUMN-FRUITING STRAWBERRIES produce smaller fruits in early summer and again in early autumn. They are sometimes called perpetual or remontant strawberries. Good varieties include:

◆ 'Aromel': produces outstandingly flavoured, conical and sometimes misshapen fruit.

◆ 'Gento': produces good yields of tangy flavoured fruits.

◆ 'Ostara': is a dependable variety producing good yields of tasty, medium-sized, pale red fruit.

◆ 'Rapella': produces heavy crops of large, bright red fruit. The fruits ripen early and can be picked before the first frosts of autumn.

ALPINE STRAWBERRIES produce tiny fruit that are aromatic and sweet. Plants grow 30cm (12 inches) tall and are perfect as border plants or for growing in containers. As with all strawberries they are self-fertile. However, unlike all other strawberries they do not form runners. Plants flower almost all season from last

the fruit garden

to first frosts. Birds tend to leave alpine strawberries alone, so netting is not essential. Plants need to be renewed every two years as they quickly lose their vigour owing to viral infections and sheer exhaustion after producing all the flowers and fruit. Crowns can sometimes be divided in autumn. Best practice is to sow seeds (spring in greenhouses; autumn in cold frames) every year to replace half your plants. Seeds can take a month to germinate. Do not cover the seeds on the surface of the compost. Bottom heat gets seeds growing quickly – 15°C (59°F). Hand-weed around plants to prevent damage by careless hoeing of crowns. Deep hoeing can also damage surface roots. Good varieties include:

◆ 'Alexandra': often called 'Alexandria', bears vigorous, bright crimson, fragrant fruits.
◆ 'Quattro Stagioni': fruits twice a year, sweet taste; sow in July or August for best results.
◆ 'Baron Solemacher': prefers partial shade; fruits are tiny, dark red and produced in large numbers.

Raspberries

These are planted in the largest bed, with summer-fruiting varieties grown against permanent supports. Raspberries prefer cool, slightly acidic conditions but can be grown in most soils. They do best in soil with plenty of moisture and therefore plenty of organic matter. They have very shallow, fibrous roots, and an annual thick mulch of well-rotted manure improves yield as well as keeping the roots cool and the weeds down.

Raspberries are divided into summer- and autumn-fruiting varieties, and in warmer, drier areas it is autumn varieties that are likely to be more successful, providing fruit from August through to November. Summer-fruiters need a moist site and can grow in shade. They will fruit on the previous year's canes for about six weeks from early July. The time to prune them is September, cutting away all the old canes that bore that season's fruit and any of the new, green canes that are too crowded. It is best to leave half a dozen healthy new canes per plant, each evenly spaced and tied firmly to the support. This is a slow but very satisfying job. Autumn-fruiters are easy to prune. All growth is cut down to ground level around the new year. Varieties at Berryfields include:

◆ 'Autumn Bliss': autumn-fruiter, good yields, firm texture, good flavour, bright red fruits from mid August to October.
◆ 'Allgold': autumn-fruiter, golden-yellow berries ripen in late summer and early autumn. Sweet flavour.
◆ 'Glen Magna': summer-fruiter, producing very large, dark red fruits from mid July to late August.

Tayberries

A cross between a raspberry and a blackberry, tayberry fruits are large, dark purple and produced from July to August. 'Buckingham Thornless' is a vigorous type, producing high yields of sweet berries. Train up a wall or fence, and heavy crops will be produced two years after planting. Tayberries require moist soil, rich in organic matter, and cool conditions. Severe winter weather can damage plants. As with summer raspberries, cut out old canes that have fruited, leaving a space of 12cm (5 inches) between new canes.

Blackberries

These are no longer the preserve of the wild hedgerows, as thornless varieties provide gardeners with delicious fruit without any pain. Fruits appear from late July to September, and plants require soil enriched with plenty of organic matter. Thornless varieties can be grown over arches, up trellis or fences or attached to wires tensioned between stout posts. Prune out old canes that have fruited to encourage production of vigorous new canes. Varieties at Berryfields include:

◆ 'Oregon Thornless': mild flavour, medium-sized fruits and thorn-free stems.
◆ 'Merton Thornless': short, thornless canes and large, good-flavoured, fruits.

Redcurrants and Whitecurrants

These are essentially different-coloured versions of the same plant. They prefer an open, sunny site with plenty of organic matter in the soil, but are amazingly tolerant of almost any conditions and will produce good yields in poor soil in semi-shade. Both red- and whitecurrants can be trained into any shape, but an open-goblet bush shape makes picking easy and, just as important, lets air and light into the centre of the bush, minimizing the risk of saw-fly damage.

Redcurrants fruit, like most apples, on mature, woody spurs rather than on new growth, and pruning is designed to encourage these as well as the shape of the bush that you require. Prune in early spring, about the same time as you prune clematis, roses and buddleja, cutting new shoots back by a third to a bud to form a strong fruiting spur. Varieties at Berryfields include:

◆ 'Junifer': the earliest redcurrant, producing fruit from early July. It crops on both one- and two-year-old wood. The fruit is richly coloured and the strings are long. Delicious.
◆ 'Laxton's No. 1': huge strings of small, brilliant red berries are produced from mid July.
◆ 'White Versailles': early whitecurrant producing long, heavy trusses of sweet, pale yellow fruit in early July. Reliable crops are produced year after year.

Redcurrants and whitecurrants are very prone to attacks by blister aphids. These cause the leaves to come out in red blisters and look seriously ill. In fact the plant does not seem to suffer and certainly the crop is untouched, so it is not something to worry about.

Blackcurrants

Although they tend to be lumped in with the other currants, blackcurrants have quite different requirements from red- or whitecurrants or gooseberries. They are very hungry and thirsty plants that need lots of sunshine. Fruit is produced on the previous year's growth, so plant deeply to ensure plenty of new shoots. In fact they have a three-year cycle – the first year's growth will have some fruit, the second

1 Raspberries can drown and die if planted too deeply and sit in wet ground, so at planting time remove a shallow trench, just 10cm (4 inches) deep. Place the bare-root raspberry plants in the trench, gently spreading the roots out to cover the soil. Then place a layer of soil over the roots, gently firm and tie the stems to a support structure. Then mulch really thickly with garden compost or well-rotted manure.

2 Never hoe raspberries – their roots are very shallow and you will inevitably damage them as you remove any weeds. Hand weed and then mulch thickly early every spring.

3 If your fig is already in the ground and growing too strongly, there is a trick to reduce the fertility of the soil, which in turn will increase the likelihood of flowers and fruit. Add a handful of sawdust to the soil around the fig. The process of rotting takes nitrogen from the soil – the same nitrogen responsible for lush leaf growth.

4 Picking apples is easy if you cup the fruit with your hand, place your thumb on the stalk and gently twist. If the fruit snaps easily, then it is ready to be harvested. If there's any resistance, it's best to leave the fruit on the tree for another few days.

5 Apples must be stored in cool, dry conditions. Store only sound apples, using bruised or damaged apples straight from the tree. Store them on slatted, wooden trays, keeping different varieties apart. Apples can be individually wrapped in newspaper and stored in tomato boxes. You can line a drawer with newspaper and store apples in there for weeks. Remember – different varieties store for differing times.

year sees maximum production that will fall in the third year and die right away thereafter. So it makes sense to remove a third of the entire bush each year (or, if you have lots of blackcurrant bushes, completely cut back a third of your bushes). The best method of pruning is to prune out complete branches at harvesting time – carrying the fruit-laden branch into the house for harvesting. This is usually at the end of July. Pruning can be left until October, but it is best done immediately after fruiting to give the new wood time to mature before winter. Cut each branch right down to the lowest bud from the ground.

An annual thick mulch with organic matter will ensure roots are moist and well fed and it reduces the competition from weeds. You can never overdo feeding or mulching when it comes to blackcurrants. Varieties at Berryfields include:

◆ 'Boskoop Giant': vigorous, spreading and certainly lives up to its name. Sweet fruits are produced early in July, provided a frost hasn't damaged the flowers. Best for a Midlands or southern garden.
◆ 'Ben Sarek': a dwarf bush growing to only 1.2m (4 feet) high. Branches need support as it crops heavily. Its large fruits are produced in mid July.
◆ 'Ben Lomond': late-flowering, avoiding the majority of frost. Heavy yields and upright growth on compact plants make this a popular variety. The 'strigs' or flower stalks are short and the profusion of plump berries are full of acidic taste.

Gooseberries

Gooseberries are fundamentally tough plants. They thrive in soil rich in organic matter with plenty of moisture but can be grown almost anywhere, alongside red- and whitecurrants. They need lots of potash, and a spadeful of wood ash every spring meets their demands. It's best to grow gooseberries either as cordons – a single stem growing from the base of the plant up wires supported on wooden stakes – or as a goblet-shaped bush from a single stout stem or leg. Both methods allow the plants to receive plenty of air and sunlight, resulting in a quality crop. In winter, the leading shoot on cordon-grown plants should be cut back to around 15cm (6 inches). All lateral shoots are cut back to 3cm (1¼ inches) from the main stem. When the top of the cane or support is reached, the leading shoot is cut back to one bud above the previous year's growth. In summer, all sideshoots should be pruned to leave five pairs of leaves from the base. This increases air circulation and reduces the risk of diseases. For goblet-shaped bushes, pruning should be done in winter. New growth produced in the current year is pruned back by a half. Sideshoots growing from the leading shoots are pruned back to about 5cm (2 inches). Varieties at Berryfields include:

◆ 'Whinham's Industry': a dessert or cooking gooseberry with upright growth and excellent taste. Dark red, medium-sized fruit is produced in late July and plants grow well in all aspects, even deep shade.
◆ 'Whitesmith': a dessert or cooking gooseberry with near-white, oval, downy fruit with good taste. A strong grower producing high yields of medium-sized fruit in late July. Grows well on most soils.
◆ 'London': a dessert gooseberry with dark crimson fruits, less hairy than other varieties, this was undisputed champion of the gooseberry show circuit between 1829 and 1867. Fruits are produced in abundance during July.

Gooseberries are prone to mildew and the best way to treat that is to use plenty of wood ash and allow lots of ventilation to the plants by growing them on a stem (or 'leg') or as cordons. They are also very prone to attacks by saw-fly, which lay their eggs at the base of the plant. The emerging larvae munch their way through the leaves, starting at the bottom, and by the time they reach the top the plant can be completely defoliated. Again, ventilation is the key, so prune to ensure that the bush is a nice open goblet with lots of air getting right down into the heart of the bush.

ORNAMENTAL FRUIT GARDEN

Not all fruit is edible. If you think of every berry, rosehip and currant as a fruit then you see that every garden has a wide range of decorative fruits, and everything in the ornamental fruit garden at Berryfields is grown primarily for its decorative value. A circular lawn is surrounded by box-edged beds filled with plants chosen for their fruits. But in order to get fruits you must have flowers, and in spring and summer this garden is filled with all kinds of blossom.

◆ *Ilex*, or holly, is invaluable in the Berryfields garden. It provides an

evergreen structure throughout the year and, if the correct varieties are planted, a display of berries in late autumn and winter. Berry colour ranges from yellow through orange and red to black. The flowers that precede the berries are usually small, insignificant and white. Most plants are unisexual – are either male or female – and berries are produced on female plants, but for berry production both male and female need to be planted, although a compatible holly in a neighbouring garden is capable of pollination and berry production. If there is room for only one variety, choose one that doesn't require a partner for berry production. *Ilex* 'Pyramidalis' is a female variety that does not require cross-fertilization to produce its scarlet berries. It grows to 6m (20 feet) high with a spread of 5m (16 feet). *I*. 'J. C. van Tol' is

a hermaphrodite plant producing red berries in autumn. The new shoots in spring are purple and plants grow to 6m (20 feet) high with a spread of 4m (13 feet).

All hollies need well-drained soil and will thrive in sun or partial shade. The few deciduous hollies and any with variegated leaves prefer sunnier conditions. Hollies respond well to pruning and are therefore great as standard specimens. However, they do not like being transplanted, so once you've planted them, leave well alone.

◆ *Hippophae rhamnoides*, or sea buckthorn, is a tough plant capable of withstanding coastal conditions. It grows best in a sunny position and dry, sandy soil. Both a male and female plant are required to produce the bright orange berries. Silvery foliage and tiny yellow flowers are produced in spring. Plants grow 6m (20 feet) high with a similar spread.

◆ *Sambucus nigra* 'Guincho Purple' produces coal-black, spherical fruits in autumn. The dark green leaves darken to blackish purple as spring and summer progress and are an excellent foil for deep colours in a border. The flowers are held on purple stalks and open from pink buds to white flowers, occasionally blushed pink. Plants grow 6m (20 feet) high with a similar spread.

◆ Quince: *Cydonia oblonga* thrive in wet soils and are perfect as pond-side plantings, but as long as they are watered in very dry weather quinces will grow in

LEFT These flowers of the elder *Sambucus nigra* 'Guincho Purple' in the ornamental fruit garden will result in a display of black berries.

any good garden soil. They produce very late blossom, so tend to be safe from frost, and the flowers are the most perfect pink. Quince jelly is a delicate but distinctive treat, and one quince, cooked with apples, will add a delicious fragrance to an apple pie or stewed apple. A sunny, sheltered position helps protect flowers and aids self-pollination in spring. The contorted, twisted growth of quinces makes training difficult, so any pruning should be restricted to removing dead, diseased or overlapping wood. Quinces grow to 6m (20 feet) high and are long-lived. They are used as the rootstock to most pear varieties, the slow growth taming the greater natural exuberance of the pear.

The ornamental quinces, *Chaenomeles*, are also edible, but are usually grown for their wonderful flowers that are produced very early in the year and range from pure white to deep, blood red. They are very happy in shade and are best trained against a wall or fence where their dense growth can be clipped to produce a neat wall covering.

◆ Fig: *Ficus carica* 'Brown Turkey' is perhaps not the most delectable of all figs but is the only reliable cropper for the Berryfields climate. It has oval fruit with rich, sweet, red flesh. Figs are ready to be picked when the fruit hangs downwards. Getting fruits to maturity is easier than many gardeners think, and correct planting is the key. Given too much root run, figs will produce large leaves at the expense of fruit. At Berryfields the fig is planted in a sunny position near a south-facing dividing fence. Fences and walls aren't vital, but sun and shelter are. The tree was planted in a pit lined with concrete slabs placed vertically around the sides to restrict root growth.

The fig produces two types of fruit simultaneously, of which one will mature and the other will not. Very small fruits, the size of peas, will over-winter or appear in early spring and develop through the year and mature in late summer and early autumn. This is called the breba crop. The second crop of fruit produced, from midsummer onwards, does not have time to mature before the onset of winter and should therefore be removed, even though it may smother the branches with good-sized fruits.

Growing figs is easy as they do not need additional fertilizer and are adapted to drought conditions. However, when conditions are very dry, the fig may jettison its breba crop of fruit. Figs are hardy down to −12°C (10°F), but extra protection is easily provided by a curtain of horticultural fleece. Pruning is best done in early spring just before growth starts and consists of removing any spindly, non-productive branches and any branches that may have become diseased.

◆ Crab apple: *Malus* × *zumi* var. *calocarpa* 'Golden Hornet' produces open, cup-shaped, white flowers in spring, before 'proper' apple trees blossom, and masses of golden-yellow crab apples in autumn, which look stunning and are also delicious when made into crab apple jelly. Crab apples prefer a sunny, well-drained

the fruit garden

tensioned across the south-facing fence panel to form a fan shape. This makes good use of the available space, allows air circulation between branches, leaves and fruit, and allows the sun to ripen the fruit. The fence itself lends some protection to the tree, and radiated heat also helps warm the air. If the flowers of nectarines are frosted there is no hope of fruit, so I made a pull-over screen out of small-gauge netting fixed to a wooden batten, for use when spring frost is forecast. Nectarines demand the slightly contrary condition of having lots of water but also being very free-draining, so plant them in soil enriched with both home-made compost and lots of grit. This will help create a free-draining soil but one that will hold water. Waterlogged soil will kill nectarines. The trick to growing nectarines (and peaches) is an adequate supply of water throughout the year. Lack of water as the fruits start to develop will stop development, and lack of water followed by a downpour later in their development will result in the skins splitting.

◆ PEARS: above all other fruit, pears are suitable for growing in a garden because they are so very much nicer to eat when properly ripe and yet reach ripeness for only about one day before beginning to rot. They must be picked carefully when they are not yet ripe but come away easily in the hand, then stored on a windowsill

RIGHT A beautifully trained nectarine growing within the protection of a greenhouse. Not ours, but perhaps one day ...

or shelf until the flesh gives gently to finger pressure, and then immediately eaten in all their juicy ripeness. Heaven!

Pears are a good fruit to train as espaliers as they respond well to hard pruning in winter and lighter pruning in summer. (Remember: winter pruning stimulates vigorous new growth and summer pruning restricts it. So winter pruning is vital in the creation of all forms of trained fruit, but summer pruning essential once they have become established.) Espalier means that one or more pairs of horizontal branches are arranged in tiers and trained to each side in a flat plane. If you start with a young feathered tree, cut off the leader and train suitable branches at 45 degrees by tying them to canes. Later, as they grow, you can gradually lower them to a horizontal position. It is a lot easier to get the structure right when the plant is young and new branches can quickly be trained to fill any gaps. Espalier training is a good way of getting a lot of fruiting branches into a narrow space such as against a fence or wall or lining a path.

There are many pear varieties worth growing, and 'Conference' is a popular choice. It reliably produces heavy crops of long, olive-green fruit. It is partially self-fertile, which means it will produce a good crop if planted solo – but if a pollination partner is close by, the yield will increase. 'Conference' flowers in the middle of the season, and so a different pear variety flowering at the same time is an ideal partner. 'Durondeau' has a compact habit and, if grown as a free-

LEFT Pears are my favourite fruit and the best for a small garden, because a ripe pear is unimaginably better than anything that you can buy. It also gives you the opportunity to grow a range of varieties in a small space – which is why we have espaliered pears in the small town fruit garden.

TOP 'Doyenné du Comice' – my first choice if I had to choose just one pear.

MIDDLE 'Conference' – tough, reliable and self-pollinating.

BELOW 'Durondeau' can be self-pollinating but is also a good partner for 'Conference'.

standing tree, is suitable for smaller gardens. It regularly produces heavy crops of large, yellow-fleshed pears with patches of russet on the skin. 'Durondeau' is also partially self-fertile, but flowers at the same time as 'Conference' and is therefore an ideal pollination partner. 'Doyenné du Comice' is, at its best, the most delicious of all pears. The fruits are large and golden-yellow, flushed with red.

◆ Cordon gages: gages are similar to plums but smaller, rounder and sweeter. They are also harder to buy in the shops, so they are a good garden choice. They are easy to grow as cordons – single stems grown at an angle of 45 degrees and tied to wires – producing good crops in the Berryfields soil. In the small town fruit garden the gages are grown against a north-facing wall in relative shade. 'Early Transparent Gage' produces gages with sweet, golden flesh. The skin is yellow and spotted red. It is a reliable variety producing a good crop every year and is self-fertile. 'Denniston's Superb' is sometimes classified as a plum, but is a large gage capable of producing heavy crops in colder areas. It is a vigorous, upright grower that produces fruit with sweet flesh with greenish-yellow, red-blushed skin. It too is self-fertile.

APPLES CASE STUDY

Apples originated in the Middle East more than four thousand years ago and arrived in England along with the Normans around 1066. Although most people would be pushed to name more than half a dozen different varieties of apple, there are literally thousands to choose from. The two main types of apple are cooking and dessert, although some varieties are dual-purpose. The amount and proportion of acid and sugar determine the taste, and cooking apples are generally larger and more acidic than dessert apples. During cooking the acids are released, which in turn breaks down the flesh. The more acidic the apple, the less likely it is to hold its shape during cooking, and the easier it is to create purée.

Given the ideal growing conditions – rich, well-drained soil; warm, dry summers, and mild, damp winters – an apple tree can be expected to grow for well over a century. The base of the tree will need regular weeding to avoid competition from weeds for water and nutrients, and an annual mulch with well-rotted manure or leafmould in autumn will ensure trees are in good health below ground.

Pruning of apple trees causes unnecessary concern for many gardeners. Pruning is done to remove diseased wood, to control the size of the tree, to improve light and ventilation in the crown of the tree and to improve fruiting by increasing the vigour of the tree. The timing of pruning has important implications for a tree's overall vigour. Winter pruning stimulates spring growth. Summer pruning (which I do whenever it is convenient in the month of July) restricts growth. Bear this in mind when considering what you want your tree to look like in your garden.

OPPOSITE There are thousands of varieties of apple and yet supermarkets sell fewer than half a dozen types. The only solution is to find out what you like to eat and what will grow well in your area and grow them at home! These are just four of the twelve varieties that we have planted at Berryfields in the past couple of years.

TOP LEFT 'Greensleeves' is a juicy desert apple, similar to 'Golden Delicious', but easier to grow.
TOP RIGHT 'Worcester Pearmain' growing in a commercial orchard. This is an excellent, early desert apple, ready in September, which ripens on the tree. Shop-bought ones tend to be picked too early, before the full flavour has developed.
BELOW LEFT Step-over apples in the small town fruit garden. These are trained as a single lateral branch about 60cm (2 feet) high and flank the path. It is a highly decorative and surprisingly productive way to grow apples in a small garden.
BELOW RIGHT 'Discovery' is a very early desert apple, ready for picking in August. It keeps much longer than most early apples.

Spur-bearing trees produce flowers and therefore fruit on small, knobbly spurs along the length of a branch. When pruning, remove most of the growth from these spurs, leaving two buds per spur. These two buds will eventually bear the fruit.

Tip-bearing trees produce their flowers and fruit on the tips of branches. Cutting back the ends of the branches in winter will remove the flower buds, resulting in no fruit. Therefore no pruning is required, except of diseased or overcrowded branches. If in any doubt about whether an existing tree in your garden is a spur- or tip-bearing variety, then don't prune.

Pollination of apple trees is important if a heavy crop of apples is required. Some varieties of apples are self-fertile, such as 'James Grieve', and will produce fruit without help from another variety, but most need at least one pollinator to be in flower at the same time. Every apple variety is categorized into a pollination group. The groups are labelled from one to seven, with one being the earliest and seven the latest to flower. So a tree from group one cannot possibly pollinate or be pollinated by a tree from group seven, although consecutive pollination groups will always have an overlap of flowering time and can therefore pollinate each other. Ideally, choose two varieties from either the same group or consecutive groups to ensure pollination. Having said all that, it's still up to the bees to do their business, and if there is an apple tree in flower within 30m (100 feet) of your chosen variety, the chances are that your variety will be pollinated anyway.

At Berryfields, in the orchard and the fruit gardens, we have the following varieties:

◆ 'Worcester Pearmain': early to mid dessert, known since 1874, mid flowering time. Pick in September, and eat immediately. Pearmains tend to be long or pear-shaped apples.
◆ 'Greensleeves': early to mid dessert, known since 1966, mid flowering time, partially self-fertile. Pick and use in October. Sweet, golden-yellow fruit with creamy-white, crisp, juicy flesh.
◆ 'Discovery': early dessert, known since 1949, mid flowering time. Pick in August, use August–October. Slightly sharp flavour. Creamy-white flesh stained pink.
◆ 'Rosemary Russet': mid dessert, known since 1831, mid flowering time. Pick in early October, use November–December. Refreshingly acidic taste, good disease resistance. One of my favourites.
◆ 'Court Pendu Plat': late dessert, known since 1613, late flowering. Pick in October, use January–April. Sweet with an aromatic flavour.
◆ 'Cornish Aromatic': late dessert, known since 1813, late flowering. Pick in October, use November–January. Spicy, aromatic flavour. Old English variety thought to have grown in Cornwall for centuries.
◆ 'Spartan': late dessert, known since 1926, late flowering. Pick in early October, use November–January. White flesh, deep crimson, almost purple skin

flushed with yellow, juicy flesh, sweet with some acidity. Leave on tree for fuller flavour.

◆ 'Peasgood's Nonsuch': dual-purpose, known since 1853, mid flowering and partially self-fertile. Pick in September, use September–December. Heavy crops of large fruits. How could you not love anything with such a glorious name?

◆ 'Calville Blanc d'Hiver': dual-purpose, known since 1598, but planted at Berryfields only in the autumn of 2003. Late flowering. Pick in October, use November–December. The yellow flesh is sweetly sharp. An old French variety considered as the best for *tarte aux pommes*.

◆ 'Reverend W. Wilks': cooker, known since 1904, early flowering. Pick in late August, use September–November. White, juicy flesh cooking to a lemon purée. I love stewed apple and this is perfect for breakfast dribbled with fresh cream.

◆ 'Grenadier': cooker, known since 1862, mid flowering. Pick in August, use August-September. Large, round fruit sometimes irregular in shape. White flesh cooks to a sharp, pale cream purée.

◆ 'Bramley's Seedling': cooker, known since 1809, late flowering. Pick in early October, use November–March. Irregular, flat-bottomed fruit. White, green-tinged, juicy flesh, cooks to a cream purée. Strong, acidic taste. Very prone to bitterpit (caused by inadequate water supply, bitterpit manifests itself as small brown areas and slight depressions on the surface of the fruit, making it inedible), so not suitable for dry areas or sandy soil.

Apple Rootstocks – Once and For All

No apple will come true from its seed. So to determine the variety they must be grafted on to a separate root – the 'rootstock'. It is this rootstock that determines the size and vigour of the tree. The variety grafted on to the rootstock determines the fruit. Rootstocks have been assigned letters and numbers. The letters show where they were bred, and the numbers are merely an indication of where in the breeding programme the rootstocks were first used and give no clue as to how big a tree will grow. It needn't be confusing – just know how big or vigorous you want your tree to be, and let the nursery people do the rest. Of all the rootstocks in use, the following are commonly used:

◆ M27: very dwarfing, mature height of tree will be 2m (6 feet), spread 1.5m (4½ feet).

◆ M9: dwarfing, mature height of tree will be 2.5m (8 feet), spread 2.7m (9 feet). Will need permanent staking.

◆ M26: semi-dwarfing, mature height of tree will be 3m (10 feet), spread 3.6m (12 feet). Used for smaller espaliers and bush forms.

◆ MM106: semi-vigorous, mature height of tree will be 4m (13 feet), spread 4m (13 feet). Good for large espaliers and bushes. Tolerant of most soils.

◆ MM111: vigorous, mature height of tree will be 4.5m (14¾ feet), spread 4.5m (14¾ feet). Used for half standards and fan-trained trees.

◆ M25: very vigorous, mature height of tree will be 5m (16 feet), spread 6m (20 feet). Used only for standard trees.

A YEAR IN THE FRUIT GARDEN

SPRING

◆ Protect nectarines and all blossom from hard frosts. Use horticultural fleece or fine-mesh netting.

◆ Remove all weeds from the fruit gardens, especially from the ground around strawberries.

◆ Mulch with organic matter after rain, when the soil is moist.

◆ Tie in young growth to supports as and when it appears. New growth is pliable, whereas older growth is harder to train.

◆ Plant out pot-grown specimens into well-prepared soil.

◆ Cover some strawberry plants to force an early crop.

SUMMER

◆ Check for any pests and diseases, picking off caterpillars wherever possible and before they do too much damage.

◆ Net everything that you want to eat. If you don't net it, you won't get it!

◆ Continue to tie in shoots to supports when growing cordon-, fan- and espalier-trained fruit trees.

◆ Remove any misshapen apples or pears. Thinning of congested fruit will also give the tree a better chance of producing quality crops.

◆ Ensure all newly planted fruit receives adequate water to ensure establishment of roots and fruit production. Use recycled water.

◆ Put up pheromone traps to capture codling moths in orchards and around fruit trees. Their larvae feed on apples.

◆ Prune espalier- and cordon-trained fruit trees.

◆ Propagate strawberry plants from runners. Simply peg the new plants on the ends of the runners into pots of John Innes seed compost or directly into the soil.

AUTUMN

◆ Order bare-rooted fruit specimens from specialist nurseries. Plant later in the season.

◆ Ensure netting is in good order to prevent bird damage.

◆ Check stakes, supports and ties are in good order in advance of autumn winds.

◆ Use or store fruit as it ripens.

◆ Cut off strawberry foliage but do not damage the crowns.

◆ Cut out summer-fruiting canes that have fruited, leaving non-fruited canes to develop.

WINTER

◆ Check stored fruit and either use or discard any overripe specimens.

◆ Plant out bare-rooted plants if the soil isn't waterlogged or frozen.

◆ Cut down autumn-fruiting raspberry canes to ground level.

◆ Cut out blackcurrant canes that are over four years old. Cut out a third of all shoots to make room for new shoots.

ABOVE Looking back from the ornamental fruit garden to the greenhouse in the soft fruit garden, before the lawn was made. Within a few weeks, without forcing the pace at all, this scene was transformed (see page 236).

OPPOSITE Mature step-over apples showing how much fruit they can bear on such a limited structure.

'At Berryfields we have made our spring garden in the **shade** of a large *hornbeam*, a *beech* and a smaller *crab apple* and *lilac*. This means that the plants grow under **deciduous cover** that creates *very light shade* in winter and spring, but the emerging leaves block out the sun from *late* spring through to *leaf fall* in October ... '

the spring garden

the spring garden

I LOVE THOSE FIRST PRECIOUS STIRRINGS OF THE GARDEN around the end of January. The weather may be atrocious – it usually is – but when I see the snowdrops and aconites tentatively begin to flower I know that for certain spring is on its way. By the end of February the garden is well and truly coming alive with hellebores, winter honeysuckle, pulmonarias, iris and the first primroses. Apart from anything else, after the grimness of midwinter the relief is enormous. My spirits lift and everything seems possible again.

The power of these early spring plants is very great, but if they are spread all over the garden they can be diffused or even lost. I think that it is better, even in a small garden, to make a concentrated area just for plants that flower and perform from early to late spring and then let it have its dormant season in summer and autumn, when there is so much else happening elsewhere in the garden.

At Berryfields we have made our spring garden in the shade of a large hornbeam, a beech and a smaller crab apple and lilac. This means that the plants grow under deciduous cover that creates very light shade in winter and spring, but the emerging leaves block out the sun from late spring through to leaf fall in October, the almost permanent shade dappled with light only when the wind shifts the branches. But by summer the garden's performance is all finished. Spring is its season. This suits most woodland plants very well, and they dominate our planting.

TREES
Trees provide:

◆ Focal points in a garden.
◆ Structure.
◆ Habitats for wildlife.
◆ Shade for gardeners.
◆ Dry woodland shade for plants.
◆ Damp woodland shade for plants.

Of all the trees in the Berryfields garden, the hornbeam (*Carpinus betulus*) is where most activity has taken place.

Hornbeam is a native and was one of the last trees to enter the UK before the erosion of the land bridge linking Britain with continental Europe. It is wild in the south-east, west to Somerset and north to Hereford.

Hornbeam grows to 25m (80 feet) at maturity and will grow in most soils, although it prefers heavier, wetter ground. The leaves are similar to beech but have serrated edges and are less glossy. In winter a trimmed hornbeam hedge will retain most of its leaves, which turn an astonishing yellow before settling to a matt coffee-colour. In spring it carries tassels of small yellow female catkins that ripen to dark green Chinese lanterns. Male catkins are minute, green and also appear in April before the leaves. Once fertilized, the female catkins elongate to around 14cm (5½ inches) and are composed of clusters of small, ribbed nutlets. Hornbeam wood is among the hardest known and was used for cogwheels in mills and the centres of cartwheels. It is still used for butchers' chopping blocks. (The hornbeam is set in the centre of beechwood. The beechwood wears away, the hornbeam doesn't, so the meat is held higher, making it ideal for cutting.)

BENEATH THE HORNBEAM
The tree roots take up lots of water from the soil, resulting in dry conditions, especially by late spring when the hornbeam is in full leaf. Regular mulching with compost and leafmould is important and, together with the natural fall of leaves in autumn, enables many

PREVIOUS PAGE, LEFT
Prunus × *yedoensis* is one of the first trees to bear blossom. In early spring it is a magical sight.

PREVIOUS PAGE, RIGHT
Magnolia stellata is one of the easiest magnolia to grow. So much the better, because I can never have too many of the snow-white flowers.

OPPOSITE The vibrant green fern *Dryopteris* grows well in the dry shade of the beech tree.

plants to grow. The edges of the spring garden, just covered by the canopy, are the areas of strongest sunlight; in the centre of the garden the light levels drop, so that is where we put those plants that are happy with the most shade. Some of the key plants are:

◆ *Helleborus foetidus*, stinking hellebore, a native evergreen, forms clumps 45cm (18 inches) high and wide. The dark green leaves are deeply divided; the pale green flowers, with red rims as though dipped in blood, are produced any time from late winter to early spring. Hardy; thriving in partial shade and well-drained soil.

◆ *Helleborus orientalis*, the toughest and most common hellebore, has been bred so that its big, downward-facing flowers span the range from almost white to almost black. The big, leathery, evergreen leaves must be removed before the flowers emerge, so as to display them well and to allow in as much light and air as possible. New leaves follow in mid spring. It grows best in deep, rich soil and is happy in full or partial shade.

◆ *Magnolia stellata*, star magnolia, a deciduous, bushy shrub growing to 3m (10 feet) high with a similar spread. Fragrant, white starburst flowers with splayed petals are produced in early spring before the foliage appears, emerging from silky buds. The leaves are narrow, deep green and appear in April. The best magnolia for smaller gardens or large containers as it grows in any soil type with plenty of organic matter. Mulch with leafmould or home-made compost.

◆ *Magnolia* × *loebneri* 'Leonard Messel' is a deciduous, upright shrub growing to

8m (26 feet) with a spread of 6m (20 feet). Fragrant, pale pink flowers are produced in mid spring. Flowers appear before the deep green leaves emerge, and often afterwards. Grows in any soil type with plenty of organic matter. Mulch annually with shredded leafmould or home-made compost.

◆ *Geranium* × *cantabrigiense* 'Biokovo' has finely divided leaves, and white flowers with light pink veins in summer. It forms loose mats of shiny foliage that turn red in autumn and winter. It grows well in partial shade and any soil type, but is well adapted to dry conditions and must never be allowed to be waterlogged. Plants grow 50cm (20 inches) high with 2m (6 foot) spread.

◆ × *Heucherella* 'Dayglow Pink', a cross between heuchera and tiarella, thrives in dry soil and partial shade. It produces masses of stems supporting pink, frothy flowers and has green, cut foliage with a distinctive central chocolate inlay that turns purple in winter. Plants grow 45cm (18 inches) high with a similar spread.

◆ *Acaena microphylla* 'Kupferteppich', sometimes labelled as copper carpet, produces carpets of finely cut, evergreen, coppery-bronze leaves. The colour intensifies in winter. Bright red, distinctive, spiny burs are produced in summer. It grows 10cm (4 inches) high and rapidly spreads to 1m (3 feet).

◆ *Alchemilla mollis*, lady's mantle, thrives in partial shade; it grows to 60cm (2 feet) tall with a spread of 75cm (2½ feet). The familiar frothy lime-green flowers, produced in summer, are good for spilling on to and softening the edge of

OPPOSITE Hellebores are among my favourite flowers of all, but they hide their glories inside flowers that hang modestly to the ground. It is not until you lift them or crouch down at pollinating level that they reveal their glorious display. They cross-pollinate very readily, especially *Helleborus orientalis*, so new colours and patterns are constantly appearing. These are known as *Helleborus* × *hybridus*.

TOP LEFT Seedling from *Helleborus* × *hybridus* 'Cosmos'.
TOP RIGHT *Helleborus* × *hybridus* 'Sirius'.
BELOW LEFT An unnamed *Helleborus* × *hybridus*.
BELOW RIGHT A double form of *Helleborus* × *hybridus*.

a path. The fan-shaped, apple-green leaves with crinkled edges die back in winter. Cut hard back for fresh growth at least once a year. It self-seeds everywhere and spreads by runners, so it can easily be divided in spring to form new plants; tough, delightful and essential.

◆ *Digitalis purpurea* 'Primrose Carousel', foxgloves, are essential for a spring garden. This hybrid produces large, claret-spotted, primrose-yellow flowers in late May/early June. Flowers are produced all around the flower spikes. Plants grow to 80cm (2 feet 8 inches), making it good for both woodland situations and containers placed out of bright sun. It is biennial but, unlike some foxgloves, comes true from seed.

FERNS

Although we tend to associate ferns with damp shade, they include an enormously varied range of plants. Different species of ferns are capable of growing in both dry and damp conditions, and there are even ferns that thrive in full sun. Ferns come in every permutation of green as well as other colours, including red, silver and black. There's also a choice in size from minute to the stately tree ferns.

Ferns are the most primitive group of vascular plants and were the dominant plant group when dinosaurs were around. But for primitive plants they have a complicated life cycle. A mature fern produces spores on the underside of its fronds. These spores are held inside structures called sori, which are released and settle on a suitable surface. The spores then germinate and form prothalli (each spore forming a prothallus) that look like green flaps or liverworts. On the undersides of each prothallus are the male and female sex organs – antheridia and archegonia respectively. Each antheridium releases antherozoids and one antherzoid fertilizes an archegonium. (I said it was complicated.) This fertilized archegonium then finally develops into a true fern, which eventually matures and the whole cycle starts again.

Rhizome-producing ferns can be split. Select a strong-growing rhizome, cut it from the parent plant and replant in the garden or in a large pot. Water both plants to encourage establishment of roots.

unnoticed here for five thousand years but is now officially a new native fern. It's not in the Berryfields garden (yet), but the following are:

◆ *Asplenium scolopendrium* 'Cristatum', hart's tongue fern, thrives in moist, slightly alkaline, well-drained soil in dappled shade. Too much sun will scorch the fronds. Fronds are evergreen, strap-shaped and crested towards the tip and can grow to 60cm (2 feet) in length.

◆ *Dryopteris affinis* 'Cristata', king of the male ferns, tolerates dry shade, but grows best in moist, well-drained soil. The dark green mature fronds can reach 1.5m (5 feet) in length. Fronds last into winter but can look ragged. New fronds are pale green.

◆ *Matteuccia struthiopteris*, shuttlecock fern or ostrich fern, needs wet soil (not waterlogged). The fronds are lance-shaped and are almost vertical as they unfurl. It rapidly forms colonies, and new plants are easily lifted and transplanted. Deciduous.

◆ *Onoclea sensibilis*, sensitive fern, prefers damp, slightly acidic soil in shade. Its fronds have wavy edges and are easily damaged by hard frosts; deciduous. The new fronds (or fiddleheads) are pinky red when they first emerge from the rhizome in spring.

◆ *Osmunda regalis*, royal fern, grows to 1.2m (4 feet) high, preferring damp soil. The fronds are exquisitely fresh green as they emerge in spring. Fronds produced in midsummer are erect and bear spores at their tips; deciduous. It spreads by rhizomes as well as spores.

◆ *Polypodium vulgare* 'Bifidomultifidum', common polypody, prefers moist, slightly

If your fern produces bulbous leaf bases, these can be split from the parent plant. Dig up the fern and wash off the soil from around the roots and leaf base. Split the swollen leaf bases from the parent plant – which can look brown and dead – and plant them upside down in trays of moist, peat-free multipurpose compost. Put the tray in a polythene bag and check after two months. Green growth shows the process has worked. Nurse the parent plant with plenty of water.

Ferns and their allies (club-mosses, horsetails and quillworts) number around ten thousand, with the last 'new' fern discovered in the UK as recently as 2003 near Wadebridge in Cornwall. *Cystopteris diaphana* is common in southern Europe but hadn't previously been seen growing in the UK. It's probably been growing

LEFT The emerging fronds of *Dryopteris* uncurl in their characteristic crosiers.

OPPOSITE The native *Helleborus foetidus* growing in woodland conditions, with daffodils.

acidic soil, but it will tolerate dry shade and even sunnier positions than most ferns; slightly acidic soil. The evergreen fronds are thick and yellowish-green. It grows to 30cm (12 inches) high.

DAMP SHADE

Dry shade is more likely in most woodlands, but damp shade is also a possibility. Plants growing at Berryfields in damp shady conditions include:

◆ *Anemone × hybrida* 'Honorine Jobert': vigorous, branching perennial capable of growing almost anywhere – full sun will scorch and shrivel plants. It thrives in damp shade, growing to 1.5m (5 feet) high and 1m (3 feet) wide. Single, cup-shaped white flowers with golden stamens are produced in late summer and autumn. Leaves are dark green and deeply cut.

◆ *Astilboides tabularis:* a native of China, this forms clumps 1.5m (5 feet) high with a spread of 1m (3 feet). Huge, rounded, slightly scalloped leaves are held on 1m

(3-foot) stalks. Plume-like white/cream flowers are produced around midsummer. It needs moisture and shade to survive.

◆ *Kirengeshoma palmata*: upright stems in loose clumps; large, light green, sycamore-shaped leaves. It appears late in spring, after the damaging frosts are over, and flowers in late summer to early autumn. The tips of the flower stems produce yellow, bell-like flowers. The plants need shelter from wind and protection from frost, so mulch over the plants in winter to assure their survival. Grows 1m (3 feet) high with a spread of 75cm (2½ feet). Prefers slightly acidic soil.

◆ *Tiarella cordifolia* 'Heronswood Mist': has cream, pink-speckled, maple-shaped leaves and masses of star-shaped, pink flowers on flower spikes from mid spring to summer. Grows to around 30cm (12 inches) with a similar spread. Displays deep pink autumn colour.

Cyclamen

Although the spring garden is, as the name suggests, focused on spring-flowering plants, we have also planted cyclamen there to provide a show in autumn, and will add to these each year.

Cyclamen are a genus of plants containing twenty species that are part of the Primulaceae family. Most are distributed around the Mediterranean, and not all are hardy, but the most common types, *Cyclamen coum* and *C. hederifolium*, are both fully hardy. Severe frost may blacken leaves, but they will recover and the tuber will survive if mulched with leafmould or grit. Most are happiest in woodland, preferring a

OPPOSITE *Cyclamen coum* are happiest in the moist shade and rich soil of the spring garden and can still be found flowering strongly in early spring.

position that is slightly shaded in summer and moist during autumn and winter. The soil must be rich in humus, and in woodland the leaf fall in autumn provides the necessary humus. If you do not have any suitable tree cover, cyclamen will grow well against a north-facing wall and in pots, troughs and rock gardens.

Before planting the tubers, fork equal parts of grit and shredded leafmould into the soil. Plant so that the top of the tuber is at soil level and mulch with a 1cm (½-inch) layer of grit. Do the same with ready-grown plants. *Cyclamen hederifolium* often produces roots from the top of the tuber, and therefore can be planted slightly deeper in the soil.

To improve the quality of your cyclamen add extra leaves as mulch in autumn. This is best if the leaves are first shredded by running a mower over them. Do not add any fertilizer to the soil or around plants, as flowering will be inhibited, the feed will only encourage soft growth prone to diseases, and the leaves will take on a cabbage-leaf appearance. Once cyclamen are planted it's best to leave them undisturbed. Flower quantity will increase and seedlings will appear around the parent plants, producing strong-growing clumps and drifts.

If growing cyclamen in pots, allow the compost to dry out before giving it a soaking. Waterlog a pot of cyclamen and they will die. The cyclamen growing at Berryfields are:

◆ *Cyclamen coum*: winter flowering, sometimes starting before Christmas and continuing into March. Flowers can be white, pink or magenta with a darker purple blotch at the base of each petal. Foliage is kidney-shaped, dark green and glossy. Sometimes the leaves are patterned with silver.

◆ *Cyclamen hederifolium*: pink flowers with a V-shaped, purple blotch at the base of each petal. Flowers in autumn; the flowers usually appear before the leaves. Young leaves look like ivy leaves – hence the *hederifolium* part of the name. Plants are variable and leaves can be almost any shape. Leaves can also vary from pale to dark green, dull to glossy. They can also be silver-patterned.

Tubers root from the top and the sides. It is a good ground-cover plant for winter when planted in sufficient numbers or when colonies establish themselves.

Primula

There are many different kinds of primula, but all are herbaceous perennials and quite a few are suitable for deciduous woodland like the spring garden at Berryfields. The only consideration is that mature trees can take up most of the available moisture and most primulas prefer slightly damp conditions, but adding plenty of compost to the soil and mulching with leafmould each year is usually sufficient to counter this.

RIGHT Primulas of all kinds are a joy that I associate with the hope and brightness of spring.

TOP The pom-pom flowers of the drumstick *Primula denticulata* var. *alba*.

MIDDLE The cowslip, *Primula veris*, grows happily in the semi-shaded woodland of our spring garden, but is at its happiest in open grassland.

BELOW The common and enduringly lovely primrose, *Primula vulgaris*, growing among *Muscari*.

Primroses (*Primula vulgaris*) dislike being exposed to strong, drying wind or too much strong sunlight. If you haven't got a canopy of overhead leaves, planting among taller shrubs will provide enough shade for primroses to grow.

Primroses should be planted deeply as they develop fresh roots annually from the crown of the plant. New roots develop in early summer when flowering has finished. The old rootstock becomes almost useless and when splitting plants it can be discarded.

It's best to split primrose plants before the new crowns become too overcrowded. The best times to split primroses are spring and early autumn, when there is plenty of root activity. This allows enough time for the plants to recover, grow new roots and establish large enough root systems to survive the immediate summer or winter.

Pick a damp, showery day when the soil is workable. Dig up the plants and ease the soil away from the plant. New crowns will be seen clearly, and these can be separated by gently pulling them apart, and replanted in soil that has been well dug with added leafmould or in pots of the same soil and leafmould mix. Water the plants in well.

Primroses in the Berryfields woodland garden are:

◆ *Primula denticulata*, drumstick primula, a robust plant growing to 45cm (18 inches) high with a similar spread, produces dense, rounded heads of purple, pink, mauve and lilac flowers on stout flower spikes.
◆ *Primula denticulata* var. *alba* produces dense heads of white flowers in early spring through to early summer. Leaves are mid green and any that turn yellow should be removed to prevent disease. Plants grow 45cm (18 inches) high.
◆ *Primula elatior*, oxlip, is a cross between the cowslip and primrose, resulting in semi-evergreen rosettes of mid green leaves. Flowers are yellow, sweetly scented and produced in umbels in spring. Plants grow 30cm (12 inches) high with a 25cm (10-inch) spread.
◆ *Primula veris*, cowslip, is one of my favourite flowers of all. It has clusters of yellow, tubular, nodding flowers on stout stems in mid to late spring. Not really a woodland plant, naturalizing on open downland or roadsides, but it does adapt

happily enough to light woodland shade.
◆ *Primula vulgaris*, primrose, is the first primrose and probably best of all flowers. A bunch of soft yellow primroses in early spring will cheer the darkest heart. It spreads quickly and prefers damp shade. Plants grow 20cm (8 inches) high, spreading to 45cm (18 inches).

BLUEBELLS CASE STUDY
A misty blue lake of the native bluebell (*Hyacinthoides non-scripta*) lapping around the trunks of a wood in spring is one the loveliest sights in nature. We can bring that into the garden, although bluebells are actually quite hard to establish and need a precise set of conditions to flourish.

Spanish bluebells (*Hyacinthoides hispanica*) are more robust, and whereas native bluebells cannot compete with grass, Spanish bluebells can. Bees pollinate both flowers and hybrids result – with a hybrid mix of the two parents' characteristics, and this is threatening stocks of native bluebells. There are many clues as to whether your bluebell is a native, a hybrid or a Spanish type. The one deciding factor is the colour of the pollen. If the pollen is cream-coloured, it is definitely native. (See the table on page 206 for other differences.)

So if you garden near woodland containing bluebells, plant only native bluebells in your garden, reducing the possibilities of cross-pollination between Spanish and native bluebells. Never collect bluebells from the wild, as this further diminishes stock, although more

NATIVE BLUEBELLS	HYBRID BLUEBELLS	SPANISH BLUEBELLS
HYACINTHOIDES NON-SCRIPTA	*HYACINTHOIDES X MASSARTIANA*	*HYACINTHOIDES HISPANICA*
Narrow leaves usually 15mm (⅗ inch) when measured half-way down	Broad leaves usually 30mm (1½ inches) when measured half-way down	Broad leaves usually 35mm (1⅓ inches) when measured half-way down
Drooping flower stem	Curved flower stem	Upright flower stem
Flowers on one side of the flower stem	Flowers mostly around the flower stem	Flowers around the flower stem
Flowers hang down	Flowers droop	Flowers stick out
Deep blue flowers	Dark blue, pale blue or white flowers	Any shade of blue, pink or white flowers
Narrow, straight-sided flowers	Open, bell-shaped flowers	Wide, bell- or cone-shaped flowers
Tips of petals rolled back on to the tube part of the flower	Tips of petals curl slightly outwards	Tips of petals flare slightly outwards
Cream-coloured pollen on unequal-sized anthers inside the flower	Pale blue pollen on equal-sized anthers inside the flower	Deep blue pollen on equal-sized anthers
Flowers are sweetly scented	Flowers are slightly scented	Flowers have little or no scent

damage is done by footfall than picking. When buying bluebells, use a reputable retailer and ensure the labelling on packaging is correct.

Bluebell leaf growth is first seen in January when the canopy cover is negligible. Flowers open in April and May. Mostly seen in deciduous woodland, bluebells can also grow on cliffs, roadsides, grassland and parkland. Conifer plantations exclude too much light for bluebells to grow, and the needles form a growth-inhibiting acidic mulch.

Native bluebell seed can be bought from responsible seed retailers. Sow the seed in autumn, sowing thinly on the surface of a peat-free seed compost mixed in equal parts with sieved leafmould, cover with a thin layer of vermiculite and put in a cold frame or plunge pots in the woodland garden. Germination will take place the following spring, and plants will be of sufficient size to flower after three years. Remember that saving your own seed is good, but if you have Spanish or hybrid bluebells near your patch of natives, you may well be nurturing more hybrids. And that's disappointing after three years of waiting. Bluebell bulbs should be planted in early summer (after flowering), 20cm (8 inches) deep in woodland soil. Water the bulbs well.

NEW TREES

Although we have the established trees already in the spring garden, we have also planted some new ones to thicken out and extend our little woodland.

The most dramatic is *Prunus × yedoensis*, or Yoshino cherry, which was planted in 2003. It is a spring-flowering cherry, producing almond-scented, white flowers 4cm (1½ inches) across. Sometimes the white is tinged with pink – and all buds are pink before they open. In summer the fruits are small cherries that ripen from red to glossy black. It's a round-headed tree with spreading, arching branches and dark green foliage that will provide dappled shade for future underplanting. *P. × yedoensis* grows 10m (33 feet) tall with a similar spread, preferring a sunny position in well-drained soil. It is native to Japan and there are apparently fifty thousand specimens around Tokyo. The Yoshino cherry is a cross between *P. speciosa*, the Oshima cherry, and *P. × subhirtella* 'Rosea'. The Oshima cherry is itself very beautiful and is often used as an understock for other cultivars, although many cherries are grafted on to wild gean, *P. avium*. This is why you often get a big lump growing at the join, where one of the two cherries is growing faster than the other. If this offends you, then you are better off going for a bush than a standard, simply because the offensive bulge will be more hidden.

There are three main options when buying a tree:

◆ Bare-root: trees that have been grown in a field and lifted with no soil surrounding the roots when the leaves have fallen in autumn. A very wide choice of varieties is available bare-root and generally at a much lower price than in a container. But the roots will dehydrate as soon as they are lifted, so must be protected at all times. Either plant immediately or heel trees in until you are ready to plant.
◆ Rootball: trees that have been lifted from a nursery with soil intact around the roots and netted or wrapped in hessian sacking. Generally applicable to

MONTY'S TIP

Heeling in, or planting temporarily, is vital to the success of bare-root trees. Planting immediately is best, but they can be planted at an angle to stop wind damage, in spare soil. Dig a hole and place the tree in it at a 45-degree angle. Cover the roots with soil and water well. Leave in this position until the planting hole is ready to receive the tree. If there is any delay between removing the tree from the heeling-in bed and the final planting hole, plunge the tree into a bucket of water and keep the roots covered and preferably damp right up until the moment of planting.

conifers, it allows large trees to be transplanted with reduced shock to the tree. Large plants are available, and there's a good choice of varieties, but rootballed trees are messy to handle and

are heavy. Cover rootballs with sacking or straw if planting has to be delayed.

◆ Containerized: trees that have been potted into containers when they were young and grown on for more than two years. Easy to handle, convenient (most garden centres stock a good range), but can be very expensive when compared with bare-root trees, and generally a more limited range is available.

It is always best to buy small. There is a number of good reasons for this, but the first is that they do not experience the same shock that larger specimens suffer from when transplanted. A larger tree stops growing while it acclimatizes to its new environment, whereas a smaller tree will soon get growing and catches up quickly. Smaller trees are also much cheaper, easier to handle, less likely to blow over and generally more healthy. Need any more convincing?

NEW PLANTING TECHNIQUE

The conventional method of planting trees is to dig a large planting hole, add plenty of organic matter to the bottom, take the tree out of the pot, teasing out the roots if they are pot-bound, place the tree in the hole, partially cover and firm the soil around the rootball. Then there is another firming in, lots of water and a mulch with organic matter to finish the job. There is now a new technique for planting trees and shrubs that has been advocated by the Royal Horticultural Society (RHS) and that we have been trialling at Berryfields. It is based on research that shows that almost all the feeding roots of any tree are within 15cm (6 inches) of the surface and that

SPRING-GARDEN BASICS
◆ Grow plants suited to the conditions in your garden.
◆ Mulch in autumn and spring with leafmould.
◆ Plant new trees to provide winter structure and summer shade.
◆ Buy small trees and plants.
◆ Plant spring-flowering bulbs.

LEFT The combination of intensely coloured sepals and pale anthers is what makes so many *Helleborus* × *hybridus* so richly beautiful.

OPPOSITE *Magnolia* × *loebneri* 'Leonard Messel' in all its flowering glory.

many trees are suffering by being planted too deeply and therefore becoming waterlogged in our wet winters. Shallow or even mound planting will counter this. So dig a shallow but wide hole, loosening and aerating the sides of the hole with a fork to help new roots grow out quickly into the surrounding soil. Then plant the tree or shrub higher than in the traditional way. Fill the shallow hole with soil to which no organic matter has been added (because that will only cause subsidence and delay the roots from growing out of the planting hole), water and mulch around the base of the tree, taking care not to pile mulch up against the trunk. Trees have been planted using both techniques at Berryfields and time will tell which works best.

A YEAR IN THE SPRING GARDEN

SPRING

◆ Repot primulas in containers.
◆ Sow primula seeds.
◆ Cut off ragged hellebore leaves, taking care not to damage flower buds.
◆ Take basal cuttings of × *Heucherella*.
◆ Divide tiarella plants.
◆ Divide large clumps of Japanese anemone.

SUMMER

◆ Order bare-root trees to ensure availability.
◆ Hand weed around cyclamen when they are dormant in summer.
◆ Divide bluebells.
◆ Take semi-ripe cuttings from geraniums.
◆ Sow Japanese anemone seed.

AUTUMN

◆ Add additional leaf mulch to the woodland garden.

◆ Sow bluebell seed in trays and place in a cold frame.

◆ Propagate ferns when spores are mature.

◆ Divide large primula clumps.

◆ Sow cyclamen seed.

◆ Repot cyclamen growing in containers.

◆ Plant bluebell bulbs.

◆ Sow seed or divide hellebores.

◆ Sow geranium seed.

◆ Sow magnolia seed.

◆ Late autumn is a good time to plant bare-root trees.

WINTER

◆ Firm in any newly planted plants after frost.

◆ Sow foxglove seed in late winter for a same-year flower display.

◆ Prune low branches from trees to increase the light reaching the woodland floor.

◆ Check tree ties and all newly planted trees and shrubs.

◆ Last chance to plant bare-root trees.

ABOVE A hellebore hybrid.

OPPOSITE *Cyclamen coum.*

'The **essential** component of any water garden is *not* the water *or* the planting but the **relationship** between the two. Clear water makes a small garden feel *more expansive* and is a *point of focus* around which everything else can revolve.'

the pond

the pond

THE POND WAS BY FAR THE BIGGEST PROJECT THAT WE undertook in our first year at Berryfields. We knew that we wanted to include a pond as a major part of the garden, but it took a little while to decide exactly what it should be like. It is not enough simply to know that one wants water as part of the garden. The choice is wide and varies dramatically, from the formality of a symmetrical piece of water framed by a hard surface that works on the same level as a parterre, to a completely natural pond that is the watery equivalent of a meadow.

The essential component of any water garden is not the water or the planting but the relationship between the two. Clear water makes a small garden feel more expansive and is a point of focus around which everything else can revolve. It creates a sense of calm and mystery, constantly mirroring the sky, the weather and thus the entire mood of the garden. Yet just clear water, without any planting, works only when done formally. At Berryfields this would not work at all. We needed lots of water wedded to lots and lots of lovely plants.

I think it a good rule to make your pond as big as space and money will allow. I have never yet seen one that is too large for the garden it is in. There is something irresistibly attractive about open expanses of water, especially when fringed by lush planting, which is why plants like *Gunnera manicata, Darmera, Rodgersia*, rheums, ligularias and hostas all look so good against a watery setting. The more space you give it, the more expansive and lush your pond can be.

The pond should certainly take in some boggy ground too, occupying that indeterminate area where the soil never dries out and yet is rarely actually water. There are not many places in the garden where mud is welcome, but bog gardens are lovely.

To encourage as much aquatic wildlife as possible you need depth in some part of the water – at least 1m (3 feet) and preferably twice that – so that fish have room to escape the worst frosts. This will

PREVIOUS PAGE, LEFT
The pond in July, just one year after the hole was first excavated, but looking as though it has been there for years.

PREVIOUS PAGE, RIGHT
Ducks make a terrible mess and eat precious plants. But ducks are also great for getting rid of slugs, so I was delighted when a family made its home on our pond.

OPPOSITE The pond in May 2004. Because none of the marginal planting had become established, the paisley shape is very clear.

MONTY'S TIP
Pond plants are best grown in open-sided baskets. Line the basket with hessian and fill with subsoil or aquatic compost. Plant firmly and top-dress the basket with a 2cm (¾-inch) layer of grit. This prevents soil from washing out of the basket and fish, if any are present in the pond, from dislodging the soil. It may seem unnecessary, but always water the pot before planting.

increase the soil to be removed by quite a bit and, unless you can afford to cart it away, the spoil has to be factored into the design: it will probably mean a slope or even a hillock as a result – at Berryfields the excavations resulted in Chris's grassy crescent that is perfectly aligned to the front door of the house across the water of the pond. So the lessons are simple: be bold, use the spoil creatively, be generous with water, margins and plants, and don't forget to leave room for a decent bog.

SITING A POND
Obviously context is vital. At Berryfields the site dictated that a naturalistic pond was likely to be more suitable and we certainly wanted to encourage as much wildlife as possible and to include in the project a wide range of marginal and boggy plants.

Before even planning the excavation, spend as long as it takes marking out proposed sites, shapes and sizes, using canes and string or hosepipe. Look at them from every angle and position in the garden. When you are sure that you are happy, live with it for a couple of weeks. We spent months doing this at Berryfields. After all, if you change your mind it is a lot easier to reposition canes and string than a finished pond!

Avoid siting a pond where it will receive sunlight all day. Sunlight will promote the growth of algae. Too much shade, on the other hand, will reduce the growth of desirable plants, such as waterlilies, so a semi-shaded position is best.

As a rule of thumb the pond should receive direct sunlight for at least half the day. It is unwise to site a pond under trees as falling leaves will decompose in the water, creating conditions advantageous to algae.

However, a sheltered position will reduce the damage that can be done by wind. Strong winds can increase water evaporation from ponds and even bow over marginal plants growing in baskets near the edge of the pond. If possible, avoid frost pockets. These are sheltered places in low-lying areas where air accumulates and can freeze in winter. Steeply sloping ground is also not ideal as it is expensive to create retaining walls.

It is well worth the expense of installing mains electricity to a point somewhere near the pond during the initial upheaval of pond construction. Even if it is never used, it is there if you ever need to pump a pond out or want to install a pump or filter.

Ensure that your pond is safe, especially if you have very young children. The only

practical way of doing this is to fence off the entire pond area – which is what we have done at Berryfields.

THE LINER
We had chosen our site, agreed on the size and shape, and work finally began in July. At first all went well. The contractors moved in with their diggers and excavated what seemed to be an enormous hole. Any kind of earth-moving operation involving mechanical diggers in a garden is always exciting and alarming in equal measure, and we watched them at work with bated breath. But after a week or so we had a wonderfully large crater with shelves and shallows. The next job was partially to refill it with a clay liner.

Once a pond is dug it needs to be lined with something. Very occasionally the natural clay of the subsoil is sufficiently water-retentive to act as a liner – but this is rare. In most cases some kind of liner is needed to stop the water draining away. There is a choice of materials that will do this for you.

BEATEN CLAY: this was our choice at Berryfields pond. It uses natural materials, looks good, will last indefinitely and is very beneficial to wildlife. However, it also has to be 'puddled', which is the process of compressing it to flatten all the clay particles and make it watertight. Traditionally this is done by penning sheep in the dry pond for a few days and letting them trample all over it. Nowadays a machine is used, although it is called a 'sheepsfoot' roller.

The downside of clay is that if the pond dries out, the clay that is exposed will crack and leak water. Tree roots can also penetrate and damage the liner. The walls of a pond to be lined with clay must be 45 degrees or less as the clay will not adhere to steep walls. You cannot use any old clay either, but special material that may be expensive to transport. Finally you need a lot of it – the liner at Berryfields is nearly 1m (3 feet) thick in places, and we used hundreds of tonnes of clay, so it is not a cheap option.

When the clay liner is finally puddled, any shelving at the margins of the pond must then be backfilled with subsoil to allow direct planting of marginal plants. Do not use topsoil as this is unsuitable both for the plants and for the balance of the water.

BUTYL LINER: butyl is very expensive but tough, flexible and relatively easy to put into place. In most cases it is likely to be the appropriate choice of liner. Most manufacturers offer a guarantee against splitting for twenty years, but in reality butyl should be good for fifty years. To calculate the size needed, measure the longest distance and add twice the maximum depth for one measurement and then measure the widest point and add twice the maximum depth for the other measurement. Before using, open the liner out and leave it in the sun for an hour. This will soften it up and make it easier to fit. Take time removing every last stone or root from the soil at the bottom of the pond and then coat the entire surface with either carpeting underfelt or 5cm (2 inches) of sand. The latter should be a clay-based builders' sand that will form a binding surface. You can also buy non-woven geotextile underlays that are very tough. Whatever you use, the purpose is the same: to protect the lining from being punctured by a stone in the soil.

Stretch the liner over the pool and gently let it ease itself into all the contours, gathering folds where possible to avoid too many creases. The water will make the fit snugger, but don't start to fill it until you are happy that it is pretty well in position.

RIGID POND LINER: this is pre-formed, rigid and often manufactured from fibreglass or reinforced plastic. Mark out the shape of the pond (in this case the shape of the liner), dig out the hole, place the liner in the hole, checking it is level, and fill with water. Infill around the liner with soil. Cover the edges and plant. Be sure to buy a liner with a ten-year guarantee against cracking and degradation in sunlight.

Concrete pond liner: this allows great flexibility as concrete can fit any shape. It also means that the base of the pond is load-bearing, which allows you to set a statue or fountain or some other ornament in the pond. To lay the concrete, first firm the soil in the hole and cover with heavy-duty polythene. A 10cm (4-inch) layer of concrete is applied to the sides and base of the hole, and wire netting is pushed into the wet concrete to act as a reinforcement. Finishing concrete is then applied to the surface, covering the netting. When the concrete is dry it has to be sealed with a concrete sealant to prevent water damage.

MARGINAL PLANTS

Marginal plants are important as they make the edges of a pond less distinct and abrupt. There is a tendency to plant at the margins of the pond and behave as though there were an invisible boundary stopping outward expansion – with the result that the water becomes increasingly invaded by vegetation. I think that ideally the planting should spread out at the expense of land rather than water. To achieve this effect you need plenty of space around the pond for marginal planting, which must look less like a perimeter border and more like the arrival of land at the water's edge. Marginal plants are also an essential component of a wildlife pond as they provide nectar in the flowers for insects

and physical protection from predators for birds, amphibians and small mammals.

The margins of a pond provide the ideal environment for plants that need plenty of water at the roots and yet can cope with being in dry(ish) soil for short periods. Most will grow in conditions ranging from mud to 15cm (6 inches) of water.

Avoid planting in regimented rows – drift different species into one another. This avoids rigid planting schemes and creates a natural look. The impoverished subsoil around the Berryfields pond is ideal for wildflower plug plants. These are small plants, one year old, and grown

from seed. Such plants do not require highly fertile soil. If planting into a grassed area around a pond, scrape away the grass surrounding any planting hole. This reduces competition from grasses.

The margins around the Berryfields pond were planted up using many good-sized plants that went straight into the submerged soil of the shallow shelving around the edge of the pond. If you use a clay lining, as we have done at Berryfields, this soil must be deep enough so the growing roots do not damage the clay. It must also be subsoil as rich topsoil will upset the eco-balance of the pond. We also used plug plants at the water's edge. Plug plants are best planted at a density of 10–15 per square metre (11 square feet).

The Main Marginal Plants

◆ *Iris pseudacorus*, or flag iris, is a rampant, beardless iris. It grows to 2m (6 feet) high with an indefinite spread. Branched stems produce golden-yellow flowers with darker veining or patches on the falls from early to midsummer. The foliage is grey-green and sword-like. Ideal conditions are semi-shade and wet soil and it is perfect for the edges of a pond.

◆ *Iris kaempferi* has rich purple flowers in midsummer and slender deciduous foliage. Cultivars provide a range of colours from white through pink and lavender to violet.

◆ *Schoenoplectus lacustris* subsp. *tabernaemontani* 'Zebrinus' is an evergreen, spreading sedge with leafless stems. It has horizontal stripes on the dark green leaves. The stripes are yellow-white. Small spikelets of brown-red flowers are produced in July and August. Plants grow to 1.5m (5 feet) and will spread indefinitely. Plants can be divided in spring and seed can be sown in both spring and autumn. They grow best in full sun and are frost hardy.

◆ *Sagittaria sagittifolia*, or common arrowhead, has familiar arrow-shaped leaves that rise above the surface on long stems and the flowers are white with black centres.

◆ *Butomus umbellatus*, or flowering rush, is happiest in water about 10cm (4 inches) deep in a sunny spot and has long sword-shaped leaves ranging in colour from green to purple. It produces stems with as many as thirty flower-heads, each one looking like an upside-down umbrella.

◆ *Caltha palustris*, or marsh marigold, is a compact, deciduous perennial thriving when planted at the edges of a pond. The round, glossy, green leaves grow 20cm (8 inches) tall and plants spread 30cm (12 inches). Yellow, goblet-shaped flowers are produced from early spring, often before the foliage. Perfect for growing at the edge of the pond.

◆ *Lythrum salicaria*, or purple loosestrife, thrives in full sun, growing to 2m (6 feet) high with a spread of 60cm (2 feet). It produces strong upright stems and poker-like heads of pink flowers in summer. Plants are vigorous and can become invasive. Flower colour can vary from the usual pink to deep purple.

◆ *Lychnis flos-cuculi*, or ragged robin, is delicate in appearance but requires only wet soil to thrive. Dark green, narrow leaves grow on stems up to 1m (3 feet) high and are crowned in summer with

OPPOSITE Boggy and marginal plants provide a rich breadth of flowering that expands our whole floral range at Berryfields.

TOP LEFT The common flag iris, *Iris pseudacorus*, rises out of the water with golden flowers in early summer.
TOP RIGHT The flowering rush, *Butomus umbellatus*, is another marginal plant. Each stem carries dozens of umbelliferous flower heads.
BELOW LEFT The distinctive flower spike of the giant South American rhubarb, *Gunnera manicata*. The flowers are a curiosity but it is for the leaves that it is grown. They are the largest that will grow in Britain and have been recorded at 2.7m (9 feet) in diameter, on stems 2.5m (8 feet) high.
BELOW RIGHT The marsh marigold, *Caltha palustris*, is a giant buttercup whose brilliant yellow flowers appear in spring.

pink flowers made up of ragged petals. Ragged robin grows wild in wetland areas around Europe.

Oxygenators

Oxygenating plants have both leaves and roots submerged below the pond surface. Their purpose is to maintain the balance of a pond and to provide food and spawning areas for fish and frogs. Despite their name, their main function is not to produce oxygen but to absorb carbon dioxide which, if allowed to build up, encourages algal growth.

Garden centres and nurseries sell bunches of oxygenating plants held together with lead strips. It is common practice just to throw these into the water, but it is best to buy a few bunches, remove the lead strips and plant in an aquatic basket filled with aquatic compost or subsoil. Place a layer of gravel on the surface of the aquatic compost or soil and place the planted basket at the bottom of the pond.

It helps to have more than one type of oxygenating plant. Here is a range:

◆ *Hottonia palustris*, or water violet, belongs to the primula family, producing bright green, feathery foliage just below the surface of the water. Flower stalks with pale lavender flowers appear in early summer, growing 20cm (8 inches) above the surface. The foliage dies down in autumn and plants over-winter as dormant buds.
◆ *Ranunculus aquatilis*, or water buttercup, has two distinct types of

foliage. The first is finely cut and is produced only below the water surface; the second is clover-like and appears on the water surface. Plants flower in early summer, producing white buttercup blooms 4cm (1½ inches) above the water surface. A good choice for smaller ponds as it doesn't become invasive.
◆ *Potamogeton crispus*, or pondweed, has wiry stems along which reddish, wavy-edged leaves are formed, not dissimilar in appearance to seaweed. Pink-white flowers are produced in early summer. Despite its name, it is not a weed and is not invasive. A great choice if you have moving water in your pond.
◆ *Lagarosiphon major*, or goldfish weed, often sold as *Elodea crispa*, is the subject

LEFT Oxygenators like this water violet, *Hottonia palustris*, may not look attractive compared to some of the flowering plants in and around the pond, but they are invaluable in keeping the balance of carbon dioxide – and algae – under control.

OPPOSITE Purple loosestrife (*Lythrum salicaria*) is another native that is at home in damp conditions, producing purple spires of flowers that can become invasive if allowed to grow unchecked.

of heated debate among pond owners. Some say it is the perfect oxygenating plant, while others stress how invasive the plant is. Both are correct. It is a great oxygenator, but where you can't get at it – in the middle of a large pond – it will quickly get out of hand. Plant it only where you can easily keep the number of long stems, packed with curled leaves, under control.

BOG GARDEN

There is a range of plants that are not strictly marginals in that they do not need to be under water and yet need a degree of wetness to prosper. These properly belong in a bog garden, and when we made the pond we created an area dedicated to these plants. A bog garden is a surprisingly rich habitat for a wide variety of plants, whose preferences in bogginess range from thick soup to moist cake, and some of which will put up with quite a lot of summer dryness as long as they get a really good soak in winter. The one real definition of a bog garden is that it is in an area of ground that never properly dries out. It can be very small and completely containable, because in the main plants that like boggy conditions will not spread to surrounding, drier areas.

The Berryfields bog garden adjoins the pond and the water keeps it permanently damp, but we have fixed a barrier, made from a roll of coir matting, to stop the soil dissolving back into the pond. This matting rots after a year, but by then the plants will be established and forming a mat of roots. The same coir matting is used to hold back the subsoil surrounding the excavated pond. Whereas pond plants require low levels of nutrients, boggy plants require high levels, so topsoil should be used as the growing medium in the bog garden while the barrier ensures that any nutrients in the bog garden do not run into the pond, upsetting the balance. An annual mulch with leafmould or compost will maintain the fertility of the bog.

The ideal is to have permanently damp soil in a bog garden but not ground that is under water, so there must be some drainage. When lining a bog garden with a butyl or plastic liner it is therefore important to puncture the liner every 10cm (4 inches) with holes. A 5cm (2-inch) layer of grit in the base of the bog garden further improves drainage.

Many bog plants are also suitable for herbaceous borders. The main requirement is moisture at the roots, with the crowns of plants above soil level. Provide the moisture and the plants will thrive.

Plants suited to bog garden conditions include:

◆ *Astilbe*: members of this genus all require moist soils and are ideally suited to bog gardens. The plume-like flowers are produced in summer and remain attractive throughout winter. *Astilbe* 'Granat' forms a clump up to 1m (3 feet) high and 60cm (2 feet) wide. The leaves are deep green, flushed bronze, broad and divided into oval leaflets. Deep red flowers are produced in summer. Once they are planted it is best to leave all astilbe plants undisturbed as they do not like being split. In favourable, boggy conditions plants will readily self-seed, although resultant plants will not produce the same-coloured flowers. Remove, pot up and use seedlings elsewhere if this detracts from the bog garden design.

◆ *Cyperus longus*, or sweet galingale, is a spreading sedge and grows up to 1.5m (5 feet) tall. It is a British native and can become invasive. The umbrella-like flower-heads are milk-chocolate brown and produced any time between June and October. It is fully hardy. Leaves are deciduous, rough-edged and glossy green. Cut back the dead foliage when plants are dormant in winter. Plants can be divided, or thinned, in autumn and spring, and seed can be sown in spring.

◆ *Eupatorium cannabinum* 'Flore Pleno', or double hemp agrimony, produces frothy heads of purple-mauve flowers on red-tinted stems between June and October. Flower-heads grow to 1.2m (4 feet) tall with a spread of 1m (3 feet) and it thrives in both sunny and partially shaded areas of the bog garden. The leaves will turn brown if the roots are allowed to dry out.

◆ *Gunnera manicata*, or giant or prickly rhubarb, produces the largest of all leaves that will grow in Britain, reaching up to 2m (6 feet) across. Conical, light green flower spikes are produced in summer followed by orange-brown seed pods. Plants can grow 4m (13 feet) high and form clumps 5m (16 feet) across and the flower stalk alone can weigh 2kg (4½lb).

Water is essential if this plant is to survive, but it is best planted on a raised mound of soil. It will be damaged by hard frost, so protect the crowns by bending back the dying leaves as a protective mulch.

◆ *Hemerocallis*, or daylily, is a clump-forming perennial with narrow, mid green, strap-shaped leaves. Delicate, trumpet-shaped, yellow flowers with reddish-brown backs are produced in early summer. Individual flowers last only a day or two, but each plant produces a succession of flowers from early to midsummer. Plants grow 75cm (2½ feet) tall with a spread of 60cm (2 feet) and grow well in sun or partial shade. Plants can be divided in spring.

LEFT The flowers of the daylily, *Hemerocallis*, only last for one day, but fortunately they are renewed for many days on end. If you have time to catch them before they fade, you will find that they are good to eat.

Foliage turns from green to the colour of gold in autumn before completely dying back.

◆ *Ligularia dentata* 'Desdemona' has large, kidney-shaped, coppery green leaves with rich purple undersides. In July wonderful egg-yolk orange flowers appear on branching stems. It is a clump-forming perennial growing to 1.5m (5 feet) high with a spread of 60cm (2 feet). Best planted in large drifts for a dramatic effect. *L. przewalskii* and *L.* 'The Rocket' both have very cut leaves and their flowers are wispy spires of flower on chocolate-black stems. *L. dentata* 'Othello' has distinct browny purple leaves and bright orange flowers rather later in the summer. All are superb plants for either a bog garden or a herbaceous border with very heavy, damp soil.

◆ *Lobelia cardinalis* is an upright plant with purple-tinged glossy foliage and brilliant scarlet flowers forming tall spikes in midsummer on top of plants growing 1m (3 feet) tall and 25cm (10 inches) across. New growth in spring is susceptible to slug and snail damage.

◆ *Lysichiton americanus*, or American skunk cabbage, grows 1m (3 feet) high with a spread of 1m. It is a herbaceous perennial, dying down in autumn and winter and reappearing in spring with banana-like spathes (with a distinct cabbagy aroma – hence the reference to skunk) pushing up through the bare mud before any leaves appear. Oval leaves are produced in late spring and are rich green and leathery with a slight sheen. The thick, fleshy rhizomes can be divided in autumn.

TOP Give *Lobelia cardinalis* the waterlogged soil of a bog and it will provide its brilliant red flowers for weeks on end in midsummer.

MIDDLE Another daylily, *Hemerocallis* 'Berlin Red', luxuriating with its roots in permanent mud.

BELOW The American skunk cabbage, *Lysichiton americanus*, is so-called because the banana-yellow spathes that appear out of the mud in early spring have a distinct fragrance of rotting cabbage. These are followed by large, upright, fleshy, bright green leaves.

AQUATIC PLANTS

So far our only aquatic plants in the pond are waterlilies. This is partly because getting the balance between clear water and plants is a delicate thing and needs to be done gradually, allowing the original planting to spread naturally, and partly because we had problems getting our lining right so had to empty the pond (twice!), taking all the plants out both times. However, the waterlilies have survived this abuse and are growing very well.

WATERLILY CASE STUDY

Waterlilies (*Nymphaea*) are a diverse genus. Some waterlilies require a few centimetres of water to grow, whereas others need 1m (3 feet) of water to thrive. All prefer an open, sunny site and still water, and most varieties produce flowers from June through to September. The large plate-like leaves float on the surface of the water, creating shade for wildlife and reducing algae populations. When purchasing waterlilies check the overall spread of the plant, as some varieties are vigorous, and do not stock your pond with waterlilies that will cover more than half of the surface. Generally the less vigorous varieties require shallow water, and the vigorous varieties require a greater depth of water to thrive – and are therefore naturally more at home in a larger pond.

Waterlilies for shallow water (45cm/ 18 inches deep) include:

◆ *Nymphaea tetragona*: foliage is dark green with purple undersides. It is the smallest waterlily, producing flowers 2cm (¾ inch) across. Each flower is star-shaped and white.
◆ *Nymphaea* 'Graziella': olive-green foliage is mottled purple-brown. Flowers are orange and cup-shaped.
◆ *Nymphaea* 'Ellisiana': small, green leaves and tulip-shaped, rose-red flowers with bright orange stamens. Early flower colour deepens within days.
◆ *Nymphaea candida*: plain green leaves and pure white, cup-shaped flowers.
◆ *Nymphaea* 'Laydekeri Lilacea': green leaves are spotted brown. Flowers are soft pink, ageing to red.

Waterlilies for medium water (75cm/ 2½ feet deep) include:

◆ *Nymphaea* 'Gonnère': young leaves are bronze, turning light green when mature. Flowers are double, open-cupped and white. Also called Crystal White or Snowball.
◆ *Nymphaea* 'Moorei': leaves are dark green spotted with purple-brown. Flowers are soft yellow.
◆ *Nymphaea* 'William Falconer': young leaves are purple, changing to olive green with age. Deep red flowers with yellow stamens.
◆ *Nymphaea* 'Helen Fowler': foliage is soft green and the scented, deep rose-pink flowers are held above the surface of the pond.
◆ *Nymphaea* 'Marliacea Chromatella': the large olive-green leaves are splashed with maroon and brown spots. Flowers are predominantly primrose yellow but can appear with pink blushing.

Waterlilies for deep water (2m/6 feet deep) include:

◆ *Nymphaea* 'Colossea': dark olive-green leaves and large pink flowers 25cm (10 inches) across, that fade to white with age.
◆ *Nymphaea* 'Escarboucle': deep green leaves can grow to 30cm (12 inches) in diameter. The fragrant flowers, equal in size to the leaves, are vermilion-crimson and deepen in colour with age.
◆ *Nymphaea* 'Picciola': red-green leaves are spotted with brown-maroon. Flowers are star-shaped, deep crimson and are held just above the surface of the water.
◆ *Nymphaea* 'Tuberosa Richardsonii': large, pure white blooms with green sepals are freely produced.
◆ *Nymphaea* 'Colonel A. J. Welch': produces young plants on flower stems, and cup-shaped, primrose-yellow blooms among the green foliage.

There are two main ways to propagate waterlilies:

PLANTING EYES: all waterlilies produce eyes along the rootstock. If left alone, waterlily eyes will remain dormant, but if removed they will develop into healthy new plants. Waterlily eyes should be cut out of the rootstock and potted into 10cm (4-inch) terracotta pots filled with aquatic compost. The pots should then be placed in a shallow tray of water and placed in a cool greenhouse or sheltered part of the garden. The eyes will produce shoots within a month and the level of the water can then be increased. When the eyes produce shoots, plants should be potted into larger pots containing the same compost formulation. When plants reach a suitable size they can be planted into the pond.

DIVISION: in late spring lift waterlilies from the pond and remove from the aquatic baskets. The crown of the waterlily has a fleshy rootstock with smaller side rootstocks. Cut off the small side rootstocks and replant in aquatic baskets filled with aquatic compost. It is best to discard the original rootstock, as it will not have the same vigour as the new plants and might not even survive.

BLANKETWEED

Blanketweed is a thin, filamentous alga that can choke a pond. Floating on the surface of the water, the filaments can accumulate to form thick green bootlaces that will reduce light levels in the pond and can be persistent. It sometimes occurs when a new pond is settling in, but the cause of persistent blanketweed could be:

◆ Lack of oxygenating plants in the pond.
◆ Topping up the pond with tap water.
◆ Too many fish in a pond, causing an imbalance of nutrients.
◆ High levels of nutrients in the water.
◆ Warming of water due to strengthening sun in spring and summer.

MONTY'S TIP
Many garden centres and nurseries sell pond plants in plastic bags. Once at home, open the bags and place the plants in buckets of either saved rainwater or scooped pond water. Plant as soon as possible after purchase.

OPPOSITE Waterlilies in the midday sun.

TOP LEFT *Nymphaea* 'Ellisiana'.
TOP RIGHT *Nymphaea* 'Moorei'.
BELOW LEFT *Nymphaea* 'Marliacea Chromatella'.
BELOW RIGHT *Nymphaea* 'Escarboucle'.

If it is any comfort, there are almost no ponds that do not have some blanket-weed, and most have radical growth for a short period of the year. Indeed, some blanketweed is desirable in a pond as water snails graze on the filaments, regulating levels of both blanketweed and general plant debris.

The best way to get rid of it is simply to weed it from the pond either by twisting it round a stick or by raking it from the surface of the water. Leave the blanketweed at the side of the pond to allow creatures to find their way back into the water overnight, and then add the blanketweed to the compost heap, where it will rot down very successfully.

MONTY'S CONFESSION
Most of the activity on *Gardeners' World* is filmed, and my tumble into the pond was no exception. Everyone watching stood open-mouthed (with delight?) except the sound recordist, who rushed forward with a cry of 'Oh no – that's my radio-mic!' I am sorry to say that although my clothes dried well enough and my pride was not too disturbed, his microphone was irretrievably sodden.

Never use any fertilizer in the pond as this will feed the blanketweed. As ever, in any part of the garden, the best long-term control is to create a sustainable balance. But the balance in a small pond is a delicate thing. Small ponds heat up and cool down quickly and are susceptible to nutrient and mineral imbalances when tap water is used for topping up. In a large pond small amounts of tap water

have negligible effects, so it can be used to top up the levels. However, it is best to store rainwater for topping up.

The following suggestions are ways to achieve a pond balance:

◆ Plant floating plants to cover half of the pond surface. They shouldn't cover more than this, as their leaves reduce light levels, which could then cause an imbalance in the pond.
◆ Clear away excess blanketweed before it chokes a pond.
◆ Submerge oxygenating plants to ensure high levels of oxygen in the pond. A quarter of the pond's volume should be made up of oxygenating plants.
◆ Never use fertilizers in or around the pond. Run-off from lawn fertilizers often finds its way into ponds, causing a nutrient imbalance.
◆ Use only aquatic or nutrient-poor subsoil when planting up aquatic plants.
◆ Remove dead and decaying leaves to prevent them from rotting. Net the pond in autumn to prevent fallen leaves from rotting in the water. If this isn't practical, it's best to check the surface of the pond daily and remove the leaves.

SHARING WITH NEIGHBOURS
To get a good stock of pond water, many people advocate adding water from a neighbouring pond. The bacteria, fungi and water invertebrates will all be adapted to local conditions and when added to a new pond will soon proliferate. But be warned: this is also a potential way of introducing weeds – including spores of algae – into your

virgin pond, so sieve out any visible material before adding 'borrowed' pond water to your own pond. This reduces the likelihood of contamination.

WILDLIFE

There is no need to introduce wildlife to a pond as water inevitably attracts wildlife into the garden. A good wildlife pond will have plenty of shade to protect wildlife and to provide nesting areas. It will also have sloping sides that allow wildlife easy access to and exit from the pond. Rough grass or meadow around a pond is good for wildlife as it acts as a refuge. Once a pond has stabilized it is best to leave it alone as far as possible. This means living with a few weeds (loved by frogs), while many insects prefer overgrown, muddy ponds.

Create piles of logs near the wildlife pond to attract insects. It's best not to add fish to a wildlife pond, as they eat the larvae of many insects. When constructing a wildlife pond ensure that the deepest part of the pond is at least 60cm (2 feet). This is the minimum depth of water required to sustain wildlife over winter, when temperatures can be below freezing point, and in summer, when anything less will heat up to intolerable levels. In large ponds it is possible to construct a small island in the centre of the pond, which can act as a fox-proof refuge for wildfowl.

A healthy pond will attract a combination – and perhaps all – of the following:

◆ Ducks: these can damage the plant growth in a pond and their droppings may cause problems to the delicate balance of the water – but you would have to be a cold-hearted person not to welcome them into your garden. Ducks need grass to feed on and a nesting box on the ground that is safe from foxes – which is where an island becomes ideal. They are avid consumers of slugs and love best of all to dabble in the mud at the edge of a pond or in a puddle. They make a mess but I love them.

◆ Tadpoles: migrating frogs should find your pond, but if they don't – and it could be that the pond isn't suitable for wildlife or simply not in their migratory path – add frogspawn from a pond within a mile of yours. Never take frogspawn from the wild. Frogspawn should float either on or just below the surface of the pond. It takes around fourteen weeks for tadpoles to metamorphose into frogs, although this process is faster in warmer weather. Tadpoles emerge from the frogspawn after two weeks, feeding on the spawn, before nibbling at algae. After nine weeks they have developed lungs, and hind leg development results in movement and feeding on insects and plants. Front legs appear after eleven weeks. The tail soon disappears and *voilà* – a frog.

◆ Frogs: these are carnivores and are renowned for their appetite for slugs. There are three types of frog in the UK – the common frog, the edible frog and the marsh frog. The common frog is the only native. Edible frogs were introduced from Paris in 1837 by a Dr Smith, who released them as an experiment. Marsh frogs escaped from a garden in 1935 and are now commonplace. Millions of frogs have been killed recently by a virus sweeping through the country. It is thought that slug pellets, vehicle emissions and warmer winters could be lowering resistance to the virus. There is no known cure – but encouraging frogs into the garden will help numbers increase.

◆ Ramshorn snails: these are 2.5cm (1 inch) when fully grown and live in the margins of the ponds. The shell of the ramshorn snail is a flat coil with no point. They are herbivores and graze on the algae that coat many pond plants (and ponds). They are also tasty treats for fish and ducks. Snail eggs are laid in the pond and are surrounded by a protective jelly.

◆ Newts: the smooth or common newt is the most likely visitor to a garden pond. It is a carnivore that eats insects (and frogspawn). The main breeding season is February to June when most are seen; at other times they hide under logs or among marginal plants. Palmate newts prefer acid soils and boggy areas. The great crested newt is the largest newt, growing to around 16cm (6¼ inches). It also has the biggest appetite, eating slugs, invertebrates and other pond life. It is widely distributed but uncommon, suffering a decline in numbers over the last twenty years. The great crested newt is protected by UK law, which makes it an offence to kill, injure, capture or disturb it in any way. It is also illegal to trade great crested newts or destroy their habitats.

◆ Whirligig beetles: these shiny black insects have yellow, oar-shaped back legs and oval, flattened bodies. They have two pairs of eyes: the top pair looks for predators above the water surface while the lower pair looks for food below the surface. Adults have wings and can fly from pond to pond. They are carnivores and will eat any insect that falls on to the surface of the water.

◆ Water snails: these feed on rotting vegetation and any decomposing food that may be in the pond. Snails may appear in a pond brought in as eggs on the feet of birds or ducks, but they can also be introduced. Plan on introducing one snail for every square metre (11 square feet) of surface water.

◆ Dragonflies: these eat virtually anything smaller than themselves. Therefore mosquitoes and flies are both food for dragonflies, but smaller butterflies can also be eaten. Eggs are laid in the water and develop into larvae that live in the water, feeding on aquatic insect larvae. The larval stage lasts for several weeks, and the larva undergoes a series of moults before emerging from the water in readiness for its final moult, when the skin splits and a winged adult emerges in all its glory. The colour of the adult is influenced by the local conditions. Warmer weather encourages stronger colours, but even the electric-blue dragonfly can first appear brown. Adults can fly at 48km (30 miles) per hour, but the average cruising speed is 16km (10 miles) per hour. They can fly forwards, sideways and backwards. Dragonflies are on the decrease because agricultural ponds and waterways are being drained, and the destruction of peat bogs has also contributed to a decline in numbers – which is yet another reason never to use peat in the garden. Fertilizers and pesticides have further compounded the problem.

◆ Water boatmen: these swim upside down using their two long legs as paddles. They grow to around 2cm (¾ inch) and feed on tadpoles, small fish and aquatic insects. They rest on the surface of the water and sense vibrations. If something – anything – disturbs the water, they will dive to investigate. Adult water boatmen can fly and soon find new ponds. The lesser water boatman is unrelated and feeds on algae in ponds. Eggs are laid singly on plant material in the pond.

◆ Pond skaters: these float on the surface of the pond, sensing vibrations in the water with sensitive hairs on their legs and bodies. When an insect falls on the water, the ripples are picked up by the pond skater and it immediately homes in on its potential victim. Pond skaters hunt any surface-dwelling insects, including nymphs of their own species. Eggs are laid on land and adults fly away from water to hibernate, emerging in April. The adult is around 2cm (¾ inch) long, dark brown or grey, with round eyes that project from the sides of its head. The body and legs are covered in dense, velvety hairs that prevent the pond skater from falling through the surface.

A YEAR IN THE LIFE OF THE POND

SPRING

◆ Propagate and introduce plants to the pond.

◆ Take established planted aquatic baskets out of the pond and examine for signs of growth or disease. Remove weak or diseased plants.

◆ Divide congested plants, replant and reintroduce to the pond.

◆ Divide congested clumps of oxygenators.

SUMMER

◆ Deadhead all flowering plants to encourage more flowers. Leave flower-heads intact if you want to attract birds into the area. The seeds will attract them in autumn.

◆ Remove dying foliage to prevent it rotting in the water and causing an imbalance of nutrients and gases.

◆ Remove unwanted oxygenators as they become congested.

◆ Watch out for the appearance of algal growth and treat accordingly.

◆ Weed margins and bog gardens.

AUTUMN

◆ Remove all marginal plant foliage as it fades. This prevents decomposition in the water. Cut above the expected winter water level. Hollow-stemmed marginals cut below this level will rot in winter.

◆ Leave waterlily foliage to rot away naturally. The oily scum on the water surface soon disappears.

◆ Allow bog plants to die back naturally.

◆ Cover *Gunnera manicata* with straw or a thick wad of horticultural fleece to prevent the crown from freezing.

WINTER

◆ Tender plants need covering with straw or fleece.

◆ Plants growing in containers should be drained, allowing just the mud to remain. Containers can then be carried to a frost-free place such as a potting shed until spring.

◆ Most floating aquatics produce bulbils or turions in early winter. Turions can be collected and placed in a container of water with a 2cm (¾-inch) layer of soil in the bottom. Put in a frost-free place, the turions will develop into plants for planting out the following spring.

ABOVE The pond in midsummer. It takes a while for any pond to attain its natural balance but gradually that's being established here at Berryfields.

OPPOSITE The cornflower, *Centaurea cyanus.*

'I think that the greatest mistake in garden design over the past ten years has been to *underestimate* the role of green. A bright blue sky can make blues, browns, pinks, ochres and even greys *look stunning*. But under a northern sky they all become *drab* and *flat*, whereas green glows and remains strong even on the wettest, darkest November day.'

the lawn

the lawn

IN A VERY SMALL GARDEN A PATCH OF GRASS CAN BECOME
a muddy chore, but it is hard to resist the call of the lawn.
A lawn gives us somewhere to play, lie, sprawl or picnic.
We like the feel of it on our bare skin and the fragrance of
it when freshly cut. Walking barefoot on grass is a summer
treat. The truth is that our British climate, even with climate
change, is perfect for meadow grasses to thrive, and we
seem to have a cultural need to clip and trim them to an
exact point of acceptability. Most people have a finely tuned
sense of when a lawn 'needs cutting' although actually it
doesn't need it at all. It is doing fine. It is *we* who need it to
be cut, so that we can still think of it as a lawn rather than as
a meadow. It seems that we have an innate need for areas of
mown grass.

Grass is also the perfect medium to link all the other plants around it. An expanse of green will harmoniously connect any of the colours that border it. It doesn't have to be perfect lawn – a mown green mix of grass, moss, clover, daisies and various so-called 'weeds' can do the job perfectly well. It doesn't have to be flat either – terraces, slopes, spirit-level flat lawns and land art all look their best in clothes of grass.

I think that the greatest mistake in garden design over the past ten years has been to underestimate the role of green. A bright blue sky can make blues, browns, pinks, ochres and even greys look stunning. But under a northern sky

they all become drab and flat, whereas green glows and remains strong even on the wettest, darkest November day. So save the decking for California or Provence and make yourself a lawn.

To get the very best from a lawn the basic rules are:

◆ Pick the right lawn for your needs. The key to success can be simplified to whether or not you need dwarf perennial rye-grasses in the mix.
◆ Ensure the soil is in good condition.
◆ Mow regularly with a sharp mower. Never scalp a lawn as this decreases the vitality of the grass and can help weeds to establish. Mowing once a week is the minimum amount of attention a lawn requires.
◆ Remove clippings and remove all fallen leaves – or other detritus – from the lawn to prevent clogging of the soil surface.
◆ Once a year remove dead grass and moss and improve drainage by scarifying and aerating.

ACTION CHOICES

The Berryfields lawn was far from satisfactory. We had three options for dealing with it:

◆ Rip the whole lawn up and start again. This could be either by seed or turf. This was a dramatic measure and would certainly have improved the situation in the long run but is often an impractical solution, especially in a working garden such as Berryfields or a large area of lawn. Seed-sown lawns cannot be walked

PREVIOUS PAGE, LEFT
The circular lawn in the ornamental fruit garden that we laid from turf in midsummer. The grass has been kept long deliberately to encourage the roots of the turf to grow and establish before it is mown shorter.

PREVIOUS PAGE, RIGHT
A dandelion. The best and quickest way to deal with large weeds in a lawn is simply to dig each one up individually.

OPPOSITE Green grass is the balancing component of the British garden. It is the background against which the whole of the garden is set.

MONTY'S TIP

Top-dressing a lawn in autumn is a good way to improve the soil structure responsible for healthy growth. Top-dressing is the addition of bulky organic matter – well-rotted garden compost or leafmould mixed 50:50 with sharp sand is ideal – to the surface of the lawn. Improvement of soil structure in turn improves drainage and the water-holding capacity of the soil. This improves growth and makes conditions less favourable to moss growth. The top-dressing is evenly spread over the surface of the lawn to a depth of 5mm (¼ inch) and raked into the lawn. On no account should the top-dressing be deeper than the length of the grass blades. The addition of grass seed to the top-dressing helps clothe bare patches. It looks scruffy – but by spring the top-dressing will have worked its way into the soil and the grass will be growing strongly.

on for weeks, and turf needs regular watering to ensure success. Neither would have been compatible with weekly filming.

◆ The other extreme would have been to do nothing and just live with it. It was, after all, green and mowable and, at a pinch, would do. We could have made a virtue of its roughness and cut into it and planted shrubs and trees. This encourages a natural feel to a lawn, with non-grass species and mosses establishing, and is a rich, diverse ecosystem for wildlife. There is much to be said for this option if you do not want all the pleasures of an open green space.

◆ The third option, a compromise between the two extremes, was to nurture and coax it back to something resembling a half-decent lawn. This involves raking out dead clippings, or thatch, aerating it to improve the drainage, increasing the frequency of mowing once the grass starts to recover, raking out moss before it smothers the grass and hand digging broad-leafed weeds. It also involves a healthy tolerance to so-called weeds.

TYPES OF LAWN

You must decide between a) a perfect lawn or b) hard wear and tear. The two are, I am afraid, completely incompatible. If you have children or do not intend to spend most of your gardening hours working on the lawn, I strongly recommend a lawn that will take wear and tear. With a little management it can look superb and cope with football, bikes, dogs and being walked across with full wheelbarrows.

LAWNS FROM SEED AND TURF

SEED	TURF
Cheap	Good turf is expensive
Extensive range of seed mixes	Very limited choice
Easy to handle	Can be muddy and heavy
Takes 6 months from sowing to a finished lawn	Turf looks good instantly and is finished in 3–4 weeks
Weeds may outgrow the grass seed	Turf smothers weeds as it establishes
Dependent on good growing weather	Requires only watering
Needs protection from birds and cats	No protection required
Seed can be stored for when the time is right for sowing	Turf has to be used within 2 days of delivery

A lawn hard-wearing enough to withstand ball games and foot traffic needs to have a high proportion of perennial rye-grass, which has a wide leaf blade that withstands rough treatment. Rye-grass grows tall and, although very tough, never makes a handsome lawn. But the introduction of dwarf perennial rye-grasses means that hard-wearing lawns can now also look good. Dwarf rye-grasses produce fine leaves and maintain their green colour well. They grow quickly, so require fairly frequent mowing. But I do not recommend just using dwarf rye-grass. A hard-wearing mix will also contain creeping red fescue grasses, which are less tough than rye-grass but bind the grasses together, helping to create a solid, hard-wearing, green mat.

A showpiece lawn or bowling green will have a high proportion of fine-leafed fescue and bent grasses. These grow into a lawn that looks good but will not withstand hard wear and tear. Great to look at and mow, but not to play rugby on. Bents and fine fescues grow more slowly than rye-grasses, but to create a top-quality lawn it will need cutting every two or three days.

Lawns do best in sunlight, but for very shady gardens specialist grasses are available. These are usually fescues and smooth meadowgrass. Such grasses will grow, but it is best to leave the grass long in shady areas. This allows a larger area of leaves to absorb a high percentage of available sunlight.

MAKING A LAWN

The most important thing to remember when making any area of grass is that it is only as good as the ground beneath it. This applies equally whether you are using seed or turf. Simply rotavating the top few centimetres of soil is no good.

Grass is a plant like any other. It will look best and recover most quickly from drought or heavy wear and tear if it is healthy. So prepare the ground as though you were preparing a herbaceous border.

First dig the area of the lawn out to a spit (the full depth of a spade), leaving it in rough clods. Spread a layer at least a couple of centimetres thick of well-rotted organic matter. This will help both drainage and water retention and is especially important on poor soils. If your soil is at all heavy, cover this with another couple of centimetres of horticultural grit or sharp sand. Do not scrimp on this – good drainage is the secret of good grass.

Rotavate this mixture well until you have a fine tilth. Most hire shops will hire out a rotavator by the day that will fit in the boot of a car. Then rake it so that it is as even as possible, working first in one direction and then at right angles to this. In the process you will gather stones or big lumps of soil that can be removed.

If you are using seed rather than turf and are in no hurry, it is a good idea to leave the ground for a week or so to let any weeds germinate. These can then be hoed off just before sowing, so that the grass has minimal competition before establishing itself.

The next stage is to firm the soil and get rid of any uneven ground. The easiest way is to tread over the whole area, using your heels in a stiff-kneed, stomping penguin-walk. Fun for all the family. This will expose any air pockets and avoid subsequent dips and hollows. Rake it smooth again.

Seed is best sown in spring or early autumn. It should be sown first in one direction and then at right angles to this to get an even covering. Resist sowing too thickly. Remember that each seed is a potential plant and needs enough space, nutrients and water to develop strongly. Too many seeds will simply compete with each other, and even though it may appear patchy at first it is surprising how quickly the gaps will fill. When you have sown, rake the seeds in, again going at right angles to yourself. Put up some protection against birds, cats and people. Cotton strung out between canes works well, especially with a few CDs dangling to catch the light. This stops birds and cats getting caught up in the cotton.

Water it well and keep it moist until the grass is growing strongly. Avoid as much footfall as possible for the first year after sowing. Water whenever necessary and be watchful for weeds trying to become established, hand weeding whenever necessary. Roll the lawn using the roller on a mower – but the blades must be set so that they do not cut the new lawn at this stage. This firms grass seedlings back into the soil. When you do mow, cut only the top 1cm (½ inch) and this first cut should occur when the seedlings are 6cm (2½ inches) high. This will encourage thick growth. Continue this regime for the first year and, in the second, the lawn will be luxuriant.

Lay turf in courses, like bricks, so that the joins do not line up. Use a wooden board to kneel on and never stand on the turf once it is laid. Use a sharp knife to cut the turfs to fit and keep all short sections in the middle, where they are less liable

to dry up. Butt the edges tightly against each other, as they will inevitably shrink a little. Water it in really well and keep it very well watered every day until it is visibly growing. Let it grow at least a couple of centimetres before walking on it or mowing – which will take at least a fortnight and probably twice as long.

Both seeded and turfed lawns can be mown when the grass has grown 4–5 cm (1½–2 inches), but just trim it lightly and keep it longer than its ultimate length for at least three months. This will give the roots a chance to develop.

Turf-buying Guide
◆ Buy turf grown from seed.
◆ Order when you know you have the time to lay the turf.
◆ Order when the conditions are right.
◆ Inspect turf on delivery for colour – dark green indicates a recently lifted turf whereas yellowing indicates a turf that has been lifted and stored for a few days. Accept only green turf.
◆ Roll out random turfs and inspect for weeds.
◆ Inspect for density of grass.
◆ Lift a length of turf by the shortest edge. A well-grown turf will not break or rip.

LAWN PROBLEMS
◆ Fairy rings and pale brown toadstools are caused by the fungus *Marasmius oreades* and occur as temperatures fall and moisture increases. Fairy rings compete with the grass for moisture and nutrients as the feeding threads (mycelium) spread outwards from the point of infection. Typically there will be

a stimulation of grass growth at the periphery of infection, causing the grass to turn dark green.

The usual cause is something organic rotting under your lawn such as a tree stump or root. Digging it up and removing it will reduce the supply of nutrients to the fairy rings, and removing the fruiting bodies will reduce the spread of spores.

If a fairy ring is accompanied by two circles of darker green grass, one on the inner edge and one on the outer edge of the ring, action may have to be more dramatic. Dig a 30cm (1-foot) trench, 45cm (1½ feet) away from the outer edge of the fairy ring. Remove the soil from your garden. Refill with clean, imported topsoil and reseed or turf.

◆ Leatherjackets are the grubs of crane-flies. They eat grass roots, causing dead patches. The simplest way of dealing with them is to aerate your lawn well to prevent stagnant soil conditions. An alternative is to cover areas of your lawn with black polythene overnight and in the morning remove it. The leatherjackets will have come to the surface at night and been encouraged to stay by the moisture beneath the polythene. It's a great breakfast for the birds.
◆ Red thread disease causes patches of grass to become bleached and the red growths of the disease appear between the bleached grass. Avoid scalping your lawn when mowing, especially if you garden on sandy soil. The healthiest height for grass is 2–3 cm (about 1 inch).

◆ Flat, curved chafer grubs eat grass roots, causing patches to turn brown and die. Encourage plenty of birds into the garden that will be happy to eat them for you. Pull away infected grass and reseed or turf.
◆ Worms produce worm casts on the surface of lawns. Worms are so essential to a good soil structure that they should always be encouraged and never considered a problem. The best way to deal with worm casts is to rake them into the surface of the soil using a besom. Worm casts are ideal top-dressing, as they are sieved and digested soil.
◆ Fusarium patch, or snow mould, is first seen as patches of a lawn starting to turn yellow. The patches then merge to

produce large dead areas, the edges of which are covered with white or pale pink mould. Avoid using nitrogen-rich fertilizers after midsummer, and ensure that air gets to the grass roots by spiking regularly.
◆ Weeds can be a nuisance in a lawn.

ABOVE A fairy ring of mushrooms – these are the fruiting bodies of the fungus spreading outwards from a central core.

Rough edges that cannot be trimmed with
edging shears ruin the appearance of an
otherwise good-looking lawn, but are easily
rectified. Cut out a square of turf that
contains the offending edge. Gently lift the
square from the soil and move it forward,
so that the ragged edge projects beyond
the border. Trim the turf in line with the
rest of the lawn, leaving a clean-cut line.
Then all you have to do is to rake over the
exposed soil behind the newly positioned
turf, remove stones and weeds and either
reseed or returf.

Broad-leafed weeds such as dandelions
and plantains are best removed
individually with a trowel. Make sure that
all the roots are removed, as plants
regrow from the smallest scrap of root.

MOSS CASE STUDY

I confess that I rather like moss. It is
green and springy and feels good to
walk on. It is not high on my list of
garden problems, but I realize that moss
is the undisputed enemy of the lawn
owner. Many hours are spent on
removing moss from lawns, but the
best long-term solution is tackling the
cause of moss. Moss is prevalent on
waterlogged lawns, and waterlogging is a
result of compacted soil. The best way to
solve this problem is to aerate the lawn.
This can be done with a garden fork, but
is very hard work, and for anything other
than a small area it is best to hire or buy
a hollow-tine aerator, which is pushed
into the ground. When pulled out of the
ground, the hollow tines each remove a
plug or core of compacted soil. These can

in turn be broken up and brushed back
into the holes along with sharp sand.
The best time to aerate is autumn.

Shaded areas, such as in the shadow of
buildings or garden structures, help
create favourable conditions for the
growth of moss. Overhanging branches
can create both shade and wet areas from
water run-off, so cut off overhanging
branches and sow lawn seed developed
for shadier areas. Regular mowing also
encourages strong grass growth, which
will not allow moss to become
established. Always collect the grass
cuttings, because if left on the lawn
surface they will reduce air circulation,
create damp areas and will encourage
moss growth. However, this removes
nutrients from the soil, and an annual
feed with seaweed extract will help put
nutrients back, producing a healthy lawn
capable of smothering moss. There are
chemicals available that kill moss in
lawns. However, if the causes of the
moss aren't tackled, it will simply return
and you will have to spend more money
on more chemicals. Treat the causes,
remove the moss by raking, and your
lawn will be moss-free.

A dry summer can lead to a mossy lawn
in autumn and spring, because moss can
withstand drought, become desiccated in
summer, but quickly rehydrate in a wet
autumn. Grass, however, suffers badly in
a dry summer and doesn't bounce back
as quickly as moss.

Moss prefers acidic conditions and these
conditions are often found in dry, sandy

soils. After testing the soil pH, you can apply ground limestone (calcium carbonate) or dolomitic lime (calcium magnesium carbonate) to a lawn to reduce the acidity.

Rake out moss in spring and autumn, collecting the moss to leave out for birds – for nesting – or to line hanging baskets.

MOLES

So far at Berryfields we have not been visited by moles. I suspect that the ground is too compacted for them. But as we improve the soil you can guarantee that they will visit, and nothing is more destructive to a lawn than a busy mole.

Moles can move their own weight in soil every minute and tunnels can stretch for 1000m (over 3000 feet). They produce a network of tunnels, mostly about 60cm (2 feet) beneath the soil surface. Mole numbers are on the increase, possibly because wet and mild winters are extending the breeding season. The same weather has increased the number of earthworms, which are the moles' favoured food. Unfortunately the better your garden soil, the more earthworms you will have and the more chance of moles. If you have an acidic soil you can skip the next few paragraphs because there will be few worms and you are unlikely to have any moles.

Adult moles stay below the surface of the soil most of their life, surfacing only to gather material for their nests (leaves, moss, grass). Nests are located under larger-than-normal molehills and are

called fortresses. But in the breeding season moles will make long tunnels just below the surface of the soil when looking for a mate. However many molehills you have on your lawn (or, just as damaging, in the border), it is very unlikely that anything other than the largest garden will contain more than two moles, as their average density is about four per acre.

Moles are solitary, meeting up only in the breeding season, which is between the end of February and May. The females can have litters of up to seven young, born between April and June. The cubs mature within six weeks and either begin being active in old networks or start their own. The mole is a carnivore, eating worms, insect larvae, beetles, slugs and invertebrates. It is well designed for living underground – tiny eyes and flapless ears mean its sight and hearing are very poor, but it has a highly developed sense of touch and scent, a thick velvet coat, and huge front paws for shovelling soil. It is hunted by owls, foxes, cats and dogs.

I am often asked how to get rid of moles, and my answer is always the same – if you know, then please let me know! The problem of how to get rid of moles from

a garden and, in particular, a lawn has taxed gardeners for centuries and here are just a few of the methods tried:

◆ Smell: garlic, chilli powder, moth-balls and urine (human or cat, take your pick) have all been used to some effect in gardens. Sprinkled in the entrance to tunnels seems to be the recommended serving suggestion.

◆ Plants: the roots of caper spurge (*Euphorbia lathyris*) exude a chemical that moles shrink away from. Make sure you carefully cut off any flowers, as once they produce seed you will have a bigger problem with the spurge than the moles. Take care doing this, as the sap can be a skin irritant. Planting bulbs of crown imperials (*Fritillaria imperialis*) is said to have the same effect on moles. They certainly smell powerfully of fox's urine, so maybe this links back to the previous suggestion.

◆ Vibration: children's windmills, open-ended plastic bottles buried in the ground and plastic bottles on the tops of bamboo canes all produce an annoying vibration in the soil that can deter moles. Try sticking any of the above in the molehill. Battery- or solar-powered sonic deterrents work on the same principle of annoyance. They blast a high-frequency sound into a tunnel that the animals feel rather than hear, and are said to deter mole activity.

◆ Sound: even the hard-of-hearing mole is apparently driven mad by some sounds. Turn a cheap radio on to an annoying radio station, turn it up loud, seal it in a plastic bag and push it into a tunnel and see what happens. Try the same with a talking/singing birthday card. Take the mechanism out of the card, ensure it is on continual play, wrap it up in plastic and place it in a tunnel. This may invite the wrath of the RSPCA.

◆ Trapping: leave this to the experts.

◆ Making a virtue from necessity:

remember that molehills make a wonderful addition to potting compost, providing the growing roots with exactly the right environment, specific to your own garden, that your young plants will eventually have to adapt to. It's an ill wind that blows no one any good.

CLOVER

Clover actually improves the fertility of the soil, and therefore the grass, because clovers are legumes and can fix nitrogen from the air. Clover is an indication that the soil is low in nutrients, as it doesn't grow well in highly fertile, nitrogen-rich soils. It grows most vigorously on alkaline soils. I would suggest that clover should not take up too much of your time and energy. But it does compete with grass and upsets serious lawn keepers. There are many plants classed as clover, but the major lawn weed is the white-flowering *Trifolium repens*.

The leaves grow from long, bare stems at ground level, which spread across the surface of the lawn, whereas the leaves of red clover shoot from the ground at the base of plants and branch from the stem. The white flowers may be flushed pink, which is especially noticeable when the buds have first opened. The top growth can die back after a few hard frosts, but it has the capability of remaining green in dry summers. You may, like me, consider this a virtue.

Controlling Clover in Lawns

Successful clover eradication is possible only if you don't let the plant get established.

◆ As soon as it's spotted, pull clover out of lawns (and soil). Put your fingers beneath the plant and rip the stems out. Go back and remove all scraps of stems, as any left on the soil surface will regrow.
◆ Hoe longer stems and remove all surface stems. Both can be composted.
◆ Rake before mowing. This lifts the surface stems, which are then cut and removed.

The alternative to fighting clover is to give in altogether and plant a clover lawn. The white flowers are irresistible to bees and your lawn will stay green all the year round. The added bonus is a lawn that is sweetly aromatic, as crushed clover leaves and flowers emit a vanilla fragrance.

LEFT Clover is one of those components of a lawn that upsets the specialist, delights the farmer and leaves me blissfully unconcerned.

OPPOSITE Moles are the greatest problem to anyone trying to maintain a lawn. Not only do they make molehills like these, but they also create furrows and potholes. However, every cloud has a silver lining, because molehills can be an invaluable part of homemade potting compost.

A YEAR IN THE LIFE OF THE LAWN

SPRING

◆ Rake to remove thatch and moss. Do not rake too vigorously as it may damage the grass.

◆ Sow seed.

◆ Lay turf.

◆ Feed with extract of seaweed.

◆ Start mowing – mow high at first, lowering blades as the season develops.

◆ Scatter worm casts when they appear.

◆ Repair broken edges.

SUMMER

◆ Mow frequently – do not scalp.

◆ Arrange for a neighbour to cut the lawn if you are away on holiday. If this isn't possible, do not scalp the lawn. On your return, mow high, then gradually lower the blades over a fortnight of cutting.

◆ Leave grass longer if conditions are dry. Long grass copes with drought better than shorter grass.

◆ If the weather is too wet for mowing, trim edges with long-handled edging shears.

◆ Dig out weeds, refilling holes with peat-free compost to which grass seed has been added.

◆ Feed with extract of seaweed.

AUTUMN

◆ Sow seed.

◆ Lay turf.

◆ Collect fallen leaves to make leafmould.

◆ Scarify (vigorous raking) to remove thatch.

◆ Aerate compacted areas with a hollow-tine aerator.

◆ Top-dress to improve soil structure.

WINTER

◆ Collect late-fallen leaves.

◆ Keep off grass in heavy frosts.

◆ Clean and service mowers.

◆ In mild winters mow the grass if it is growing.

ABOVE The orchard at the end of the hot, dry summer of 2003, showing how parched the grass had become. But it always amazes me how quickly grass will recover from this kind of situation and become a lush green sward again. In the end, grass is tough stuff.

OPPOSITE The turf maze that Chris created graced the garden for a month.

index

Page numbers in *italic* refer to the illustrations

Acacia baileyana 'Purpurea' 102
Acaena microphylla
    'Kupferteppich' 198
Achillea 'Fanal' 24
    A. Summer Pastels 51, *52*
acid soil 57–8, 65, 137–8
aconites 195
aerating lawns 244, 245
Agapanthus 103
    A. 'Snowy Owl' 102–3
Agastache rupestris 48
Alchemilla mollis 198–200
alecost 108, 109
alfalfa 133
algae, in ponds 215, 221, 227–8
Allium 77, 98–101, 102
    A. hollandicum 'Purple
        Sensation' 99, *99*
    A. karataviense 99
        A.k. 'Ivory Queen' 99
    A. schoenoprasum 116
    A. sphaerocephalon 38, 99–101,
        99
Aloysia triphylla 121, *123*
Alyssum 45
Anchusa azurea 'Loddon Royalist'
    23, 76, *79*
Anemone × *hybrida* 'Honorine
    Jobert' 202
angelica *106*, 110, 113
annuals 17
    cottage garden 76–7
    herbs 110
    sowing 47–8
    £20 border 44, 45, 50–1
Antirrhinum 77, *88*
aphids 116, 135, 169, 178
apple mint 113, *119*, 120
apples 116, 126, 173, 179, 185,
    188–91, *189*, *192*
aquatic plants 225–7
Aquilegia 44, 76, 83
    A. 'Winky' *82*
arrowhead, common 219
Artemisia 11
    A. dracunculus 113
        A.d. dracunculoides 113
    A. ludoviciana 'Valerie Finnis'
        22
    A. schmidtiana 'Nana' 96
artichokes, globe 144, *145*
asparagus 126, 127, 130, 135–7,
    136
Asplenium scolopendrium
    'Cristatum' 201

Astelia chathamica 39
Astilbe 222–3
    A. 'Granat' 222–3
Astilboides tabularis 202
aubergines 167–8

basil 107, *107*, 109, 110, 112, 113,
    135, 162, 168
baskets: hanging 60–2
    pond plants 214
bay 109
beans 130, 137, 138
bedding plants 56, 65–9
beds *see* borders; raised beds
beech trees 196, *197*
bees 116
beetroot 130, 144, *145*
bellflowers 62, 76
Bellis perennis 69
biennials 17, 45, 76–7
bindweed 75, 86–7
birds 139, 176, *177*, 231, 243
blackberries 178
blackcurrants 178–9
blackfly 135
blackspot 116
blanketweed, in ponds 227–8
bleeding hearts 76
blight 162
blister aphids 178
blood grass, Japanese *14*, 16
blossom end rot 162
bluebells 205–7
bog gardens 64, 214, 222–4
borage 109, 110, 113, *121*
borders: cottage garden 76–85
    long borders 10–41, *10*
    Rachel's garden 37–9, *38*, *40*
    £20 border 42–53, *45*
botanical names 17
botrytis 116
box balls *14*, 39
Brachyscome 62
brassicas 65, 130, 137–41
Briza media 'Limouzi' *15*
broad beans *130*, 144
broccoli, purple sprouting 65,
    137, 139–41, *140*
Brugmansia arborea 'Knightii' 56,
    57
brussels sprouts 137
buckwheat 133
bulbs 17, 28–37, 77, 168
Butomus umbellatus 218, 219
buttercup, water 221
butyl liners, ponds 216
Buxus sempervirens 14, 39

cabbage aphid 135
cabbage moth 135
cabbage root fly 135, 138
cabbage whitefly 138–9
cabbages 65, *125*, *130*, 135, 137,
    139
    ornamental 69, *71*
calabrese 137
Calamagrostis × *acutiflora* 'Karl
    Foerster' 16
Callicarpa bodineiri var. *giraldii*
    184
Caltha palustris 218, 219
Camellia 57–60
    C. japonica 58–9, 60
        C.j. 'Adolphe Audusson' 58,
            59
        C.j. 'Apollo' 58
        C.j. 'Mathotiana Alba' 60
    C. saluenensis 59, 60
    C. × *williamsii* 60
        C. × *williamsii* 'Anticipation'
            60
        C. × *williamsii* 'Donation' *59*,
            60
        C. × *williamsii* 'Jury's Yellow'
            59, 60
Campanula 76
    C. grandiflora 77
candytuft 50
Canna 11, 24, 27
    C. 'Durban' 24
    C. × *ehemanii* 24
    C. 'Musifolia' 24
    C. 'Striata' 24
Canterbury bells 77
caper spurge 246
caraway 110, *120*
cardoons 11
Carex muskingumensis 16
Carpinus betulus 196–8
carrot fly 135
carrots 130, *130*, 135, 144
caterpillars 138, 139
catmint 76
cauliflowers 65, 137, 139
celery 130
Centaurea cyanus 77
    C. nigra 76
Cerinthe major 'Purpurascens' 20,
    21–2
Chaenomeles 182
    C. speciosa 'Geisha Girl' *183*
chafer grubs 243
chamomile 109
chard 144
cherries 116
cherry, flowering 207

chervil 109, 135
chicory 144
chillies 151, 163–6, 163, 164
Chinese cabbage 137
chives 109, 109, 110, 112, 113, 116
chocolate cosmos 26, 27
chocolate mint 120
Choisya ternata Sundance 14
Cistus × crispatus 'Warley Rose'
  96
citrus fruit 169
clay, lining ponds 215–16, 219
clay soil 46
Clematis 17–21
  C. 'Abundance' 19
  C. alpina 21
  C. 'Barbara Jackman' 21
  C. 'Chinook' 18
  C. 'Daniel Deronda' 18
  C. 'Etoile Violette' 21
  C. 'Gazelle' 18
  C. henryi 21
  C. 'Jackmanii' 21
  C. 'Marie Boisselot' 18
  C. 'Miss Bateman' 21
  C. montana 21, 105
  C. 'Nelly Moser' 21
  C. 'Niobe' 18, 19
  C. 'Perle d'Azur' 18, 19, 76
  C. 'Polish Spirit' 18
  C. 'Princess Diana' 18
  C. Victor Hugo 17
  C. 'Ville de Lyon' 21
  C. viticella 11, 21
    C.v. 'Purpurea Plena Elegans'
    18, 19
  C. 'Vyvyan Pennell' 21
clematis wilt 21
climbers 16–21, 80
clover, in lawns 247, 247
club root 65, 138
coir 48
cold frames 159
colours: cottage garden 76
  long borders 12, 21–8
  Rachel's garden 39
columbine 76
comfrey 110, 113, 122
companion planting 115–16, 135
compost 131, 132, 133
compost, potting 44, 48, 57–8,
  60–1, 64
concrete, lining ponds 217
coneflower 23
containers: courtyard garden
  56–71
  dry garden 102–3, 104
  herbs 108–9, 112, 115

lilies 85–6
  vegetables 142, 161
cordons 188
coriander 109, 110, 112, 135
corms 17
cornflowers 77
Corylus maxima 'Purpurea' 13, 184
Cosmos 28, 45, 77
  C. atrosanguineus 26, 27
  C. bipinnatus 65–6
    C.b. 'Dazzler' 72
Cotinus coggygria 'Royal Purple'
  13
cottage garden 72–89, 72, 75, 89
  calendar 88–9
  hard landscaping 74–5
  preparation and pruning 75
  site 74
cotton thistle 45
courgettes 130, 144
courtyard garden 54–71, 54
  bedding plants 65–9
  calendar 70–1
  dry containers 62–5
  east-facing wall 56–60
  hanging baskets 60–2
cowslips 204, 205
crab apples 182–4, 196
cranesbills see Geranium
cress 137
Crocosmia 28, 77
  C. 'Emily McKenzie' 23
  C. 'Lucifer' 23
  C. 'Zeal Tan' 23
Crocus 31, 36, 77
  C. tommasinianus 36
crop rotation 129–31
crown imperial 34, 35, 246
cuckoo spit 115
cucumbers 152, 166–7, 167
cuttings 60, 80, 118–20
Cyclamen 202–4
  C. coum 202–3, 203, 210
  C. hederifolium 202–4
Cydonia oblonga 181–2
Cyperus longus 223
Cystopteris diaphana 201

daffodils 28, 31, 75, 77
Dahlia 11, 28, 77
  D. 'Bishop of Llandaff' 24, 25
  D. 'Black Monarch' 25
  D. 'Friendship' 25
  D. 'Grenadier' 24, 25
daisies 69
damp shade 202–7
Darmera 214
datura 56, 57

daylilies 223–4, 223, 224
de Thame, Rachel 37–9
deadheading flowers 61
Delphinium 23, 51, 73, 76, 78
  D. elatum 78
    D.e. Hybrid 'Fenella' 78, 79
Deschampsia 16
Dianthus (pinks) 51, 73, 73, 77
  D. barbatus (sweet William)
    45, 73, 77
Dicentra scandens 'Golden Tears'
  50
  D. spectabilis 76
Dichondra micrantha 'Silver Falls'
  61
digging 45–6, 87
Digitalis (foxgloves) 45, 77, 79, 83
  D. × mertonensis 83
  D. purpurea 79, 83
    D.p. 'Primrose Carousel' 200
dill 109, 110, 112, 135
diseases: herbs 115, 120
  vegetables 129, 138, 143, 162
division, waterlilies 227
dragonflies 232–3
drainage: bog gardens 222
  herbs 115
  lawns 241
drought-resistant plants 92–4
drumstick primula 205
dry garden 90–105, 90, 105
  calendar 104–5
  plants 96–102
  preparation and planting 94–6
Dryopteris 197, 201
  D. affinis 'Cristata' 201
ducks 231

Echeveria 64
  E. lindsayana 63
elder 13, 181, 181
electricity 155, 215
Elodea crispa 221–2
Epiphyllum 64
  E. 'Kanchenjunga' 64
Equisetum scirpoides 65
Eragrostis curvula 'Totnes
  Burgundy' 16
ericaceous plants 38
Eryngium giganteum 23
  E. × oliverianum 23
espaliers 187
Eucomis comosa 'Sparkling
  Burgundy' 36–7
Eupatorium cannabinum 'Flore
  Pleno' 223
Euphorbia lathyris 246
eyes, propagating waterlilies 227

fairy rings 242–3, 243
fan training 185–6
fennel (herb) 108, 109, 110, 111,
  112–13, 119, 121
ferns 200–2
fertilizers: brassicas 137
  dry garden 94
  hanging baskets 61
  and ponds 228
Festuca 16
  F. glauca 93
feverfew 113
Ficus carica 'Brown Turkey' 182
field beans 132, 133
figs 179, 182
fish, in ponds 231
flame flower 28
Foeniculum vulgare 113
  F.v. 'Purpureum' 119, 121
forget-me-nots 44, 75, 77
forsythia 75
foxgloves 45, 77, 79, 83
French beans 135, 144
Fritillaria 35–6, 77
  F. imperialis 34, 35, 246
  F. meleagris 35
  F. persica 35
frogs 231–2
frost 46, 215
fruit garden 172–93, 175
  calendar 192–3
  companion planting 115–16
  ornamental fruit garden 180–5,
    193
  site 175
  small town fruit garden 108,
    185–8
  soft fruit garden 175–80, 193
fungus diseases 115, 120, 138,
  162
fusarium patch 243

gages 185, 188
Gaillardia Goblin 49, 51
galingale, sweet 223
garlic 107, 109, 110, 112, 113, 116,
  135
Gaura lindheimeri 'The Bride'
  48–50
Gazania 27–8
Geranium 83–4
  G. × cantabrigiense 'Biokovo'
    198
  G. cinereum 'Rothbury Gem'
    83–4
  G. endressii 76, 82
  G. × oxonianum 'Claridge
    Druce' 76

G. × *riversleaianum* 'Russell Prichard' 76
Geum rivale 65
gingers 11
Gladiolus 28, 77
global warming 92
goldfish weed 221–2
gooseberries 174, 180, 185
grass: paths 127
    see also lawns
grasses, ornamental 14–16
gravel *38*, 102
green manures 132–5
greenfly 135
greenhouses 127, 150–71, *150*, *158*, *168*, *169*, *171*
    benches and shelving 155
    calendar 170–1
    edible crops 159–69
    electricity 155
    frames 152–3
    glazing 153
    heating 156–9
    insulation 157–9
    shapes 152
    siting 154–5
    ventilation 156
    water supply 155, 156
Griselinia littoralis 14
Gunnera manicata 214, *218*, 223

Hakonechloa macra 'Alboaurea' 16
half-hardy plants 17, 45
hanging baskets 60–2
hardening off 68, 159
hardy plants 17, 45
hart's tongue fern 201
hazel 13, 184
hazel hurdles 12, 37, *41*, 154
heating greenhouses 156–9
hedges 12, 37, *37*, 127, 154
heeling in 207
Helenium 11, 28, *29*
    H. 'Moerheim Beauty' 28
    H. 'Rauchtopas' 28
    H. 'Sahin's Early Flowerer' 28
Helictotrichon 16
Helleborus 195, 211
    H. foetidus 198, *200*
    H. × *hybridus 199, 209*
        H. × *hybridus* 'Cosmos' *199*
        H. × *hybridus* 'Sirius' *199*
    H. orientalis 38, 198
Hemerocallis 223–4, *223*
    H. 'Berlin Red' *224*
hemp agrimony, double 223
herb garden 106–23

calendar 122–3
companion planting 115–16
containers 115
diseases 115, 120
transplanting herbs 108–9, 118
herbicides 87
Hesperis matronalis 77
Heuchera 96
    H. 'Plum Pudding' 39
    × *Heucherella* 'Dayglow Pink' 198
Hippophae rhamnoides 181
holly 180–1
hollyhocks *47*, 73
honesty 45
honey bush 22
honeysuckle 56–7, 80, 195
hornbeam 196–8
Hosta 22, 214
    H. 'Halcyon' 39
    H. sieboldiana 22
    H. 'Snowden' 22
    H. 'Sum and Substance' 22
Hottonia palustris 221, *221*
Houttuynia cordata 'Chameleon' *64*, 65
hoverflies 135
hurdles, hazel 12, 37, *41*, 154
Hyacinthoides hispanica 205–6
    H. × *massartiana* 206
    H. non-scripta 205–7
hyacinths 77
hyssop 108, 109

Ilex 180–1
    I. 'J.C. van Tol' 181
    I. 'Pyramidalis' 181
Imperata cylindrica 'Rubra' *14*, 16
insects: and ponds 231, 232–3
    see also pests
insulation, greenhouses 157–9
Ipomoea 'Purple Haze' 50
Iris 93, 195
    I. germanica 76
    I. kaempferi 219
    I. pseudacorus 218, 219
    I. sibirica 76

Jasione laevis 'Blaulicht' 96

kale 137
Kirengeshoma palmata 202
kitchen garden 124–49, *124*
    calendar 148–9, *149*
    crop rotation 129–31
    location 127
    planning 127–8
    raised beds 127, 128–9
    soil 126, 131–5

see also vegetables
knapweed 76
Knautia macedonica 94, 95, 96
Kniphofia 23
    K. 'Bees' Lemon' 23
    K. uvaria 'Nobilis' 23
kohl rabi 137

labels 51
lady's mantle 198–200
Lagarosiphon major 221–2
larkspur 50
Lathyrus latifolius 'Red Pearl' 84
    L.l. 'Rosa Perle' 84
    L.l. 'White Pearl' *82*, 84
Lavandula angustifolia 116
    L.a. 'Hidcote' *114*, 118
    L.a. 'Lavender Lady' 118
    L.a. 'Lavenite Petite' 118
    L.a. 'Loddon Pink' *117*, 118
    L.a. 'Munstead' 96–8, 118
    L. stoechas 118
        L.s. 'Madrid White' 118
Lavatera 75, 77
lavender 109, 110, 112, 114–15, *114*, 116–18, *117*
lavender shab 115
lawns 236–49, *236*, *239*, *248*, *249*
    calendar 248–9
    edges 244
    mowing 238
    problems 242–7
    sowing seeds 238–40, 241–2
    top-dressing 238
    turf 240, 242
    types of 240–1
    weeds 237, 242, 243–4, 247
leatherjackets 243
leaves, drought-resistant plants 92–3
leeks 129, 144
lemon balm 108, 109, 116
lemon mint 120
lemon verbena 121, *123*
Leonotis leonurus 27
lettuces 135, 141–3, *141*, *142*
Leucojum 77
lewisia 103
Ligularia 214
    L. dentata 'Desdemona' 224
        L.d. 'Othello' 224
    L. przewalskii 224
    L. 'The Rocket' 224
lilac 196
Lilium candidum 77
    L. longiflorum 'White Elegance' 39
    L. regale 85–6

lime-hating plants 38
liners: bog gardens 222
    hanging baskets 60
    ponds 215–17, 219
Linum perenne 'Blau Saphir' 48
Lobelia 61, 66
    L. cardinalis 224, *224*
long borders 10–41, *10*, *33*
    backbone shrubs 13–14
    bulbs 28–37
    calendar 40–1
    colours 21–8
    grasses 14–16
    height 16–21
    site 12–13
Lonicera 80
    L. × *brownii* 'Dropmore Scarlet' 80
    L. henryi 80
    L. hildebrandiana 56–7
    L. japonica 'Halliana' 80
    L. periclymenum 'Graham Thomas' 80
loosestrife, purple 219, *220*
lovage 109, 110, 113
love-in-a-mist 77, *77*
Lunaria 45, 77
lupins 50, 51, 73, 78
Lupinus 'The Governor' 77, *78*
    L. polyphyllus 76
Lychnis flos-cuculi 217, 219–21
Lysichiton americanus 224, *224*
Lythrum salicaria 219, *220*
    L.s. 'Robert' 39

Magnolia × *loebneri* 'Leonard Messel' 198, *208*
    M. stellata 195, 198
male fern 201
mallow 49, 51, 75
Malus 'John Downie' 184
    M. pumila 'Cowichan' 184
    M. H zumi var. *calocarpa* 'Golden Hornet' 182–4
Malva moschata f. *alba* 49, 51
manure 44, 127, 129, 131
marginal plants, ponds 217–22
marigolds, French 66, *134*, 135
marjoram 108, 109, 113
marsh marigold *218*, 219
Matteuccia struthiopteris 201
meadows 229
Meconopsis betonicifolia 77, *77*
    M. cambrica 77
Mediterranean herbs 108, 110–12, 115
Melianthus 11
    M. major 22

Melissa officinalis 116
membrane, permeable 87, 102, 127
Mentha × *piperita* 120
   M. × *piperita* f. *citrata* 'Chocolate' 120
   M. × *piperita* f. *citrata* 'Lemon' 120
   M. requienii 83
   M. spicata 119, 120
      M.s. var. *crispa* 'Moroccan' 120
   M. suaveolens 119, 120
mice 50
mildew 116, 180
mint 83, 107, 109, 110, 113, 115, 118–20, 135
mint rust 120
Miscanthus 16
   M. sinensis 'Ferner Osten' 16
   M.s. 'Silberfeder' 15–16
mizuna 137
modules, buying plants 69
moles 245–6, *246*
Molinia caerulea subsp. *arundinacea* 16
monkshood 23
morning glory 50
moss, in lawns 244–5
mowing lawns 238
mulches 17, 46, 87, 94, 95–6, 102
mushroom compost 131, 138
mustard 132, 133, 137

names of plants 17, 22
Narcissus (daffodils) 28, 31, 75, 77
   N. 'Golden Harvest' 31
   N. 'King Alfred' 31
   N. 'Mount Hood' 31
Nasturtium 62, 135
   N. 'Double Gleam Mixed' 62
   N. 'Jewel of Africa' 62
nectarines 116, 185–6, *186*
nematodes 135
Nemesia 66
   N. 'Honey Girl' *67*
Nepeta 76
   N. × *faassenii* 49, 51
Nerine 'Virgo' *92*
newts 232
Nicotiana 45, 66, 77
   N. sylvestris 66
Nigella 45, 50
   N. damascena 77, *77*
nitrogen 130, 137, 138, 247
Nolana 62
Nymphaea 225–7
   N. candida 225

N. 'Colonel A.J. Welch' 227
N. 'Colossea' 227
N. 'Ellisiana' 225, *226*
N. 'Escarboucle' *226*, 227
N. 'Gonnère' 225
N. 'Graziella' 225
N. 'Helen Fowler' 225
N. 'Laydekeri Lilacea' 225
N. 'Marliacea Chromatella' 225, *226*
N. 'Moorei' 225, *226*
N. 'Picciola' 227
N. tetragona 225
N. 'Tuberosa Richardsonii' 227
N. 'William Falconer' 225

onion fly 135
onions 135, 144–6
Onoclea sensibilis 201
Onopordum 11, *53*
   O. acanthium 22, 94
oregano 109
organic gardening 8, 74, 126, 131
organic matter 46, 94, 131, 133, 238
Origanum onites 113
   O. 'Thundercloud' 98
   O. vulgare 113
      O.v. 'Aureum' 113
Osmunda regalis 201
oxlip 205
oxygenating plants, ponds 221–2, 228

pak choi 137
Panicum 16
pansies 68
Papaver (poppies) 45, 51, 76
   P. nudicaule 'Meadow Pastels' *42*
   P. somniferum 77, *87*
parsley 107, 109, 110, 112, 113, 114
parsnips 130, 146
paths 38, *38*, 74, 127, 128–9, 154–5
paving 44, 74–5
peaches 186
pears 185, 186–8, *187*
peas 126, 130, *130*, 137, 138, 146
peat 57
Pelargonium 62, 84–5
   P. 'Atomic Snowflake' 85
   P. crispum 'Variegatum' *84*, 85
   P. 'Decora Lilas' *55*
   P. Fragrans Group 85
   P. 'Lady Scarborough' 85
   P. 'Lara Jester' 85
   P. 'Mabel Grey' 85

P. odoratissimum 85
P. 'Old Spice' 85
P. 'Pink Capricorn' 85
P. 'Royal Oak' 85
Pennisetum 15, 16
   P. glaucum 'Purple Majesty' 11, 15, 27
Penstemon heterophyllus 50
peonies 76
peppermint 113, 120
peppers 163
perennials 17
   long borders 21–8
   sowing 46–7
   £20 border 44–5, 48–50
perlite 60
pests: companion planting 115–16, 135
   crop rotation 129
   herb gardens 115
   vegetables 138–9, 143, 162
Petunia 66–8
   P. 'Prism Sunshine' 68, *68*
pH values, soil 8, 38, 57, 131, 138
phacelia 132
phlox 73
pigeons 139
pinching out tips 76
pinks 51, 73, *73*, 77
Pittosporum tobira 39
plant names 17, 22
plug plants 69, 217–19
plums 116, 185
polyanthus 69
Polypodium vulgare 'Bifidomultifidum' 201–2
pond skaters 233
ponds 212–35, *212*, *215*, *235*
   aquatic plants 225–7
   blanketweed 227–8
   bog gardens 222–4
   calendar 234–5
   liners 215–17, 219
   marginal plants 217–22
   oxygenating plants 221–2, 228
   siting 214–15
   wildlife 231–3
pondweed 221
poppies *42*, 45, 51, 76, 77, *87*
Potamogeton crispus 221
potato blight 162
potatoes 126, 129, 130, *130*, 146
pricking out seedlings 47, 66
primroses 195, 204–5, *204*
Primula 204–5
   P. denticulata 205
      P.d. var. *alba* *204*, 205
   P. elatior 205

P. veris *204*, 205
P. vulgaris 204–5, *204*
propagation: cuttings 60, 80, 118–20
   waterlilies 227
   see also seeds
propagators 44, 46–7
pruning: clematis 18–21
   fruit trees 187, 188–90
   lavatera 75
Prunus avium 207
   P. speciosa 207
   P. × *subhirtella* 'Rosea' 207
   P. × *yedoensis* *194*, 207
pulmonarias 195
pumpkins *145*, 146–7

quaking grass 15
quinces 181–2, *183*

Rachel's garden 37–9, *38*, *40*
radishes 65, 137, 139
ragged robin 217, 219–21
rainfall 86, 92, 132, 154, *155*
raised beds 93, 94–5, 103, 127, 128–9
Ranunculus aquatilis 221
raspberries 126, 177, 179
Raven, Sarah 32, *170*
red cabbage 139
red hot poker 23
red thread disease 243
redcurrants *173*, 178
rheum 214
rhubarb 130
   giant *218*, 223
ribes 75
rocket 137
Rodgersia 214
Rootrainers 48
roots, drought-resistant plants 93–4
rootstocks, apple trees 191
Rosa 'Charles de Mills' *81*, 82
   R. 'Königin von Dänemark' 82
   R. 'Madame Grégoire Staechelin' 184–5
   R. 'Madame Knorr' 82
   R. moyesii 184, *184*
   R. pimpinellifolia 184
   R. Rhapsody in Blue 39
rose hips 184–5
rosemary 103, 107, 108, 109, *109*, 110, 112, 118
roses 73, 75, 80–3, 116, 184–5
rotation of crops 129–31
royal fern 201

Royal Horticultural Society 92, 209
Rudbeckia 11, 23
  R. fulgida var. *deamii* 23
  R. 'Herbstsonne' 23, 28
  R. laciniata 'Goldquelle' 23
rue 110
runner beans 147
rush, flowering *218*, 219
rye, grazing 132, *133*

safety, ponds 215
sage 107, 108, 109, *109*, 110, 112
Sagittaria sagittifolia 219
salad crops 130
Salvia 45
  S. lavandulifolia 112
  S. nemorosa 'Rose Queen' 98
    S.n. Select Rose 50
  S. officinalis 112
    S.o. 'Purpurascens' 112
Sambucus nigra f. *porphyrophylla*
  'Gerda' 13
  S.n. 'Guincho Purple' 181, *181*
Sanvitalia 62
savory 109
saw-fly 178, *180*
Scabiosa atropurpurea 'Chile
  Black' *97*, 98
scale insects 169
Schoenoplectus lacustris subsp.
  tabernaemontani 'Zebrinus'
  219
Scotch thistle 22
sea buckthorn 181
seakale 137
Sedum 64, 103
  S. 'Purple Emperor' 98
seedlings 47, 66, 69, 159
seeds: annuals 44, 46, *46*, 47–8
  herbs 113
  lawns 238–40, 241–2
  mixed packets 50–1
  perennials 46–7, *46*
  vegetables *128*, 139, 141
sensitive fern 201
shade, damp 202–7
shallots 147, *148*
Shirley poppies 77
shrubs 13–14
shuttlecock fern 201
skunk cabbage, American 224,
  224
slugs 18, 139, 141, 142, 202
snails 18, 141, 142, 202, 232
snake's head fritillary 35
snapdragons 73, 77, *88*
snow mould 243

snowdrops 31, 77, 195
snowflakes 77
soil 8
  acidic soil 57–8, 65, 137–8
  bog gardens 222
  cottage garden 74
  crop rotation 129
  double digging 45–6, 87
  dry garden 94–5, 102
  in greenhouses 154
  herb garden 112, 113
  kitchen garden 126, 129
  lawns 241, 245
  mulches 17, 46, 87, 94, 95–6,
    102
  pH values 8, 38, 57, 131, 138
  planting around ponds 219
  soil conditioners 131–5
Solomon's seal 77
sorrel 113
sowing *see* seeds
Spartina 16
spearmint 113, *119*, 120
spinach 130, 147, *147*
spring garden 194–211, *194*
  beneath the hornbeam
    196–200
  calendar 210–11
  damp shade 202–7
  ferns 200–2
  new trees 207–9
squashes 130
star jasmine 57
Stephanandra incisa 'Crispa'
  13–14
stepover apples 185, *192*
Stipa 16
  S. gigantica 15
  S. tenuissima 15
stocks, Brompton 77
strawberries 116, 126, *172*, *174*,
  175–7
succulents 62–4
sulphur chips 57
sunflowers 77, 135, *145*
supports, climbers 80
Swan River daisy 62
swedes 137
sweet cicely 110
sweet peas 48, 50, 77, 80, 84
sweet rocket 77
sweet William 45, 73, 77
sweetcorn 126, 127, 147
Symphytum officinale 122

Tanacetum vulgare 116
tansy 116
tares, winter 133

tarragon 109, 113
Taxus baccata 37
tayberries *176*, 177–8
tender plants 17, 27, 56, 102–3
Teucrium × *lucidrys* 98
thermometers, greenhouse 159
thyme 103, 107, 109, 110, 112
Thymus vulgaris 112
  T.v. 'Silver Posie' 121
Tiarella cordifolia 'Heronswood
  Mist' 202
Tithonia rotundifolia 27
toadstools 242–3
tobacco plant 66
tomatoes 113, 126, 130, *134*, 135,
  152, 159–63, *161*, 168
Trachelospermum jasminoides 57
training fruit 185–6, 188
transplanting herbs 108–9, 118
trees 196, 207–9
Tropaeolum speciosum 28
tubers 17
tulip fire 35, 102
Tulipa 'Abu Hassan' 32
  T. 'Ballerina' *30*, 32
  T. 'Black Parrot' *30*, 35
  T. 'Blue Parrot' 32–5
  T. clusiana var. *chrysantha* 101
  T. 'Flaming Parrot' 35
  T. 'General de Wet' 30
  T. humilis 'Eastern Star' *100*,
    101
  T. linifolia 101, *102*
  T. 'Little Princess' 101
  T. 'Negrita' 32
  T. 'Orange Emperor' 30
  T. 'Prinses Irene' 32
  T. 'Queen of Night' 32
  T. 'Queen of Sheba' 32
  T. 'Recreado' 32
  T. 'Red Riding Hood' 101
  T. 'Rococo' 35
  T. 'West Point' 32
  T. 'White Triumphator' 32
tulips 28, 31–5, 77, 101–2
turnips 65, 137
£20 border 42–53, *45*

vegetables 124–49
  companion planting 135
  in containers 142
  crop rotation 129–31
  pests and diseases 138–9, 143
  sowing *128*
ventilation, greenhouses 156
Verbascum 46, 78–9
  V. chaixii 78
    V.c. 'Gainsborough' 78

  V. 'Clementine' 80
  V. 'Helen Johnson' 78–80, *79*
  V. phoeniceum 49, 51
  V. 'Virginia' 80
vermiculite 46, *46*
vervain 109
Viola tricolor 17

wallflowers 45, 65, 77, 137
walls 74, 94, 103
wasps 135
water, ponds 228–31
water avens 65
water boatmen 233
water violet 221, *221*
watering 92, 95
  containers 61, 62–4
  greenhouses 127–8, 155, 156
  herbs 115
  water butts 127–8, 154, *155*
waterlilies 215, 225–7
weeds: annual weeds 47
  bindweed 75, 86–7
  crop rotation 129
  green manures 132, *133*
  kitchen garden 138
  in lawns 237, 242, 243–4, 247
whirligig beetles 232
whitecurrants 178
whitefly 135, 138–9, 162
wildflowers 217–19, 229
wildlife 214, 231–3
windbreaks 154
wood chippings, paths 127
worms 243, 245

yew hedges 12, 37, *37*

Zantedeschia aethiopica 64–5
  Z.a. 'Crowborough' 64, *65*
zinnia, creeping 62

Acknowledgements

This book, as with every programme of Gardener's World, is the fruit of the labour of a dozen or more skilled people that include researchers, camera crews, runners, gardeners, producers, directors, production assistants and so on. I am just a single element in that team and I have enjoyed and benefited from their help and skills immensely. But I would like to thank the two series producers, Gill Tierney and Sarah Moors in particular, for encouraging and supporting me at every stage and for making my job so interesting and enjoyable.

I should also like to thank my fellow presenters Rachel de Thame, Chris Beardshaw and Sarah Raven for their professional and horticultural skill, and the pleasure of their company. They are a joy to work with.

But my overwhelming thanks are to Phil McCann, who did a huge amount of work researching and preparing this book. Without his expertise and unfailing help this book would never have been completed on time.

Monty Don, 2005

The Gardeners' World team

Head of Programmes, BBC Birmingham
Tessa Finch
Executive Producer
Nick Patten
Series Producer
Sarah Moors
Series Producer (2003 – May 2004)
Gill Tierney
Producer
Andy Vernon
Assistant Producer
Louise Hampden
Directors
Mark Scott, Sharon Fisher, Ewan Keil (2003), Oliver Clark (2003), David Leighton (2004)
Horticultural Researchers
David Henderson, Richard Holmes, Phil McCann
Production Manager
Jacque Brown
Production Executive
Tracey Bagley
Production Executive
Caroline Morgan-Fletcher
Production Team
Marcus Chiltern-Jones, Kerry Preston-Jones, Alan Brough, Kevin Line, Ed Thornton, Kay Tudor, Julie Field, Christine Hardman, Judy Sampson, Matthew Stewart

Phil McCann would like to thank Jack McCann for being the best production manager in the world.

BBC Books would like to thank the whole BBC Gardeners' World Magazine team, and Lucy Hall in particular, for their considerable input, enthusiasm and advice.

Picture credits

BBC Worldwide would like to thank the following for providing photographs and for permission to reproduce copyright material. While every effort has been made to trace and acknowledge all copyright holders, we would like to apologize should there have been any errors or omissions.

Mark Bolton: 95, 145tl, 204t & c; Torie Chugg: 67, 73; John Glover: 77t, 100, 117, 123, 145bl, 172, 173, 187t, c & b, 189tl, 192, 246, 247; Harpur Garden Library: 19tr & br, 34, 42, 49tr & b, 59b, 64c & b, 71, 77b, 79t, 82c, 97, 99, 102, 114, 121, 125, 136, 140, 147, 161b, 174, 176, 181, 183, 184, 218t, 220, 223, 224, 226t; Jason Ingram: 25bl, 36, 77c, 88, 106, 109c, 130t, ca & b, 167, 199, 203, 204b, 209, 211, 218br; Andrew Lawson: 19tl, 25tr, 26, 49tl, 52, 55, 59t, 63, 64t, 68, 70, 79b, 81, 82b, 84, 87, 109b, 111, 119t & br, 120, 122, 130cb, 145br, 148, 186, 189tr & br, 218bl, 221, 226b, 243; Steven Wooster: 194, 195, 200, 201, 208, 210.

All other photographs © BBC Worldwide: Jason Ingram 1, 2, 4, 5, 7, 10, 11, 14, 15, 19bl, 20, 25tl & br, 29, 30, 33, 38t, 40, 41, 46tr & br, 47, 51, 53, 54, 57, 72, 75, 82t, 89, 90, 91, 96, 103, 104, 105, 107, 109t, 119bl, 124, 134, 141, 142, 145tr, 146, 149, 150, 151, 153, 155, 158, 161t & c, 163, 164, 169, 170, 189bl, 193, 197, 212, 213, 215, 217, 229, 230, 233, 234, 235, 236, 237, 239, 248, 249; Giles Park 38c, 171; William Shaw 38b, 43, 45, 46cr, 93, 128, 132, 168, 175.

This book is published to accompany the television series, *Gardeners' World*, produced for BBC2 by BBC Birmingham.

Published by BBC Books, BBC Worldwide Limited, Woodlands, 80 Wood Lane, London W12 0TT

First published 2005
Text © Monty Don 2005
The moral right of the author has been asserted

Specially commissioned photography by Jason Ingram (see page 255 for full picture credits)

ISBN 0 563 52172 4

Horticultural researcher
Phil McCann

Commissioning editor
Vivien Bowler
Project editor
Sarah Reece
Copy editor
Steve Dobell
Designer
Andrew Barron @ Thextension
Illustrator
Nancy Nicholson
Picture researcher
Joanne Forrest Smith
Production controller
Kenneth McKay

Set in FF Scala and FF Scala Sans
Colour origination and printing by Butler & Tanner Ltd, Frome, England

For more information about this and other BBC books, please visit our website on www.bbcshop.com or telephone 08700 777 001.